IRISH ROOTS IN COUNTY DOWN

Stories of Family & Place

EDITED BY STANLEY R. MEGRAW

LYNETTE NUNN & BRENDA ANDERSON
ASSOCIATE EDITORS

AINSLEY PUBLISHING

2014

Library and Archives Canada Cataloguing in Publication

Irish roots in County Down : stories of family & place / edited by Stanley R. Megraw ; Lynette Nunn & Brenda Anderson, associate editors.

Includes bibliographical references and index.
ISBN 978-0-9939188-0-3 (pbk.)

1. Down (Northern Ireland : County)--Genealogy.
I. Megraw, Stanley R., 1952-, author, editor

CS448.D68I75 2014 929.3416'5 C2014-906698-8

Cover Photo: Ulster Folk and Transport Museum, Holywood, Co. Down; photographed by S.R. Megraw (August 2010).

Book design and production: Ainsley Publishing

Dedicated to the memory of two family historians who have provided exceptional support and encouragement to so many others researching their Irish heritage in County Down—Fiona Doyle Jones (1964-2012) and Sheila Phillips (1951-2012).

County Down

County Down is situated in the northeast of Ireland (left) and is divided into civil parishes (below). It covers an area of about 2,450 square km (945 square miles) and ranks third as the most populated county in all of Ireland.

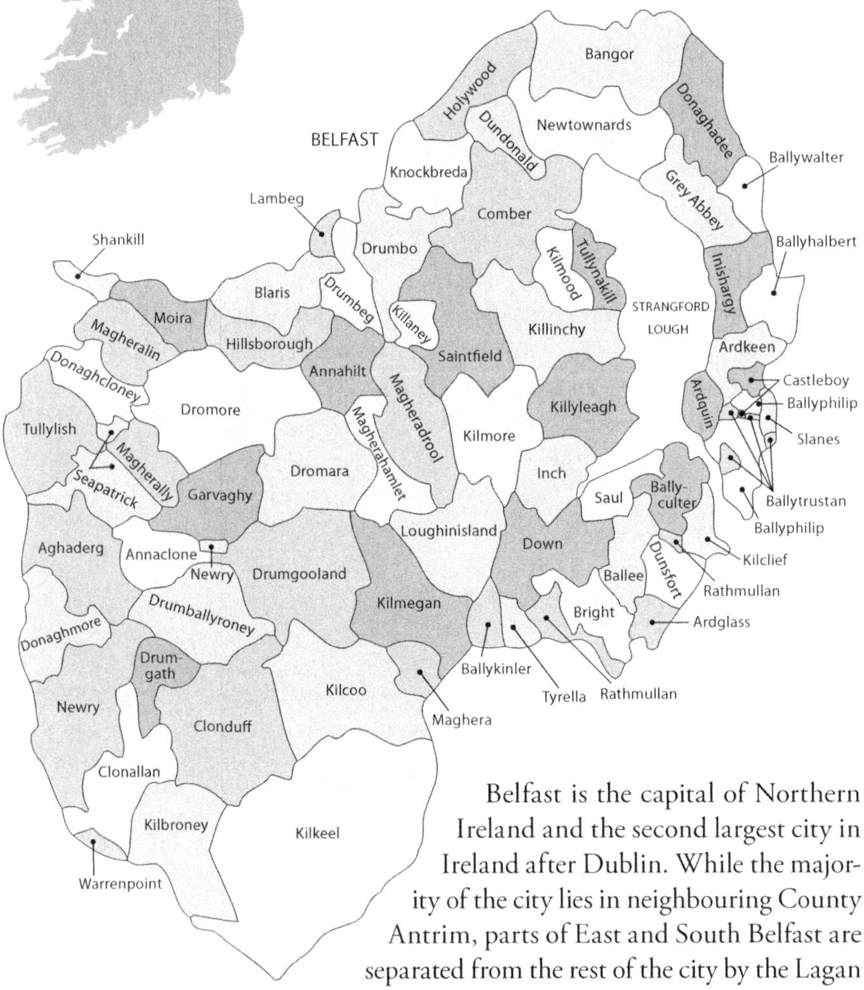

Belfast is the capital of Northern Ireland and the second largest city in Ireland after Dublin. While the majority of the city lies in neighbouring County Antrim, parts of East and South Belfast are separated from the rest of the city by the Lagan River and are situated in County Down.

Towns and Townlands

The map below shows the locations of the towns and townlands of County Down that are mentioned in this publication.

(Illustrations by Stanley R. Megraw, 2014)

Contents

Preface

THE IDEA FOR PUBLISHING *Irish Roots in County Down* originated with the late Fiona Doyle Jones, a gifted writer and editor whose enthusiasm for any and all things related to the people and places of Ireland is legendary among those who knew her. The book was written by family historians and members of Fiona's County Down Genealogy (FCDG) Group, a special-interest group on the web portal Yahoo!.

Fiona Doyle Jones started her freelance writing career as a medical writer, but later branched into writing about genealogy and family history. Examples of her latter work include the *Down Star* newsletter and an e-publication, simply titled *Kilkeel*. She also maintained a number of websites, including "The Miners of Mourne", which immortalized her paternal grandfather Henry Joseph (Harry Joe) Doyle, and the Ireland Genealogical Projects (IGP), County Down website, a resource to assist those tracing their elusive Irish ancestors. Fiona was also the founder of the County Down Genealogy Group on Yahoo!, which was later renamed in her honour.

However, Fiona's most ambitious endeavour was the publication of *A Mourne Townland: The History & People of Aughnaloopy*, a book that took five years to complete. It was inspired by Fiona's great-grandmother Anne Doyle (nee Quinn) and was a collaborative effort with another well-respected and knowledgeable County Down researcher, the late Sheila Phillips.

Sheila Phillips was a tireless worker who gave freely of her time to help countless others in breaking down their County Down brick walls. Every Wednesday, she would travel from her home in Ballymartin, Co. Down, to the Public Record Office of Northern Ireland (PRONI) in Belfast to comb their records on behalf of researchers from all over the world. She would also make regular trips to the General Register Office (GRO) in Dublin in search of elusive documents that would prove (or disprove) ancestral relationships. These and other acts of kindness were carried out selflessly and often at her own expense. To members of the FCDG Group, Sheila was known as "our genealogy angel".

Sheila passed away on 12 January 2012, only six months before the publication of *A Mourne Townland.* Her co-author, Fiona Doyle Jones, wrote to the FCGD Group to inform us of her passing, and to remember a close and very dear friend:

> It is with great sadness that I have to pass on the news that today Sheila Phillips lost her battle with cancer. She died peacefully at home surrounded by her family … Sheila worked away quietly and diligently and her work was always to the highest level of professionalism. I, like many, used to eagerly await her return from PRONI on a Wednesday night … Even after a long day traveling to and from Belfast and peering through a microfiche reader, Sheila would sit up writing emails to let you know what she had discovered. Her energy and enthusiasm were boundless.
>
> – Fiona Doyle Jones, January 2012

A Mourne Townland: The History & People of Aughnaloopy was released on 5 July 2012. It was a bittersweet moment for Fiona who was not able to share in the experience with her collaborator Sheila Phillips.

In the book, Fiona proudly acknowledges that "This project would not have been possible without the tremendous support and encouragement of all members of the Yahoo County Down Genealogy Group". It was Fiona's intention to give back to the group by offering to take our family research and turning it into a "published compilation". It was also her way of paying homage to the memory of Sheila Phillips. As Fiona explained,

> ... [this initiative] would be especially appropriate for anyone who has had the benefit of Sheila helping them with their research to publish what they have learnt. ... I know many folks are reluctant to write up their research either because they don't feel confident or perhaps don't have time which is why I have offered to take this on. So if we get enough people willing to donate their research, I am happy to move the project forward.
>
> – Fiona Doyle Jones, July 2012.

Sadly, Fiona was unable to follow through with her proposal. Not long after the publication of *A Mourne Townland*, she took ill and passed away on 6 October 2012. The outpouring of grief and sympathy that followed was unprecedented.

Members of the FCDG Group expressed an interest in pursuing Fiona's original plan for a "published compilation" and so the project was re-launched in July 2013. During the course of the next few months, manuscripts were solicited and the task of putting together a collection of family research stories commenced. It took another several months to complete the project and *Irish Roots in County Down* is the end result of that effort.

Fiona Doyle Jones and Sheila Phillips were two very special people who gave generously of their time, knowledge and hearts. As one member of the FCDG Group so aptly remarked, "We were blessed to have Fiona's vision to start this group, and doubly blessed to have Fiona's and Sheila's hard work to help so many of us."

It is our hope that this publication fulfills Fiona's original vision for the book and serves as a worthy legacy of her and Sheila's exceptional contributions to the County Down genealogical community.

Stanley R. Megraw (Quebec, Canada)
Lynette Nunn (Queensland, Australia)
Brenda Anderson (Ontario, Canada)

September, 2014

CHAPTER ONE

A Tinsmith's Daughter from Newry

The Americanization of Sarah Baxter (1883–1963)

BY DAVID GRIFFITH (UNITED STATES)

COUNTY DOWN. THOSE WORDS MIGHT be the first words my grandmother spoke to me. In all likelihood they were not, but when I think of her, those two words are the first to enter my mind. For some reason, she never dwelled on specific places like Belfast, or Newry, or Killyleagh, or even Ireland for that matter. County Down was sufficient to identify her homeland. She was proud of that fact and announced it to anyone who asked. In her mind, everyone must have heard of County Down! To her, no maps or explanations were needed.

My grandmother was born in Newry, Co. Down, on 1 April 1883 and christened Sarah Baxter. The coincidence of being born on April Fools' Day was fortuitous. We all remember the corny jokes like "there is a hole in your pants – oh, April Fools," but the jokes served as a reminder that it was Grandma's birthday. I never forgot it.

The Baxter Family in Newry

Grandmother was the third oldest of eleven children born to William Baxter, a tinsmith, and his wife, Sarah Beattie. William and Sarah married in the summer of 1878 in Newry and were blessed with five boys and six girls:

- William Baxter, born 1879.
- Jane Baxter, born 1881.
- Sarah Baxter, born 1883.
- Thomas Baxter, born 1885.
- Selena Baxter, born 1887.
- Margaret Baxter, born 1889.
- Isaac Baxter, born 1891.
- Albert Baxter, born 1893.
- Florence Baxter, born 1895.
- Nora Baxter, born 1898.
- Robert Baxter, born 1900.

Unfortunately, Isaac died at age 5 months and Thomas at age 19 years.

There is no record of what life was like as the family of a tinsmith, but I can imagine it was meager. It was an urban rather than rural upbringing, and the family lived above the tinsmith shop. After Isaac's death, there would have been two adults and ten children confined to a few rooms, and there was probably a lot of sharing of clothes (hand-me-downs) and chores between the siblings.

Thanks to the preservation of the 1901 and 1911 census of Ireland records and their availability online, a little more is known about the family. In 1901, the oldest son, William, is listed as a tinsmith, Sarah's occupation is a shirt maker, and Thomas appears as a mechanic. The younger children, ages 4 to 14, are described as scholars.

By 1911, the family had started to shrink as the older siblings married and moved away and some of the younger ones went with them. For example, only the two youngest, Nora and Robert, were still living at home in Newry. Margaret was living with her older brother William and his family in Belfast, Albert was with his older sister Selena and her family in Newry, and Florence had joined her sister Sarah's family in America.

Of the nine Baxter children who lived to adulthood after the deaths of Thomas and Isaac, four would call Ireland home (William, Jane, Selena, Albert), one accompanied her husband to Australia (Nora), and four immigrated to America (Sarah, Florence, Margaret, Robert).

Based on the Baxter presence in Newry, I was surprised to discover that my great-grandfather William was not born in Ireland, but in Liverpool, England, on 9 May 1857.

William Baxter standing outside his tinsmith shop in Newry, Co. Down, with two unidentifed girls (photo: date unknown).

William was the son of Isaac Baxter, also a tinsmith, and Jane Reid. In the 1881 census of England, both Isaac and Jane listed Ireland as their birthplace, but I have not been able to find a birth record for either of them. They were definitely living in Liverpool when William was born in 1857, and they appear in the 1861 and 1881 census records for England, but I have not been able to locate them in the census records for 1871 or 1891.

Isaac Baxter died in Newry on 4 January 1892 and his wife Jane followed on 22 January 1895. I am not sure why Isaac and Jane settled in Liverpool for a time, but I suspect it was related to the large Irish emigration due to the Great Famine and poor economic conditions during the period of 1845 to 1852. Family lore mentions that Isaac had a job as a tinsmith on the boats going back and forth from Liverpool to Ireland, although it is not clear when this happened or where he resided when not on board a boat.

Great-grandmother Sarah Beattie was born about 1860 in Newry, the daughter of Thomas Beattie and Selena (last name unknown). As might be surmised by the missing surname, little is known about this side of the family. A lack of Irish records from the 1800s have hindered my research efforts.

Sarah Baxter's Marriage

As listed on the marriage certificate, Evan Griffith and Sarah Baxter were wed in the parish church in Newry, Co. Down, on 27 March 1905. Their ages were shown as "full," but based on their birthdates, he was 27 years old and she was 21. Evan's profession was listed as a "sett maker", which is a quarry job that requires hammers and chisels to form small, rectangular blocks of stone used to pave streets. Sarah's profession was left blank on the form, but I suspect she was still working as a shirt maker as was listed in the 1901 census of Ireland.

When or where my grandmother met my grandfather Evan Griffith is unknown. Family history has it that Evan's mother died in Wales when he was young and that he went to live with relatives who abused him. So he ran away as a teenager, joined the merchant marines, and spent time sailing the seas. If that was the case, perhaps Evan and Sarah met in Newry or Belfast when his ship made a port of call.

I do know that Evan was the first of the two to set foot on American soil, arriving at Ellis Island, New York, on 2 April 1903 aboard the ship *Oceanic*. Along with other Welshmen, he made his way to Berlin, Wisconsin, to work as a stone cutter in the granite quarry. I believe that he probably

Sarah Baxter with her husband Evan Griffith in Newry, Co. Down (photo: ca. 1905).

knew Sarah before he made this trip and that he immigrated to find a job and place to live, save up money for Sarah to travel, and prove to the Baxter family that he was a responsible young man worthy of marrying their daughter. Because I have not yet found a record of his travel from America back to Ireland, I do not know exactly how long he lived and worked in Berlin. He definitely made his way back to Newry before his wedding in March of 1905.

Sarah's First Trip to America

At the age of 24, Sarah Baxter Griffith sailed aboard the *Compania* from Liverpool on 29 June 1907 on a voyage that lasted seven days. She arrived by herself at Ellis Island, New York, on 6 July 1907. According to the ship's manifest, Sarah stated that her husband had paid for her passage and that she was there to join him. It appears that after the wedding, Evan returned to America alone. With no record of his return trip yet discovered, it is unknown whether he stayed in Newry for a few years with his new wife, or if he returned soon after the marriage to continue to save money and secure a house for Sarah and his future family.

My grandmother never discussed her travel experiences with me, but I imagine she experienced some anxiety and perhaps outright fear on the voyage. She travelled steerage class, which is commonly defined as accommodations at the lowest or cheapest rate. First-hand reports from passengers describe such travel as an ordeal with no privacy, limited toilet use, poor food, and hundreds of people crammed into a single compartment with bunk beds for what little sleep could be had amid the clamor. In my mind, she had to have had a strong will and courage to be separated from her husband and endure such travel.

One change awaiting Sarah when she arrived in the United States was that Evan had moved from Berlin to Redgranite, Wisconsin. A new granite quarry had opened in Redgranite (about 10 miles to the northwest of Berlin), and Evan and other quarry workers relocated there because the granite was softer and could be worked year around [see "Life in Redgranite" below]. I have found no written record of their early years in Redgranite, but can assume they settled into married life together and that they were glad to be starting anew in a country that promised equality and opportunity for all.

Return to Newry

As many young married couples do, they decided to start a family. That decision, it appears, also led them to return to Ireland, probably in late 1908. On 20 September 1909, Sarah gave birth to the couple's first son, William Griffith, in Newry, County Down. Apparently, Sarah elected to return home to be with her mother and sisters when the baby was born. But Evan did not stay for the birth. He returned alone via Ellis Island on 12 March 1909 aboard the *Mauretania* and left Sarah in the care of her Baxter family. Again, she had to deal with being separated from her husband for a long period of time.

Sarah's Second Trip to America

About five months after the birth of her son in Newry, Sarah returned to America with infant William. On 26 February 1910, Sarah and William left Liverpool aboard the *Lusitania* (yes, the same ship that was later sunk by the Germans in 1915) and they did not arrive in New York until 5 March 1910. Their final destination listed on the ship's manifest was, of course, Redgranite; but I have no information about how they travelled from New York to Wisconsin. Most likely it was by rail to Chicago, Illinois, and then up through Milwaukee, Wisconsin. I know they arrived successfully because the whole family—Evan, Sarah, and young son William—is listed in the 1910 census of the United States for Redgranite, Wisconsin, which was enumerated on 21 May 1910. The house they lived in was about one block east of the quarry, and Evan, who listed his occupation as paving stone cutter, had just a short walk along a dirt path to arrive at work every day.

Whenever I think about this phase of my grandmother's life, I am amazed at her strength, courage, and resolve. She not only made the trip across the Atlantic three times, but also travelled alone for one of those trips and with a 5-month old baby on another. Travelling steerage class with an infant must have been very difficult. Yet she did it. She was separated from her husband on at least two occasions, and the second time was for a period of almost a year.

Sarah Baxter (seated, far left) at her home in Redgranite, Wisconsin, with young son William and husband Evan Griffith (standing, far left). Also shown are members of the Shields family, neighbors of Evan and Sarah (photo: 1910).

The Griffith Family in Wisconsin

After Evan, Sarah, and William settled into their new home in 1910, four other children were born—Albert (b. 1911), Flora (b. 1912), Walter (b. 1915), and Nora (b. 1916).

Although Sarah's trips across the Atlantic suggest that she may have had a strong sense of adventure and independence, the Baxter family ties remained strong. When Sarah was pregnant with her second son (my father Albert), she summoned her younger sister Florence Baxter to come from Newry, Co. Down, to assist with the birth and to stay on and help care for the two young boys.

Despite being about 16 years old, Florence travelled alone on the *Laurentic* and arrived at Ellis Island on 19 February 1911. Again, I am not sure how long it would have taken to travel from New York to Redgranite, but my father was born on 23 March 1911 and Florence was there to help Sarah. I am sure this was a win-win situation for both Sarah and Florence. Sarah got the help she needed from a trusted sibling, and Florence got to leave Newry for a new start in life with unlimited possibilities in America.

Baxter family ties also affected another of Sarah's younger sisters. In 1912, Margaret left Ireland for Philadelphia, Pennsylvania, where she married Joe Hanna in 1913. Their first child, daughter Eveline, however, was born in Redgranite in 1915. I have no knowledge of the specifics of this situation, but Margaret may have chosen Redgranite when her first child Eveline was born so that she would be near family and have her sisters to help if needed.

So three of the six Baxter sisters who were born in Newry, Co. Down, were reunited for awhile in Wisconsin, but eventually, Margaret, Joe, and young Eveline returned to Philadelphia. Florence, however, remained in Redgranite where she met and fell in love with a Welsh quarryman. On 4 June 1917, Florence Baxter and Hugh Jones were married and settled down to raise their family of two sons.

Life in Redgranite

The village of Redgranite is located in Waushara County, Wisconsin, a rural and predominantly agricultural area that began to be settled by farmers in the 1850s. The wider area was called the Indian Lands in the 1850 census of the United States. In later years, the location where Redgranite developed was called Sand Prairie because of the sandy, well-drained soil that was present. That was about to change, however, when a group of quarrymen from Berlin purchased a farm in 1889 that had a granite formation with a color described as being red, pink or mahogany. The significance of this new granite was that it was not as hard as the granite in Berlin, and it could be cut, split and worked in the winter (winters in Central Wisconsin are cold and snow covered). While the Berlin quarry had to close for the winter months, this new quarry with "red granite" could operate all year long.

Like many other settlements that grew into villages and small towns in America, development flourished. Quarrymen and paving stone cutters moved to the area. Boarding houses and general stores were built. Doctors, dentists, tailors, and shoemakers opened up shop. The railroad added a spur to enable the granite paving stones to be shipped to Milwaukee and Chicago and other major cities where they were used to pave the streets. Redgranite was incorporated in 1904 and became quite a boom town during the period from about 1905 until 1918.

Quarry workers cutting paving stones in Redgranite, Wisconsin (photo: 1911).

Despite the boom-town atmosphere, earnings were meager for the stone cutters. If I recall the family story correctly, the workers received one cent for each paving block (approximately 9" x 5" x 5") they shaped. Since the more you produced the more you were paid, some workers stayed after hours to cut and dress additional paving blocks and earn a few more pennies a day.

This was the environment in which Evan and Sarah found themselves raising their family of five children. It was definitely a more rural setting than what Sarah had experienced in Newry, Co. Down.

In addition to his paving stone-cutting skills, Evan proved to be a good carpenter. As more children were born to the family, Evan built new rooms onto the house. It started with one bedroom for him and Sarah. Then a bedroom was added for William and Albert. When the first daughter Flora arrived, an additional bedroom was constructed. When Walter was born, the three boys not only had to share one bedroom, they also had to share one bed! Finally, Nora joined the family, but no new construction was needed. She simply joined Flora in the "girls' bedroom".

Sarah Baxter Griffith with her daughters Flora (left) and Nora (right) outside the family home in Redgranite, Wisconsin (photo: ca. 1923).

The Griffith house had no running water, only a common hand pump to retrieve cold water from the local aquifer below the village. There was no plumbing, so everyone had to venture outside to the two-hole outhouse which was described as terribly cold during the winter months. A cast iron stove that could burn coal or wood served to warm one end of the house, but the boys bedroom at the other end of the house could only muster some residual heat from the wood burning kitchen stove if Sarah was cooking or baking.

Life for the children was challenging. The boys were expected to go to the train depot to round up any stray chunks of coal that might have tumbled off the rail cars, and they spent time at the local fishing holes in an attempt to bring home as much protein as they could. At the beginning of the school year, each child was outfitted with a new pair of shoes and blue jeans that were expected to last the entire year. Any holes in garments or shoes ran the risk of punishment, and had to be repaired by hand by Sarah. When school was out the next spring, heads were shaved and shoes were kicked off, and the kids went barefoot all summer long until the next school year began.

To make ends meet, Sarah maintained a garden and a cold cellar to store as much produce and canned goods as she could. Lots of potatoes and rice were served for meals, but local blueberries and apples often made their way to the table in the form of pies and muffins. She enjoyed baking, her favorites being bread and custard pie.

Perhaps because of her Irish heritage, Sarah preferred drinking tea rather than coffee, and she joyfully demonstrated "saucering"—the practice of pouring a small amount of hot tea out of the cup and onto the saucer below to allow for air to be blown over the surface to cool it down. The cooled tea could then be poured back into the cup, or drunk directly from the saucer!

Sarah was very skilled at sewing, knitting, and crocheting. It was easy for her to make something for the children to wear, and it was cheaper to mend the holes and tears in existing garments than to buy new clothes. By the time her family had grown, Sarah turned her attention to the grandchildren. It became a Christmas tradition for me to find a pair of her hand-knitted mittens wrapped under the tree.

One tranquil morning, the normal breakfast routine in the Griffith household was interrupted when tragedy struck. While priming the wood burning kitchen stove with kerosene, there was a small explosion that flared up and burned Sarah's neck and face, and destroyed her black hair. She slowly recovered from the painful burns, but when her hair grew back it was white, a trait that all of us descendants seem to have inherited (it is often noted that some elderly people have gray hair, but the older Griffith children and grandchildren have white hair). How she survived is a miracle, because even with the local doctor's care, the only remedy seemed to be towels wrapped in petroleum jelly that were changed constantly to prevent infection.

With Redgranite booming from the influx of all nationalities from Europe and elsewhere, Sarah was one of the many immigrants who started life in America as a non-citizen. And the motivation to gain American citizenship was strong for many of these immigrants. I am not sure what kinds of study or tests were required back then, but Sarah prevailed and became a naturalized citizen on 18 April 1927.

Perhaps her biggest accomplishment was raising five children who turned out to be happy, productive adults. The family was not rich monetarily, but it was blessed with love, respect, and loyalty that kept them together. Evan and Sarah never owned an automobile or a television, but they did not need material things for their happiness. They had the courage to risk starting a life in America, and were successful at it.

There were bumps in the road, however. The quarry in Redgranite closed when cities turned to concrete for their streets instead of granite blocks. Facing unemployment, Evan sought work in other quarries. He left the family and found work in Waukesha, Wisconsin, and even labored at Stone Mountain in the State of Georgia, where he rented rooms and sent money back home to Sarah. This marked another time when Sarah was separated from her husband, but she endured the separation for the good of the children. It took hard work and sacrifice, but the family survived. While they struggled at times, I am sure that if given the chance, they would make the same decisions all over again.

Kudos to County Down

County Down … To Sarah, those two words were a source of pride. To me, those two words evoke memories of a wonderful grandmother; a kind, gentle and compassionate person with a wonderful sense of humor and a smile that would warm any heart. When she held you on her lap, or looked you in the eye, she made you feel like the only person in the world. She seemed wise beyond her years, and her advice was always sought. I am convinced that a childhood in County Down, under the tutelage of her parents of course, helped to create such a wonderful human being.

Sarah Baxter Griffith died at the age of 80 years on 9 March 1963.

My grandmother Sarah Baxter, shown here with her husband Evan Griffith (photo: ca. 1952), was a gentle, compassionate person with a strong sense of pride in her County Down heritage.

She broke her hip when she fell while making her bed, and after a stay at the hospital, she was later cared for at a nursing home for a short time. I believe she may have finally lost her will to live because she was confined to bed. She never attempted physical therapy, or tried to use a walker or other form of assistance. She is buried at the Foster Road Cemetery in Redgranite, Wisconsin, next to her husband, Evan, who preceded her in death on 23 January 1954.

CHAPTER TWO

Three Townlands in Kilmore Parish

A Brief Historical Account

BY ROSALIND DAVIES (AUSTRALIA)

IN THE 1990S, AFTER I had finished researching my own family, I turned my sights on my husband's Marner family in County Down. He emigrated to Australia in 1971, but still has family in the parish of Kilmore.

I was initially appalled by the lack of records available in Ireland compared with those in the other five countries I'd been researching. This was before the internet, and it's somewhat better nowadays. I tried the church records in PRONI[1] and found that the ones I wanted from Loughinisland Catholic parish went back to 1805. I was disappointed, however, to find that the original records were barely readable before 1825. As a result, I could only piece the Marner family tree back to 1830; the rest was speculation. Moreover, the Catholic records for Kilmore parish were "in local hands," and to this day, after lots of asking around, I still haven't seen them.

It was at this point that I decided that if I couldn't name the people specifically, then I could at least find out what was happening in their lives. Thus was born my "One Place Studies" of three townlands in

[1] Public Record Office of Northern Ireland.

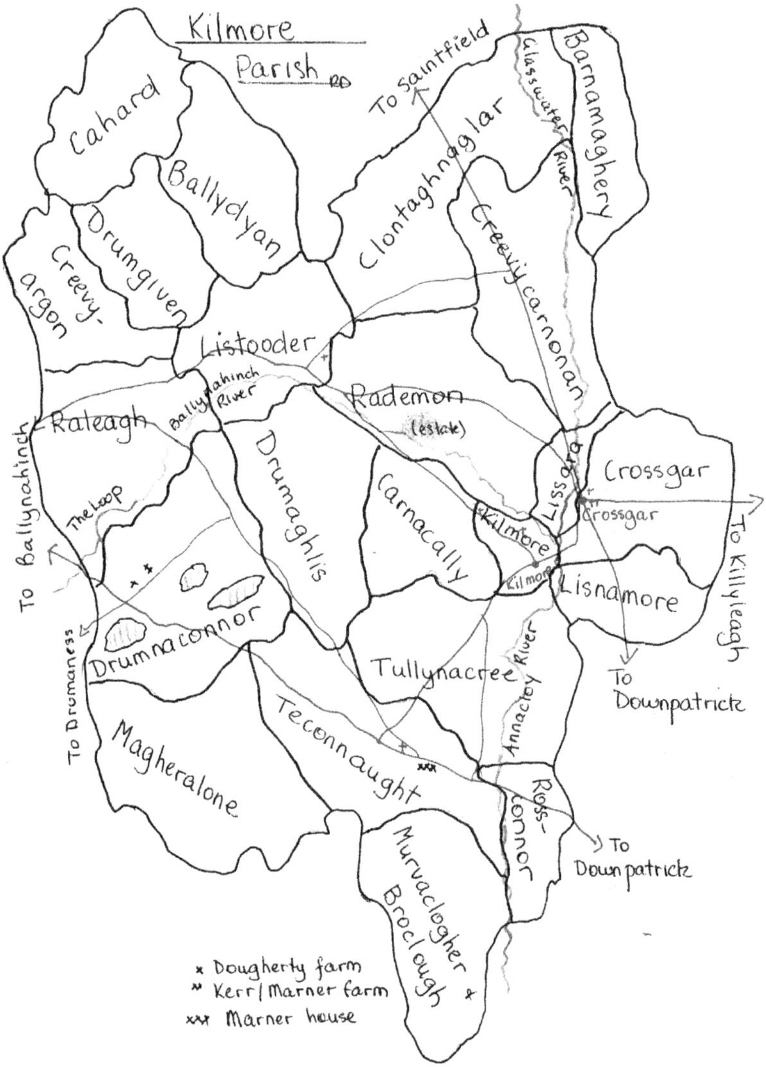

A sketch of Kilmore parish showing the location of its townlands and principal roads. (hand drawn by Ros Davies).

Kilmore parish, namely Drumnaconnor, Magheralone and Broclough/ Murvaclogher. The families in these townlands intermarried, so there's still a lot of family tree branches yet to be explored.

* * *

The name "Marner" is an anglicized spelling of the Irish surname *Marinan,* and it seems to be localised to the Ballynahinch area of County Down. We still have the family farm in Drumnaconnor townland, so I started by collecting all the information that I could find which included early land leases in PRONI, Tithe Applotment Books, Griffiths Valuations, wills, newspaper articles, talking with older members of the community, church and civil registration records, and census material.

My husband's grandmother Mrs. Mary Marner outside the family home in Drumnaconnor with her brother Ned Kerr (photo: ca. 1960). The house, now demolished, was part of a clachan of seven houses on a hill overlooking the Heron Lough. It had three rooms with a flagged stone floor and a lovely old fireplace in the kitchen with a hook for the cooking pot and kettle. There was a well just to the side of the house.

Then I realised that my husband's Marners centred on the nearby townland of Magheralone. So I also began collecting any information that mentioned Magheralone. The earliest I could find was Patrick Maranan leasing land in 1769 from the Forde Estate. This is a family name, so I made assumptions.

My husband's great-grandparents (the Carrs) came from the townland of Broclough, and the family still owned the farm there until 1960s. So I decided to research this townland as well to try and find out how far back the Carr family went. The earliest records show 1821.

All three of these townlands are rural areas without villages. So they would probably never rate very highly on anyone else's research list, but they do typify what was going on in so many other rural areas in Ireland ... ordinary people leading ordinary lives as best they could.

Drumnaconnor[2]

This townland is five kilometres southeast of Ballynahinch near the Downpatrick road[3] and comprises 904 acres.

There are four roads through Drumnaconnor: the Drumnaconagher Road, from Teconnaught to Raleagh; the Cumber Road, from the Downpatrick Road to Drumnaconagher Road; the Ballynahinch to Crossgar Road; and the road from the Drumnaconagher Road near to Drumaghlis, ending at the Ballynahinch to Crossgar Road. The Cumber Road was known in olden times as the "Rocky Road to Dublin" which was the main road from Comber, Co. Down, to the city of Dublin. It was later known as "Rocks Road" and then "Cumber Road".[4]

Drumnaconnor was originally held by members of the McCarten family—Phelemy McCarten and then Patrick McCarten in 1641. In 1657, Ever Magenis held 387 acres.[5] That same year, the Commonwealth, by right of conquest and law of arms, granted Drumnaconnor (along with

---

[2] My choice of spelling. Also known as: Drumnaconagher, Dromnaconagher, Drumnatticonnor, Dromonticonor, Dromonticonner, Droman Iknogher, Drumtitonor, and Drumnavoniher.

[3] Ordnance Survey of Northern Ireland, Irish Discovery Series 21. Strangford Lough 1 : 50,000.

[4] personal communication; Billy McCaughey of Drumnaconnor, Co. Down..

[5] The Down Survey of Ireland (http://downsurvey.tcd.ie/).

the townland of Raleagh) to Lieutenant Colonel James Trail of Tullychin in Killyleagh parish who had rendered active service in the suppression of the 1641 Rebellion. According to a deed, dated 25 May 1657 and 15 February 1657, Cornelius and Samuel Rock, troopers in L.D. Fleetwood's troop of horse, sold the townland (except for 12 acres of Demesne) to Lieutenant Colonel Trail for £80.[6]

After Trail's death on 18 May 1663, Drumnaconnor and Raleagh passed to his younger son Hans Trail. Hans died in Dublin in 1692, leaving his "corn-mill and tuck-mill" to his eldest son, James Trail.[7] In 1770, Reverend Hamilton Trail of Killinchy owned the townland. He subsequently put Drumnaconnor in the hands of Reverend James Mant, Lord Bishop of Down & Connor, and Reverend James Hamilton Clewlow in September 1775 prior to its sale to Alexander Stewart of Newtownards in December 1775 for approximately £3600.[8] Other part landlords listed in the Freeholders' records were Lord Londonderry (1789) and Marchioness of Downshire (1818) .

View of Heron Lough (top middle) in Drumnaconnor looking southeast towards Downpatrick (top right).

In 1836, there were three watermills in Drumnaconner belonging to J. Hill Silcock: a corn mill, with a wheel diameter of 17 feet, and two flax

[6] Placenames Database of Ireland (www.logainm.ie/en/).

[7] David Stewart, *The Story of Kilmore Presbyterian Church* (Belfast, 1932), pp. 12, 19.

[8] FamilySearch, "Transcripts of memorials of deeds, conveyances and wills, 1708-1929," Vol. 280, 1769-1771; FHL film no. 530913.

mills, with wheel diameters of 13 feet and 14 feet each. They could only be operated for part of the year, however, because there was insufficient water for any of these mills to work in the summer season.

There is a small, very ancient bridge called Lyons Bridge which spans the Ballynahinch River in Drumnaconner. It has one arch measuring 66 feet by 9 feet from one buttress to the other and is covered almost entirely in ivy. There is another bridge over the same water with two arches and a dimension from one buttress to another of 129 feet by 20 feet. It is also very old and was repaired in 1833 at the expense of the county.

The main road from Ballynahinch to Downpatrick passes through the townland, but it was not in very good order in 1836. The average width was 24 feet, and in some places it was dangerously narrow, not exceeding 18 feet in width. When the road crossed a bog, it was raised about three feet without fences on either side.

The Ordnance Survey Memoirs[9] comment that the farmers of Drumnaconnor in the early nineteenth century appeared to be quiet and industrious, and that their diet was strong and good. The farms, generally speaking, had a degree of cleanliness about them, which showed that some attention has been paid to their individual comfort. The farmhouses were mostly thatched, but there were many exceptions. The crops were generally in the haggard by the last of October.

The earliest farming families in the area with continuous residence were the Carvills, Greens, Kellys, Marners, Montgomerys, Silcocks and Savages, with the Stewarts being the major land owners. The other families moved into Drumnaconnor at various times from neighbouring townlands in the parish, or from parishes surrounding Kilmore. The Kerrs, for example, possibly moved from Broclough whilst still retaining the lease on the land there.

There were ten new farming families between 1830 and 1864, which shows the population was reasonably transient at the time. Those replaced could have been evicted for nonpayment of rent (the famine years), and those replacing them could have been younger sons from nearby who wanted their own land to farm, but still be within easy travelling distance to their parents and wider family. Alternatively, the newcomers could have

[9] Ordnance Survey Memoirs of Ireland 1830-1840 (Angélique Day and Patrick McWilliams, editors).

been workers who had been hired at the mill.

Between 1864 and 1911 there were 25 new families that moved into the neighbourhood. Most of the farm servants mentioned in the 1911 census were from families within the parish.

Surnames of people who have lived in Drumnaconnor:

Alderdice, Bailie, Bain, Bell, Boyd, Brannan/Brennan, Campbell, Carvill, Cleland, Coupland/Copeland, Craig, Cranney, Davey, Dorian, Doherty, Dumigan, Dunn, Ellison, English, Fagan, Farley, Gormley, Graham, Green, Hardy, Hunter, Hutton, Johnston, Kelly, Kerr, Lenaghan, McCance, McCartan, McCartney, McCaherty/McCaugherty, McClean, McClements, McClurg, McConnell, McCoubry, McCullough, McGrath, McGraw, McKeown, McManus, McMaster, McNeill, McRobert, McVey/McVeigh, Maffet, Mageean, Maguire, Marner, Martin, Mon, O'Hare, Poland/Pullien, Renton, Rice, Ringland, Rogan, Rodgers/Rogers, Savage, Silcock, Smith, Stewart, Thomas, Thompson, Trail, Welshman, Wilson.

Magheralone

The Blackstaff River runs through this townland, which is about seven kilometres southeast of Ballynahinch town. It consists of 871 acres and is the site of an ancient Catholic chapel from the penal times.[10] This chapel was called Shankill and in 1870 was in James McGauran's field. It was also called Killylone.[11]

The name Magheralone means "Owen's plain" or "Plain of Luan" (the grass plain or plain of the lamb). In the land leases of 1770, the townland was divided into four quarters (named Drumind, MaGwire, Bighouse and Wood) and was owned by the Forde family of Seaforde before the tenants were able to purchase their own land around 1890.

Magheralone was transferred from Loughinisland parish to Kilmore parish in 1718, and again in 1897 when Father Crickard transferred both

[10] The penal times refer to the period during the sixteenth and seventeenth centuries, when laws were passed to prevent Catholics from practicing their religion.

[11] Rev. James O'Laverty, *An Historical Account of the Diocese of Down and Connor, Ancient and Modern* (Dublin: James Duffy and Sons, 1878), Volume 1.

Magheralone and Teconnaught townlands to Kilmore. This provided Father James McArdle, parish priest of Kilmore, with a magnificent site on Annacloy Road for the Holy Family Church, which was blessed and dedicated on Easter Sunday in 1899.

In 1659, there were no English/Scots and 12 Catholic families living in the townland. On his tombstone of 1774 in the old graveyard of Downpatrick Cathedral, John Savage is noted as being "leat of Mahavaloon"[12] (late of Magheralone).

In the census of 1911, there were 53 inhabited houses and 6 uninhabited houses in Magheralone. The population that year was made up of 53 families comprised of 117 males and 123 females, of which 98 were Catholic, 18 Protestant, and 7 Presbyterian.

There were quite a few new families represented since the 1901 census, with some of the older families having moved or died out. Most inhabitants now owned their homes and farms, and a few of the larger landowners had swallowed up the smaller holdings and were leasing out the original cottages without any land attached. We also see the appearance of council houses[13] in the 1911 census.

A few of the families travelled to the mills in Drumaness for work. Some of the children were working in the mills at the age of 14, whilst others were still at school at 17.

Other notable obervations from the 1911 census:

- Several inhabitants were born across the water in Scotland and England and married to locals, which hints at seasonal work migration.
- There was sometimes a large gap in the ages of spouses where the woman was often older than her husband.
- The child death rate was reasonable.
- Many of the Catholic children spoke both Irish and English, a sign of effective schooling.

The Carvill, Grieve, Cleland, Dorrian, Magoran, Maguire, Marner,

[12] *Association for the Preservation of the Memorials of the Dead, Ireland*. Journal for the Year 1907, p. 288.

[13] A type of public or social housing.

Nelson, Reid, Rice and Rogan families had continuous occupation in this townland from the early 1800s to 1911 and beyond. My husband's Marner family leased land in 1769, and it was still in the family in 1915.

Surnames of people who have lived in Magheralone:

Agnew, Anderson, Bailie, Bingham, Brennan, Canavan, Carr, Carvill, Casement, Cleland, Coghlan/Cochlan, Connor/Conagher, Craney/Creeney, Davidson, Dorian, Dornan, Dougan, Fitzpatrick, Forde, Graffin, Graham, Green, Grieves, Hall, Hanvey, Harper, Herald, Kelly, Kennedy, Kerr, Lewis, McAllister, McCleland, McCormick, McCoy, McGauran/Magoran/McGoran, McGraffin, McGrath, McGuire, McLeagh, McLean, McMullen, McNamara, Madine/McDine, Maguire, Marner, Martin, Mulholland, Mullan, Murdock, Murnin, Nelson, Nixon, Orr, Pray, Reid, Rice, Rodgers, Rogan, Savage, Thompson, Turner, Walsh, Willis.

Broclough/Murvaclogher

This townland of 648 acres is located just north of the road between the villages of Loughinisland and Annacloy, and south of the road from Teconnaught to Loughinisland, and is centred around Tareesh Lane. It was transferred from Loughinisland parish to Kilmore parish in 1771.

Broclough and Murvaclogher were separate townlands at one stage, then merged and known by both names until more recently when the townland became known as just Broclough. The name Broclough means "margin of the lake" and the name Murvaclogher was originally Murnaclogheth, or in Irish, *Muir ba clochair*, meaning "stony place under sea". This was probably when the nearby Loughinisland Lough was flooded.

Edmond Savage owned the townland in 1659 when it was occupied by six English/Scots and six Catholic families.[14] By 1863, the land was owned by William B. Forde of Seaforde Estate.[15] A dispensary[16] was located here

[14] Seamus Pender, *A Census of Ireland circa 1659, with Supplementary Material from the Poll Money Ordinances* (Belfast: Irish Manuscripts Commission, 1939).

[15] AskAboutIreland, "Griffith's Valuation," database and images (www.askaboutireland.ie/griffith-valuation/index.xml).

[16] A place where medical advice and care was available and where medicines were prepared.

that same year and it is mentioned again in the 1911 census, the remains of which can still be seen today on the Loughinisland Road.

There is an old, undated document from about 1750 at PRONI in Belfast which gives the acreage for "Murbacloghah" as 380 acres in total, with 104 acres in the Big House Quarter, 75 acres in "Croleys" Quarter, 79 acres in "Crafords" (and partners) Quarter, and 120 acres in John M'Mullen and "Inenses" Quarter.[17] The landlord then was Matthew Forde Esq., whose family had come to the area in 1636. The McMullens were still represented in 1828 and the "Crafords" (Crawfords) in 1833. I'm thinking that "Inenses" could be Jennings, but "Croley" is a mystery. I do know, however, that the surname Crolley was prominent in the Downpatrick/Ballykilbeg area since 1177 in Norman times.

In the 1901 census, there were 23 inhabited houses and 4 uninhabited houses. There were 99 people (51 males and 48 females), and one family occupied each house. Most residents were Catholic. One female belonged to the Church of Ireland, and two males and two females were Presbyterians.

All houses were made of stone with thatched roofs and were identified as mainly second or third class homes with just two rooms and generally two windows facing the front. John Savage had the largest house with five rooms, and James Crawford had the most outbuildings ... eleven.[18]

The oldest resident was James Crawford who, at the age of 84 years, was still farming. The prize for "most children living in a small house" goes to John Carlin and his wife Rose with eight children in two rooms. John's uncle also lived in the house.

The majority of heads of household were farmers. The only other occupations listed were for unmarried daughters who worked as seamstresses; a coach builder, who was probably employed by the Forde Estate; and the only Presbyterian family in the townland, the Magowans, who ran a small grocery business out of their front room.

There were three residents who listed their place of birth as outside the county: a cousin/housekeeper named Mary Ann Jennings who was born

---

[17] Public Record Office of Northern Ireland (PRONI), " A survey of the Town Land of Murbacloghah," Lands: Murvaclogher or Broaghologh Co. Down (c.1750), microfilm, PRONI Reference: D1529/1/4a.

[18] The outbuildings consisted of two stables, one coach house, two cow houses, two piggeries, one fowl house, one barn, and two potato houses.

in Liverpool, England; Mrs. Anne Jennings, a widow who was born in County Wexford; and Henry Magowan's mother-in-law, who was born in County Cavan.

There were six widows listed, most of whom were still farming, and thirteen unmarried adults. Multi-generational families were common. Four households employed servants, either domestic or agricultural. Two occupants were listed as disabled. Margaret Crawford, aged 60 and working as a domestic servant, was deaf, whilst John McNamara, aged 69 and brother to the head of the house, was both deaf and dumb, but working as a farmer to assist his younger brother. .

Interestingly, there were three children aged 14 still at school. There wasn't a high school available and it was unusual for children this age to not be out working, or at least helping on the farm.

Also in 1901, there were three married women living with their families and running the farm, but without a husband present. They were probably working elsewhere to supplement the family income.

In the census of 1911, there were 23 inhabited and 5 uninhabited houses in the townland. There were 23 families comprised of 60 males and 40 females, and all were Catholic. Many of the adult children could speak Irish, and some of the husbands appeared to be away from the area for work .

The older residents from 1901 had died off by 1911, and 11 new families had moved into the area, such as the households of Patrick Burns and Daniel Gordon from Annacloy, and the John Flynn family from Teconnaught. All were newlyweds. County Louth native Patrick Halfpenny, whose wife Catherine (nee Hanvey) was living with her children and mother (Rose) in Broclough in 1901, had joined his family by 1911 as a retired policeman..

The earliest family names of farmers mentioned in documents are Maxwell (1790) and Savage (1726). The Crawford, Jennings and Maguire families had continuous occupation in this townland from the early 1800s to 1911 and beyond. My husband's father still owned the Carr family farm in the 1960s.

Surnames of people who have lived in Broclough/Murvaclogher:

Brown, Burns, Carlin, Carr, Carvill, Clarke, Crawford, Davy, Donegan/Doonigan/Dunigan, Duff, Fitzpatrick, Flanaghan, Flynn,

Forde, Gordon, Grant, Gribben, Halfpenny, Hanvey, Hazard, Herrold, Irvine, Jennings, Johnson, Kelly, Kerr, Killen, McCashin, McCurry/McCorry, McMullen, McNamara, McShane, Madine, Magowan, Maguire, Martin, Maxwell, Milligan, Mitchell, Montgomery, Morgan, Murphy, Pray/Oprey, Rea, Savage, Trainor.

* * *

And so concludes my brief account of three townlands in the parish of Kilmore, Co. Down. For more details on these and other families, please see my website "Ros Davies' Co. Down, Northern Ireland Family History Research Site" (freepages.genealogy.rootsweb.ancestry.com/~rosdavies).

CHAPTER THREE

Irish Immigrants to Canada

The Beattie Family of Ards, County Down

BY JIM BEATTIE (CANADA)

I HAVE RESEARCHED MY PATERNAL ANCESTRY IN County Down for the better part of thirty-five years, and this is but a brief overview of our Irish roots. It's a story about one of countless families who immigrated to other countries from the only home that they ever knew—Ireland.

Many families left Ireland in the early to mid-1800s due to the lack of food, at a time when staying meant almost certain death to many of the very young or elderly. Our branch of the Beattie family left home much later, coming to Canada in the mid-1920s with little more than the clothes on their backs, a few pictures of their loved ones they left behind, and the family Bible that my grandmother carried with her.

Irish Roots

The search for my family roots began in an area of County Down called the Ards Peninsula, which is now part of the borough of Ards. As I researched our branch of the Beatties, I found family living in the northern part of the peninsula south-east of Bangor in townlands such as Cotton, Ballyminetragh, Herdstown, and Ballyfotherly. All were within twenty kilometres (twelve miles) of each other, much the same as how we have lived and grown up here in Canada.

The earliest ancestor I have found is my paternal great-great-grandfather, Charles Beatty/Beattie. He was a widower and a labourer living in Ballyminetragh, parish of Bangor, when he married Christian Davis, daughter of John Davis, on 31 October 1846 in Newtownards, Co. Down.[1]

Charles and Christian had seven known children, all born in Herdstown, parish of Donaghadee, Co. Down.[2]

- Rachel Beatty, born 10 February 1850; baptized 5 June 1850.
- Anne Beatty, born 11 February 1852; baptized 2 February 1853.
- Charles Beatty, born 12 November 1855; baptized 28 June 1857.
- Christian Beatty, born 9 May 1857.
- Hugh Beattie (my great-grandfather), born 20 March 1860.
- James Beattie, born ca. 1861.
- Eleanor Campbell Beatty, born 16 June 1863.

In 1863, the family was living on a small parcel of land that was leased from Ferris Campbell in Cotton, parish of Bangor, near Six Road Ends. Times were extremely tough for the folks of that area as money was very scarce and, at times, so was food.

Charles Beatty died on 21 October 1883 in Cotton at the age of 59 years. His wife, Christian, died between 1901 and 1911.

My great-grandfather Hugh Beattie married Agnes Gilmore, who was three years his senior, on 10 April 1882 in Ballycopeland, parish of Donaghadee. Agnes, the daughter of Hugh Gilmore and Sarah Davis,[3] was from Herdstown, Donaghadee. Witnesses at their wedding were John and Annie Gilmore, and the minister was John Beatty.

Hugh and Agnes had several children; four who came to Canada and others who we can only assume stayed, had families and died in Ireland. They were James (born 1883), John Nelson (born 1888), Charles (born ca.

[1] Lookup of original church register by Doreen Walker, Northern Ireland Family Historical Society (NIFHS).

[2] Sent to me through NIFHS.

[3] Sarah Davis was the sister of Christian Davis, wife of Charles Beatty.

1889), Elleanor Jane (born 1894), Agnes (born 1896) and Christina (born 1900). Their eldest son, James Beattie, was my grandfather. Further details are given in the Appendix.

In 1901, the Beattie family was living in Ballyfotherly, Co. Down, on the farm of Thomas Hanna. Hugh Beattie, age 40, and his sons James, age 18, and John Nelson, age 16, were employed as agricultural labourers. Charles, age 13, and Elleanor, age 7, were attending school.

On 24 September 1906, my grandpa James ("Jim") Beattie married my grandma Margaret ("Maggie") Allen in the town of Donaghadee, Co. Down. The witnesses were grandpa's brother John Nelson Beattie and John's first wife, Leah Isabella Conway. John and Leah were married at the same church earlier that year on 3 May 1906.

Marriage Transcription—James Beattie, full age, bachelor, labourer, Ballyfotherly, son of Hugh Beattie, labourer; married Maggie Allen, full age, spinster, The Primary, Bangor, daughter of John Allen, labourer; witnesses: John Beattie and Leah Isabella Beattie; Shore Street Church, Parish of Donaghadee; 24 September, 1906.

In the 1911 census of Ireland, grandpa and grandma were living in the townland of Cotton, Co. Down. The family was listed as:

- James Beattie, head of family, Presbyterian, could read and write, age 29, agricultural labourer, married, born in Co. Down.
- Maggie Beattie, wife, Presbyterian, could read and write, age 23, seamstress, married (6 years), born in Co. Down.
- John A. Beattie, son, Presbyterian, could not read or write, age 5, scholar, born in Co. Down.
- Charles Beattie, son, Presbyterian, could not read, age 2, born in Co. Down.

By 11 December 1916, my great- grandfather Hugh Beattie was living at Ballymaconnell, Bangor, as recorded on his daughter Ellenor's marriage license. At this time, there is no sign of great-grandmother Agnes, so we can only assume that she had passed away sometime earlier.

Farewell to Ireland, Family, and Friends

My grandfather Jim was a kind and gentle man who worked at the farm in Cotton. This farm was owned by Mrs. Campbell, a cousin of Jim's father, who by 1920 was widowed. Grandpa not only worked the farm but family lore has it that he also drove a team of horses for the local undertaker--or at least that's what my father said.

Mrs. Campbell must have been a kind lady as my dad remembered going there as a little child and playing in her yard while grandfather did the chores. He often told of the day that they were to leave for Canada.

It appears that Mrs. Campbell had a huge gander on the farm as well as several geese, and the gander was a very protective beast. It had attacked dad and likely the other children many times before, and would bite and beat them with his wings until they would either run away, or someone would chase it off.

Well, on their last day in Ireland, grandpa and family went to the farm they had known so well to say their farewells. The gander, being the bully that he was, commenced to tear into dad, who was all of six years of age, and gave him a terrible thrashing. Grandpa and Mrs. Campbell had to chase it away from dad. It must have been a good beating to remember it so clearly seventy-odd years later.

This must also have been a sad time for all as they said their goodbyes to their loved ones and prepared to embark on the journey of a lifetime. It would be the last time that grandpa would see his father and sisters, and the last grandma would see of her parents, John and Agnes Allen, as well as her brother Archie, his wife Maggie Allen, and their two daughters, Nellie and Sadie. I'm sure that many a tear was shed by all, knowing in their heart that this would be the last time they would see their parents. I'm also sure that the family worried about the life that lay ahead.

Settling in Canada

The family left Belfast Harbour with grandpa's brother Charlie Beattie aboard the Cunard RMS *Alaunia* on 27 March 1926 and arrived in Halifax, Nova Scotia, eight days later on Easter Sunday. They travelled by train to Kingston, Ontario, and settled in the Hay Bay area of Adolphustown, while Uncle Charlie stayed in Kingston.

At the time of their emigration from Ireland, there were eight children with my grandparents: Charlie (born 1909), Eleanor (born 1911), Hugh (born 1913), Archibald (born 1916), William (born 1918), Robert (born 1920), Agnes (born 1923) and a third daughter (still living). Their oldest son, John Joseph (born 1906), had come ahead to Canada aboard the Cunard liner *Lancastria* and landed in Quebec City on 10 May 1925 with grandpa's brother John Nelson Beattie, or "Jack" as he was known.

Grandpa's sister Elleanor and her husband Bob Moore left Ireland at about the same time, but first went to Scotland and arrived in Canada aboard the *Doric* at Quebec City on 26 April 1926. One of their daughters, Mary Agnes, chose to stay in Scotland with family, but followed at a later date.

After the family arrived in the Adolphustown area of Ontario, grandpa quickly got a job working for one of the local farmers.

Grandpa Jim Beattie and his wife Maggie Allen (photo: ca. 1940). The photo on the left was carried by Jim's sons Archie, James and Robert while serving overseas during the Second World War.

My father, Robert Moore Beattie, married my mother, Dorothy Helen Lyman, in Enterprise, Lennox and Addington County, Ontario, on 10 August 1948 after his return from the Canadian Army where he served as a gunner with the Canadian 13th Field Regiment.

My dad Robert Moore Beattie shortly after enlisting in the Canadian Army where he served as a gunner overseas in the Second World War (photo: 1942).

My dad lived a wonderful life, was loved dearly, and passed away peacefully on 1 February 2003. My mom followed him three years later on 16 July 2006.

* * *

Researching our family has been an adventure for me; rewarding, but very difficult and frustrating at times, to say the least. It is unfortunate that some important Irish records have been lost, but such is life. All in all, I have had great help from some wonderful people who spent many hours assisting in my research, and I am truly grateful to all.

Appendix

Descendants of Hugh Beattie (1860–)

Hugh Beattie, my great-grandfather, was born on 20 March 1860 in Herdstown, parish of Donaghadee, Co. Down, and married Agnes Gilmore on 10 April 1882 in Ballycopeland, Donaghadee. Agnes was born on 26 January 1857 in Herdstown, Co.Down, Ireland

It is not known when Hugh died, but my Aunt Ellie, dad's sister, said that he was at the dock in Belfast when her family left for Canada on 27 March 1926. His wife Agnes had passed on before the marriage of their daughter Nellie on 11 December 1916 in Newtownards.

Children of Hugh Beattie and Agnes Gilmore:

1. James Beattie, born 31 August 1883 in Cotton, Bangor, Co. Down, Ireland; died 31 August 1953 in Strathcona, Lennox and Addington. Ontario, Canada; married Margaret Allen on 24 September 1906 at Shore Street Presbyterian Church, Donaghadee, Co. Down, Ireland.

   Children of James Beattie and Margaret Allen:

   i. John Joseph Allen Beattie, born 8 April 1906 in Cotton, Bangor, Co. Down, Ireland; died 24 June 1952 in Cleveland, Cuyahoga, Ohio, United States.
   ii. Charles ("Charlie") Beattie, born 25 March 1909 in Cotton, Bangor, Co. Down, Ireland; died 1962 in Newburgh, Lennox and Addington, Ontario, Canada; married Theresa Baldwin on 22 July 1932 in Morven, Lennox and Addington, Ontario, Canada.
   iii. Eleanor ("Ellie") Hilda Beattie, born 17 April 1911 in Cotton, Bangor, Co. Down, Ireland; died 31 October 31, 2008 in Selby, Lennox and Addington, Ontario, Canada; married Solomon Elgin Baldwin on 16 March 1942 in Camden East, Lennox and Addington, Ontario, Canada.

Eleanor Beattie (photo: 1927).

iv. Hugh Beattie, born 5 November 1913 in Cotton, Bangor, Co. Down, Ireland; died 13 November 1974 in Napanee, Lennox and Addington, Ontario, Canada; married Alma Marjorie Alkenbrack on 4 May 1939 in Camden East, Lennox and Addington, Ontario, Canada.

v. Archibald ("Archie") Beattie, born 1 March 1916 in Cotton, Bangor, Co. Down, Ireland; died 12 May 2007 in Amherstview, Lennox and Addington, Ontario; married Marjorie Violet Brant on 3 October 1941 in Tyendinaga, Hastings, Ontario, Canada.

vi. William James Beattie, born 3 February 1918 in Cotton, Bangor, Co. Down, Ireland; died 19 October 1993 in Napanee, Lennox and Addington, Ontario, Canada.

vii. Robert Moore Beattie, born 5 June 1920 in Cotton, Bangor, Co. Down, Ireland; died 1 February 2003 in Napanee, Lennox and Addington, Ontario, Canada; married Dorothy Helen Lyman on 8 August 1947 in Enterprise, Lennox and Addington, Ontario, Canada.

viii. Agnes Jane Beattie, born 29 October 1923 in Cotton, Bangor, Co. Down, Ireland; died 30 June 1979 in Kingston, Frontenac, Ontario, Canada .

ix. [private]

x. Sidney Beattie, born 20 February 1928 in Adolphustown,

Lennox and Addington, Ontario, Canada (died same day).

2. John Nelson Beattie, born 16 August 1888 in Co. Down, Ireland; died 25 May 1949 in Yarker, Lennox and Addington, Ontario, Canada; married Leah Isabella Conway on 3 May 1906 at Shore Street Presbyterian Church, Donaghadee, Co. Down, Ireland; next married Leita Marion Allen McWilliams on 19 May 1932 at Newburgh United Church, Newburgh, Lennox and Addington, Ontario, Canada.

   Children of John Nelson Beattie and Leita Marion Allen McWilliams:

   i. Roy McWilliams Beattie, born 4 October 1933 in Camden East, Lennox and Addington County, Ontario, Canada; died 7 April 2001 in Stone Mill, Lennox and Addington, Ontario, Canada; married on 30 August 1952 in Switzerville, Lennox and Addington, Ontario, Canada.
   ii. Ross Nelson Beattie, born 24 September 1934 in Camden East Township, Lennox and Addington, Ontario, Canada; died 21 August 2011 in Cobourg, Ontario, Canada; married on 24 May 1958.

3. Charles ("Charlie") Beattie, born ca.1889 in Co. Down Ireland; died Cataraqui, Frontenac, Ontario, Canada.

4. Ellenor ("Nellie") Jane Beattie, born 11 March 1894 in Ballyfotherly, Bangor, Co. Down, Ireland; died 3 June 1951 in Cataraqui, Frontenac, Ontario, Canada; married Robert Gaw Moore on 11 December 1916 in Newtownards, Co. Down, Ireland.

   Children of Elleanor Jane Beattie and Robert Gaw Moore:

   i. Mary Agnes Moore, born 28 June 1917 in Co. Down, Ireland; died 17 August 1965 in Niagara Falls, Ontario, Canada.
   ii. John Beattie Moore, born 29 June 1919 in Ballyalicock, Newtownards, Co. Down, Ireland; died 26 September 1977

in Tamworth, Lennox and Addington, Ontario, Canada; married Lois Vale Nixon on 31 August 1941 in Peterborough, Ontario, Canada.

iii. Christina Beattie Moore, born 14 January 1921 in Cotton, Bangor, Co. Down, Ireland; died 29 October 1960 in Toronto, Ontario, Canada.

iv. Robert Gaw Moore, born 24 January 1924 in Glasgow, Scotland; died 26 October 1982 in Deseronto, Hastings, Ontario, Canada.

v. Charles Beattie Moore, born 2 April 1927 in Canada; died 27 December 2000 in Napanee, Lennox and Addington, Ontario, Canada; married Kathleen Frances Hanaghan on 15 November 1948.

vi. Margaret Edna Moore, born 3 February 1929; married Harvey John Jelley on 4 June 1945 in Cataraqui, Frontenac, Ontario, Canada.

vii. Hughena Eleanor Jane Moore, born 31 October 1931; died 22 April 1990 in Kingston, Frontenac, Ontario, Canada; married John Lewis Robinson on 25 September 1952.

viii. William Frederick Alexander Moore, born 19 April 1933; died 30 September 1993.

5. Agnes Elizabeth Beattie, born 25 August 1896 in Ballyfotherly, Bangor, Co. Down, Ireland; died before 1915 in Newtownards, Co. Down, Ireland.

6. Christina Beattie, born 1899 in Cotton, Bangor, Co. Down, Ireland.

CHAPTER FOUR

Working in the Belfast Shipyards

My Story

BY SAMUEL J. STEWART (AUSTRALIA)

The following recollection was written in 2006 by my father Samuel James Stewart (1931-2007) just before he was diagnosed with lung cancer. I had asked him to write about his life in Harland and Wolff for the Titanic Society, which he was interested in joining. Sadly, he never got the chance—lung cancer took his life within fourteen weeks of diagnosis. Possibly the cancer was contracted while he worked in the yard. As an apprentice electrician, he was routinely covered in asbestos powder that insulated the hulls. – Alison Aldersea

MY GRANDFATHER SAMUEL STEWART[1] WAS a holder-on[2] in H&W [Harland and Wolff] and worked on board the Titanic. His nickname was "Hard Egg" because his piece [sandwich] everyday in the yard was 2 slices of buttered bread and one or two hard boiled eggs.

During the First World War, he was sent to the port of Seaforth to

[1] Samuel Stewart started his working life at the shipyard in Barrow-in-Furness, England, later famous for building submarines. He lived there with his aunt Margaret Stewart McBride and her family for a short while and can be found with them in the 1901 census.

[2] A "holder-on" places a heated steel rivet into a hole drilled through a metal plate and jams the head of the rivet in place while the other end is hammered flat against the plate by a riveter.

be sent to the Somme. Boarding the ship he slipped on the gangplank and broke his leg. He went to hospital. All of his mates were later killed on the Somme.

Samuel "Hard Egg" Stewart (front row, left) in England training for action in Somme, France during World War 1.

During the Second World War, we had a house at 26 Clandeboye Place, Bangor, and my grandfather spent time in Belfast and some time in Bangor. He travelled to Harland's on a train during and after the war. One day he was in the last compartment together with one other traveller [and] for some reason the train stopped at Sydenham. The Holywood train, unaware that the Bangor train had stopped at Sydenham, ploughed into it, killing my granda and his fellow traveller. They were so badly mutilated that the only way to tell them apart was the contents of their pockets.[3]

When the funeral took place—horse-drawn of course—the crowd was very big because everyone knew "Hard Egg". When the tail of the

[3] This accident took place on 15 January 1945. Nineteen people were killed and forty one injured. Most of the dead were from Bangor. Samuel Stewart was the only one from Belfast. According to family history, he always sat in the last carriage of the train with two mates to play cards. They were all killed.

procession was leaving Saunders St. [where he lived off the Newtownards Rd], the start of the funeral had passed the Holywood Arches over a mile away.

In the Stewart family, my granda & granny had 5 sons and one daughter. All the sons worked in H&W—3 shipwrights and 2 drillers. [One of them], my uncle James ("Jamsie"), left the yard to join the Navy. He was put on board the HMS *Hood*. Early [in his stint] on the *Hood* he fell and had to go to hospital. He was lucky because the *Hood* was later sunk.[4]

When I was born in 1931, my name was sent in to H&W to be an apprentice electrician. At 16, I began work at Harland's. Our first learning period was the school. There you were taught by 5th-year apprentices to wire simple circuits. You were there for about 3 months. During that period I worked with Billy Bingham of football fame.[5] His father and mine were mates.

The next part of our training was in the temporary light shop, making temporary lights for use during the building of ships.

When I finished my period on temporary lights I was moved on to a tanker called "Lotoreium". I was put into Joe Brown's squad and was told to work with, of all people, Danny Blanchflower.[6] I was with Danny for a few weeks. During that time, on Monday lunch, he would draw the shape of a football [soccer] ground [field] on the bulkhead and work out why somebody had got past him on Saturday and how he should have done it. I knew he was going places.

I then went to Davy Balnave's squad at the deep water on board 1220 or the *Eagle*—probably the only boat ever where some apprentices had all their 5 years on one boat. The *Eagle* aircraft carrier was docked on the left wharf of the deep water and had been in that place for many years. It was a very complicated ship to find your way around, having 2

[4] On 24 May 1941, early in the Battle of the Denmark Strait, the HMS Hood was struck by several German shells and exploded.

[5] Billy Bingham was a professional footballer (soccer player) who played for Glentoran in Belfast before moving to England where he played for a number of teams. Between 1951 and 1963, he won 56 caps for Northern Ireland, scoring 10 international goals, and played at the 1958 FIFA World Cup.

[6] Robert Dennis "Danny" Blanchflower (1926–1993) was born in the Bloomfield district of east Belfast and gained international fame as a professional footballer in Great Britain.

hangar decks. The powers that be decided to move *Eagle*—known by all as 1220—to the right wharf, meaning that the gangway would be on the other side of the ship and I believe the gangway could no longer be placed on the same deck, making things a bit complicated. From memory, it was moved during working hours. Men who had been on it for years couldn't find their way off, and the next morning couldn't find their way to their "dugout"—that is where they kept their tools. This confusion lasted for weeks with some of the workers.

I was later transferred with Davy's squad to the ship *Edinburgh Castle*, on which I went on trials.

I finished my time as an apprentice on tankers and as a journeyman was given an apprentice called Derek Duggan[7]. When I look back—learning with Billy Bingham, my first journeyman was Danny Blanchflower and my first apprentice was Derek Duggan—and I never played football!

One of the most horrific things I experienced during my time at H&Ws was going past the *Reina Del Pacific* after the gangplank broke. There were bodies everywhere, including people I knew.[8]

A story which I think as funny was about Joe Brown, my first gaffer [foreman]. Joe and his wife had over 20 children. I knew some of them who worked in the yard. People who knew Joe found it hard to imagine how he achieved over 20 children because he was always on overtime.

The house he lived in just off the Newtownards Rd—Josephine Street I believe—was 2 houses knocked into one. Joe was, for some reason, not working overtime. His wife was not pregnant. She asked Joe would he mind the kids while she and her mate went to the "POP", the Popular Cinema.[9] Joe agreed. When the picture session ended, she walked home with her mate, but coming to Josephine St., there were cops everywhere. People in the street had alerted the police when their kids went missing.

---

[7] Alexander Derek Dougan (1938–2007) was born in east Belfast and had a successful career as a professional footballer in Ireland and England.

[8] Dad may be getting this mixed up with a different incident. The *Reina Del Pacifico* was damaged by an engine room explosion off the Belfast coast on 12 September 1947. On 31 January 1955, the gangplank on the *Juan Peron* collapsed, killing around eighteen people. Apparently Dad's uncle Tommy Stewart jumped into the water to save someone's life and was rewarded with £100.

[9] The Popular Cinema, now closed, was located at Bridge End, Lower Newtownards Road in Belfast.

Joe had put them to bed thinking they were his!

I was the first of the family to leave the yard. I became a photographer and eventually bought over John Bell's shop in Garfield St.[10] During that period, I was founder of 'The Professional Photographers Association of Northern Ireland.' That was in 1966.

The author shortly after he started his photography business in Belfast (ca. 1960).

As a photographer, I was involved with car companies, especially Houston and Williamson[11] of Crumlin Rd. Archie Williamson told me

[10] Before this, my dad had a studio on High St and later a shop on the Shankill Rd.
[11] A funeral parlour.

a funny story one day. It seems his firm was so busy one day they phoned up another major car company to borrow 5 cars. They asked that it be delivered to Houston & Williamson. They never arrived. It seems the man who took the request ordered "5 cars for H&W." They were at Harland and Wolff's all day!

Working in Harland's taught me more about life than any other job I have worked at. I will always remember my first wage in H&W—£1, 1s, 1d per week.

* * *

Before we close my dad's story, one more famous name must be mentioned—Alex ("Higgy") Higgins, world champion snooker player. Dad got to know him when a very young and broke Higgy started making the rounds of the clubs. Dad was a very good snooker player himself and took the young Higgy under his wing after he got to know him at the YMCA. He bought him his first cue and paid for his entrance into a few competitions. My grandfather Sammy Stewart didn't approve of Higgy, who even then was a bit of a wild one. After we had emigrated to Australia, Dad got a letter from Higgy asking him to come back to Belfast and be his manager. Dad didn't do this, but remained friends with Higgy for some years. And when Higgy toured Australia, Dad caught up with him. –A.A

The author (shown here) was a good friend of world champion snooker player Alex "Higgy" Higgins.

CHAPTER FIVE

In Search of Lost Kin

The Megraws of Magherascouse, County Down

BY STANLEY R. MEGRAW (CANADA)

IN THE FALL OF 1845, a disease infected much of Ireland's potato crops, leading to one of the bleakest times in Irish history. During the next several years, hundreds of thousands of deaths occurred as a result of the "Great Hunger" (*an Gorta Mór).* For those that survived, many were sent to overcrowded workhouses, while others felt compelled to emigrate and seek a better life. Among those to leave Ireland was John Megraw, a farmer from County Down.

In 1849, John and his wife Isabella Wallace, along with two young children, sailed for North America to settle in an area that was then known as the Province of Canada (present-day Ontario).

A century later, in 1949, a nineteen-year-old named William ("Bill") Stanley Megraw left his family home on Ladas Drive in Belfast to begin a new life in Northwestern Ontario, Canada.

Nearly sixty more years would pass before someone would discover how two Irish immigrants, who came to Canada one hundred years apart, shared a common past. That person was me, son of Bill Megraw, and this is the story of how I traced my Irish heritage back to a small townland in the parish of Comber, Co. Down.

The Mystery of John Megraw

I first became aware of John Megraw during a family vacation in Southern Ontario in 1962. That was when I met three of his granddaughters—-Winnifred, Edna and Viola ("Ola") Megraw

One of the granddaughters had in her possession a copy of the *Paisley Advocate*, a weekly newspaper dated 20 February 1890. This particular issue was a special edition celebrating the 25th anniversary of Paisley, a small settlement in Bruce County, Ontario where John Megraw raised his family after immigrating to Canada.

The owner and editor of the *Advocate* was John's son Ainsley Megraw, who wrote about the history of Paisley as well as some details of his father's early days in the area. Included was this interesting fact, which would greatly help me in my research later on:

> The oldest mason in Paisley is Mr. John Megraw who was initiated in Union Lodge, No. 136, Ballygowan, Ireland … in 1842, and who it will thus be seen is nearly a half century mason, of whom there are few in Canada today.
>
> – *Paisley Advocate*, 20 February 1890

We were also shown a copy of John's Megraw obituary, which provided a little more information about his Irish origins:

> Mr. Megraw was born at Balleygowan [sic], Ireland, on Nov. 15th, 1819. While still a young man of 30 years, he emigrated to Canada with his wife and two small children.
>
> – *Paisley Advocate*, 15 March 1906

I was immediately intrigued that someone from so long ago shared the same, rather uncommon surname as me (Megraw) and came from the same country as my dad (Ireland). But while I was told there was a family connection, no one knew what that relationship was. So, for more than four decades I would often wonder, "Who was John Megraw?" and "How are we related?"

This portrait of John Megraw (1819-1906) was included in a special edition of the Paisley Advocate *that was published by his son Ainsley Megraw on 20 February 1890.*

The Search Begins

Schooling, a family, and a career had taken priority in the interim, but the mystery of John Megraw was eventually pursued with determination in the spring of 2006.

I started by researching family papers and other records that were available in Canada. While much was discovered about John Megraw's life and family in this country, I found nothing about his Irish roots other than he was born in Ballygowan, Co. Down.[1]

In January of 2007, I turned my attention to Ireland and decided to start with my father's immediate family and trace his ancestors backwards in an attempt to determine how we may be related to John Megraw. It

[1] Although no birth or baptismal record has been found, later research suggests John Megraw was born in Magherascouse, Co. Down.

didn't take long, however, to realize that this would be no easy task.

I had very little knowledge of my paternal Irish roots when I first started to research John Megraw. All I knew was that my grandparents were Bertram Stanley Rutherford Megraw (known as "Stanley") and Eleanor Lucinda Simpson, and that they once lived on Ladas Drive in Belfast before moving to Lisburn sometime before 1963. So my first step was to contact the Ulster Historical Foundation (UHF) in Belfast to see if they could assist in any way. I provided them with the names of my grandparents and what little I knew ahout John Megraw.

The UHF found the original marriage registration for John Megraw and Isabella Wallace, which showed they were married in the Ballygowan Presbyterian Church in the parish of Killinchy on 17 February 1846. It recorded that John was a farmer living in Magherascouse and that his father's name was Robert Megraw.

The UHF also located a record of my grandparent's marriage, which is transcribed below:

Marriage Transcription—Bertram Stanley Rutherford Megraw, full age, bachelor, manager of hardware store, 5 Ormiston Gardens, Belfast, son of James Megraw, boiler maker; married Eleanor Lucinda Simpson, full age, spinster, Hillcrest, Saintfield, daughter of W.G. Simpson, teacher, witnesses: Samuel Stewart & Louisa Maud Simpson; First Saintfield Presbyterian Church; 18th April 1922 .

Unfortunately, this information did not get me any closer in determining whether there was an ancestral link between John Megraw and my family. However, it did bring home the fact that I needed to learn a lot more about my ancestors if I was ever to be successful in finding this link. Therefore, I temporarily abandoned my research on John Megraw and set about to learn what I could about my family roots in Ireland.

I again contacted the Ulster Historical Foundation (UHF) for assistance and they were able to provide me with another key piece of information—the marriage record for the parents of my grandfather Stanley Megraw:

Marriage Transcription—James Megraw, full age, bachelor, shipbuilder, 48 Lagan Village, son of James Megraw, blacksmith; married Emily

Lowry, full age, spinster, dressmaker, 133 McClure Street, Belfast, daughter of Thomas Lowry, builder, witnesses: William Megraw & William Lowry; Cliftonpark Congregational Church; 6 October 1882.

I now knew the name of my grandfather (Bertram Stanley Rutherford Megraw), my great-grandfather (James Megraw Jr.) and my great-great-grandfather (James Megraw Sr.).

The UHF also located testamentary records that showed James Megraw Sr. had died on 15 December 1870 at the age of 41 years and that his wife's name was "Jane". Unfortunately, they could not locate a registration of their marriage, so the name of my great-great-great-grandfather remained unknown. And I was still no wiser as to the identity of John Megraw.

About eighteen months after beginning this research journey, I caught a lucky break.

Solving the Mystery

When my dad emigrated from Ireland, he carried with him an address book, which I had scanned as part of my family records. One day, while idly googling "megraw" as a keyword, I got a hit that matched an entry in my dad's book.

I checked Google Maps and found that the residence was located just on the outskirts of Liverpool, England. I searched a little further and found an email address that appeared to have some connection to the occupant. With nothing to lose, I decided to write the person, explaining who I was and describing my interest in researching the Megraw family tree.

Within a short time, I received a reply and learned that I was now in contact with a second cousin. The address I had found was his mother's house where my dad had spent his last night before boarding the RMS *Ascania* in Liverpool to immigrate to Canada in 1949.

During the next few weeks, my cousin provided me with details about the siblings of my grandfather Stanley Megraw, and I made contact with other cousins, who helped to fill in other parts of the family tree. We all shared the same great-grandfather (James Megraw Jr.) and so the information I received was all related to his descendants. No one knew anything about his ancestors.

As I continued to correspond with my cousin in England, certain facts came to light that greatly advanced my research, including the following snippet that led to the mystery of John Megraw finally being solved.

> … [a] loss to our search has been a book published privately in the early 1920s - a history of the Saintfield Masonic Lodge. This included a section on families whose links with the lodge spanned several generations, including of course the Megraws … But I just don't know what happened to the book.
>
> – Email from a cousin in England, 24 September 2007

The book, as it turned out, was *The History and Antiquities of Freemasonry in Saintfield, County Down*, and it was written in 1924 by William George Simpson, the father-in-law of my grandfather Stanley Megraw.

It took a few weeks to track down a copy of the rare, out-of-print book and the effort was well rewarded. One section of it describes Stanley's involvement in the Masonic organization and includes this passage about his father (my great-grandfather):

> Bro. JAMES MEGRAW, P.M., P.R., father of the above named Bro. Stanley Megraw, is secretary of Lodge 436, Ballymacarrett, and an enthusiastic Mason of nearly 40 years' service. His uncle, Bro. JOHN MEGRAW, was Master of Lodge 136, Ballygowan; and R.W. Bro. Major AINSLEY MEGRAW, son of the last-named, was District Deputy Grand Master of British Columbia, deceased 1923. The latter's father served Masonry for 65 years, his own service reaching 40 years.
>
> – W.G. Simpson, 1924[2]

After more than four decades of wondering, I now had my answer. John Megraw was the uncle of my great-grandfather James Megraw Jr., which meant he was the brother of my great-great-grandfather James Megraw Sr.

Now I was faced with another question—who was James Megraw Sr.?

[2] W.G. Simpson, *History & Antiquities of Freemasonry in Saintfield, Co. Down* (Downpatrick, Co. Down: Down Recorder, 1924).

At this stage in my research (October 2007), all I knew was that James Megraw Sr. was a blacksmith (from his son's marriage registration) and that his wife's name was "Jane" (from testamentary records).

Digging Deeper into my Family History

My first task was to find the marriage registration for my great-great-grandfather James Megraw Sr. I soon located a transcription online at the Ulster Historical Foundation website (now AncestryIreland).[3] His family name was recorded as "McGraw".[4]

MARRIAGE TRANSCRIPTION—JAMES MCGRAW [SIC], FULL AGE, BACHELOR, BLACK SMITH, BOND ST., BELFAST, SON OF ROBERT MCGRAW [SIC], FARMER; MARRIED JANE PATTERSON, FULL AGE, WIDOW, BOND ST., BELFAST, DAUGHTER OF WILLIAM MCMILLIN [SIC], FARMER, WITNESSES: HUGH BLAIR & MARGARET MCWILLIAM; ALFRED PLACE CHURCH; 12 NOVEMBER 1853.

I now had confirmation that my great-great-great-grandfather was Robert Megraw, and so my next task was to find out more about him. That was when I first became acquainted with Fiona Doyle Jones and Sheila Phillips.

Fiona had just started the County Down Genealogy group on Yahoo![5] and was the coordinator for the Ireland Genealogy Projects, Co. Down website.[6] The latter featured a "brickwall" page for people to post requests for assistance in finding their elusive ancestors. On it, Fiona had written "… we have a very kind researcher who picks names from those listed on the brickwall and conducts some research at PRONI [Public Record Office of Northern Ireland] to help breakdown your brickwalls."

The "Secret Researcher," I later learned, was Fiona's good friend Sheila Phillips. When I found that PRONI held a copy of the will for my great-great-great-grandfather Robert Megraw, I approached Fiona to see if

[3] Ulster Historical Foundation (www.ancestryireland.com).

[4] I later obtained a copy of the marriage registration which showed that James signed his name as "Megraw".

[5] Now known as Fiona's County Down Genealogy Group (http://groups.yahoo.com/neo/groups/CountyDownGenealogy/info).

[6] Ireland Genealogy Projects (http://www.igp-web.com/).

Sheila could assist in transcribing it for me. It didn't take long to get a response:

> Hello Stan. This is Sheila Phillips – I believe you would like me to take a look at a couple of Wills for you! … I just LOVE looking at Wills – as I'm sure Fiona must have told you!! It is absolutely no problem at all – and they are on my list for next Wednesday (that's when I make my weekly pilgrimage to PRONI!).
>
> – Email from Sheila Phillips, 29 January 2009

True to her word, Sheila tracked down the will for Robert Megraw at PRONI and transcribed it for me.

Robert was a farmer from Magherascouse, Co. Down, and he died on 18 September 1864. His will identified three sons: James Megraw (my great-great-great-grandfather), Robert Megraw Jr., and Ansley Megraw. I can only surmise that the reason he didn't bequeath anything to his son John Megraw was because John was now living in Canada. Nevertheless, I now had two additional ancestors to research and learn about—Robert Megraw Jr. and Ansley Megraw.

Also not mentioned in the will of Robert Megraw Sr. was his wife, who had most likely predeceased him. This was a major disappointment because I had no clue who she was, and I held little hope of ever learning her identity. She would have married Robert before the start of civil registration of non-Catholic marriages in 1845 and died prior to 1864 when the civil registration of deaths commenced. Many of the other records that are available in this time period (early to mid-nineteenth century) focus on documenting males as land tenants or owners (e.g. Tithe Applotment Books, freeholders lists, etc).

So while I had solved one mystery (the identity of John Megraw), I now had another—who was the wife of Robert Megraw Sr.? Since I had resigned myself to the fact that it would be very difficult, if not impossible to learn her name, I more or less forgot about her and continued on with researching the other parts of my family tree. That is, until January 2009, when I stumbled across a book that was self-published by a family historian living in New Zealand.

An Unexpected Discovery

Beyond Ballygowan: The Adair-Moore Story was written and published by Janet Benfell in 2008. I first came across a reference to it on WorldCat, an online library catalogue of books and other materials.

From my research of church records, I knew that Ballygowan was a townland in the parish of Killinchy, County Down, where some of my Megraw ancestors had been baptized or married. However, I was also aware that Ballygowan was the name of several other townlands, both in Down and elsewhere in Ireland. What caught my eye with this particular publication was that "Sara Megraw" was listed as a keyword.

I wrote to the author and learned that she was the great-granddaughter of Sarah Ann Megraw who had married James Adair on 28 December 1847 in the Ballygowan Presbyterian Church in the parish of Killinchy. Sarah Ann and James Adair immigrated to New Zealand aboard the *Chariot of Fame* in 1862 where, for reasons unknown to their descendants, they adopted the surname of "Moore"; hence, the subtitle of the book.

I was also told that the church minister had not recorded the fathers' names on the marriage registration for Sarah Ann Megraw and James Adair. However, the author had a copy of Sarah Ann's death certificate and it records her parents as Robert Megraw and Martha Megraw (nee Bowman).

Something else I learned from the author was that Sarah Ann (Megraw) Adair/Moore had a sister named Agnes Megraw. She married Thomas Gourley on 3 February 1862 in the Ballygowan Presbyterian Church and they also immigrated to New Zealand.

So as a result of finding the book *Beyond Ballygowan*, I not only had a name for the wife of my great-great-great grandfather Robert Megraw Sr., but I discovered that he had two daughters in addition to the four sons I had found through my own research.

Completing the Story

I opened this chapter by introducing two characters—John Megraw and my dad William ("Bill") Stanley Megraw—who emigrated from Ireland to Canada exactly one hundred years apart. I then described my journey to learn more about John Megraw and how it led me to discover the details

Following the death of Robert Megraw Sr. in 1864, his son Robert Megraw Jr. inherited the family farm in Magherascouse, Co. Down (shown above in the background). Robert Jr. married Agnes Bowman and together they were blessed with six daughters. With no sons to take over the farm, however, Robert Jr. had instructed his executors to sell out everything he owned after he died on 9 July 1908. The farm was taken over by his son-in-law Robert Townley (ca. 1873-1948) and today is occupied by one of his great-granddaughters (photo: 2010).

of my Irish heritage. In this section, I summarize my findings.

What I have learned is that my great-great-great-grandfather Robert Megraw Sr., a farmer, and his wife, Martha Bowman, raised a family of six children in the townland of Magherascouse, Co. Down, during the first half of the 1800s:

- Sarah Ann Megraw (ca. 1818–1916)
- John Megraw (1819–1906)
- James Megraw Sr. (ca. 1825–1870)[7]
- Agnes Megraw (ca. 1827–1911)
- Robert Megraw Jr (ca. 1830–1908)
- Ansley Megraw (ca. 1833–1878)

The two youngest children, Robert Jr. and Ansley, remained in Magherascouse where they started their own families, while the others left the family farm and began a new life elsewhere. Sarah Ann and her sister Agnes immigrated to New Zealand, John immigrated to Canada, and James Sr., my great-great-grandfather, moved to Belfast where he worked as a blacksmith.

James Megraw Sr. married Jane (McMillan) Patterson in 1853 and they had four sons. The second eldest was my great-grandfather James Megraw Jr. (ca. 1860–1934), who was employed as a yard manager in the Belfast shipyards.

James Megraw Jr. married Emily McCreary Lowry in 1882 and they raised a family of four daughters and four sons. Their youngest son was my grandfather Bertram Stanley Rutherford Megraw (1894–1968).

Stanley Megraw worked as a hardware store manager and married Eleanor Lucinda Simpson in 1922. They had two sons—Robert Annesley Megraw (1923–1988) and my dad, William Stanley Megraw (1929–2003)—who were both born in Portadown, Co. Armagh. The family later resided on Ladas Drive in Belfast, where my dad left home at the age of 19 years to immigrate to Canada; a century after another Megraw left his family's farm in Magherascouse, Co. Down to immigrate to Canada. That would be John Megraw (1819–1906), who I now know to be my dad's great-granduncle.

---

[7] My great-great-grandfather.

* * *

When I first set out on my research journey, it was not with the intention of learning about my Irish heritage. I was simply curious—"Who was John Megraw?" and "How are we related?" I never envisioned that I would discover so much about my family's past. And it all began more than fifty years ago when I was shown an old newspaper that had been published almost seventy-five years earlier.

Along the way, other publications have proven invaluable in helping me to break through my brick walls, most notably a book written by my great-grandfather William George Simpson,[8] and another written by Janet Benfell,[9] a third cousin. It is my hope that the chapter I have written here will also be of some value to others interested in learning more about their own family history.

---

[8] W.G. Simpson, *History & Antiquities of Freemasonry in Saintfield, Co. Down* (Downpatrick, Co. Down: Down Recorder, 1924).

[9] Janet Benfell, *Beyond Ballygowan: The Adair-Moore Story* (Ashburton, New Zealand: 2008).

CHAPTER SIX

Family Roots

The McClurgs of Killinchy in the Woods, County Down

BY NANCY MCCORMACK SCHAALJE (CANADA)

KILLINCHY IN THE WOODS—I love the sound of that name—is a townland in County Down located on the western edge of the parish of Killyleagh and consists of about 988 acres. In some of the older records, it is also referred to as "Killinshey in the Woods" and "Killinsha of the Woods". The appendage distinguishes it from another townland in County Down called Killinchy, which was occasionally referred to as "Killinchy on the Plain".

In the early days, Killinchy in the Woods probably had more trees before they were removed to facilitate the growing of crops and the raising of cattle or sheep. Perhaps it looked like the picture on the next page which was taken in 2009 on Glasswater Road which runs east-west through the townland. The property of Thomas McClurg, my great grandfather, is located on Derryboy Road near the junction of the Glasswater Road.

Killinchy in the Woods has always been special to us and used by our family to name homes and cottages here in Canada. It is the birthplace of my mother, Maud Watts Gibson Morrow (married surname of McCormack), as well as her mother, Christiana McClurg, and perhaps her grandfather Thomas McClurg.

The earliest record I have found of the McClurg name is a registered deed recorded in 1755. The grantor of the deed was Hamilton Clewlow, and the lease was granted to James McClurg (sometimes spelled "McLurg"). The deed is for the lease of land consisting of 22 acres[1] in "Killinshey of the Woods" for either twenty-one years or for the lives of James McClurg's two sons, William and Thomas. I do not as yet have documented proof, but I believe that Thomas may be the father of my great-grandfather James McClurg.

Glasswater Road near the junction with Derryboy Road in Killinchy in the Woods, Co. Down (photo: 2009).

James McClurg (or McLurg) was born about 1782 and married Ann Morrow of Ballyalgan about 1812. Ann died on 11 December 1871 in Killinchy in the Woods. I have not found a death record for James, but I speculate he died sometime in the early 1860s. His name appears in the 1827 Tithe Applotment Book for the parish of Killyleagh, but not in the 1864 Griffith's Valuation. In the family Bible, he recorded the birth of a grandchild born in 1860, but not the birth of another born in 1863.

[1] Cunningham Measure (1 acre = 6250 square yards)..

James McClurg and Ann Morrow raised a family of six children:

- Thomas McClurg (ca. 1814–1888)
- Hamilton McClurg (ca. 1818–)
- Robert McClurg (1821–1908)
- Mary Ann McClurg (ca. 1823–1896)
- Joseph McClurg/McLeod (1826–1898)
- William McClurg (ca. 1830–)

Thomas McClurg (ca. 1814–1888)

Thomas McClurg, my great-grandfather, was born about 1814 in Killinchy in the Woods. He married Jane Wallace who was born about 1814 on Simmy Island in the parish of Killyleagh. She was the daughter of Thomas Wallace and Agnes Carroll (see "Chapter Sixteen" for details on the Wallace family).

Thomas was a farmer and a carpenter. His children were born in a house whose current address is 173a Derryboy Road. I have not been able to establish the age of the house, but it may been built by Thomas or by

House on Derryboy Road where the children of my great-grandfather Thomas McClurg were born (photo: 2009).

his father, James McClurg.

Thomas was involved with the local school and was chairman of the board at one time. Two of his daughters taught in the school, which had the possibility of adding income to the McClurg family. However, the school board decided not to pay them since they were not certified as teachers.

Thomas may also have been involved with the building of Raffrey Presbyterian Church in 1843 where some of his children were baptised. He and his wife, Jane Wallace, are buried in the Raffrey churchyard. Their tombstone is visible in the photo below, just at the bottom of the far right window.

Raffrey Presbyterian Church where Thomas McClurg and his wife Jane Wallace are buried (photo: 2009).

Thomas McClurg and Jane Wallace had nine children, five of whom immigrated to Australia. Family oral history indicates that Jane stood on a hill overlooking Strangford Lough and watched as some of her children sailed to England where they would board a ship for Australia. She knew she would never see these children again. Eventually, two of them did return just for visits, but not before their mother's death in 1881. Their father, Thomas McClurg, later died in 1888.

The children of Thomas McClurg and Jane Wallace were:

1. Jane McClurg (1838–1908) married James Martin on 30 October 1855 in the Raffrey Presbyterian Church. They were the parents of three children:

    i. Thomas Martin (ca. 1858–1895)[2]
    ii. Jane Martin (ca. 1863–896)
    iii. Georgina Martin (1865–)

2. Hamilton McClurg (1841–1926) immigrated to Australia and married Harriett Ann Hay in 1875. They were the parents of twelve children:

    i. Thomas William Wallace McClurg (1877–1959)
    ii. Hamilton John McClurg (1879–1963)
    iii. William McClurg (1881–1958)
    iv. Ethel May McClurg (1884–1957)
    v. Jane Wallace McClurg (1886–1972)
    vi. Daisy Victoria McClurg (1888–1959)
    vii. Gertrude Mary Eleanor McClurg (1890–1962)
    viii. Amy Alice McClurg (1891–1971)
    ix. Francis Ann McClurg (1892–1893)
    x. Wallace Gordon McClurg (1894–1894)
    xi. Lottie Josephine Mcclurg (1895–1966)
    xii. Lily McClurg (1898–1898)

    Some of the children were born in New South Wales, Australia, and others in Victoria, Australia. There are many descendents of Hamilton McClurg in Australia today.

3. Agnes Wallace McClurg[3] (1844–1915) immigrated to New York

[2] Thomas Martin (1838-1908) married Sarah Coulter on 22 August 1888 in Saintfield, Co. Down. Ireland, and they had two children—Jane Martin, born in 1891; and James Martin, born in 1893. James invented the Martin ejector seat which is still saving the lives of jet pilots who must abandon their aircraft. He was knighted in 1965.

[3] On the birth records for Agnes' children, she is sometimes recorded as "Nancy

City in the United States about 1865 where she married John Morrow about 1866. He was also from Ireland, and it is possible they knew each other before immigrating, but I have not been able to find his parents or birthplace.

Agnes Wallace McClurg and John Morrow had eleven children:

i. Jane Wallace Morrow (1869–1902)
ii. James Hamilton Morrow (1870–1942)
iii. Maria MacCullough Morrow (1873–1895)
iv. Agnes W. Morrow[4] (1874–)
v. Agnes A. Morrow (1875–)
vi. John Hamilton Morrow (1877–1879)
vii. unnamed infant Morrow (1879–)
viii. Margaret G. Morrow (1880–aft 1915)
ix. John Francis Morrow (1884–1885)
x. John Russel Morrow (1887–1940)
xi. Frank B. Morrow (1889–1918)

4. Thomas McClurg (1847–1891) immigrated to Australia, where he died on 11 December 1891 near Cootamundra, New South Wales, as a result of drowning during a period of bad floods. He was unmarried.

5. Margaret Ann McClurg (1849–) married Edward Patman Coulter in 1885 in Belfast, Ireland. Edward was born in County Down about 1855. They later immigrated to Australia and had one son, Edward Dhu Coulter, who was born in 1890 in New South Wales and died about 1955.

6. Alice McClurg (1851–1934) was another child who immigrated to New South Wales, Australia, where she supported herself as a school teacher. She remained unmarried.

McLeod" (various spellings). However, the correct surname of McClurg is recorded on the marriage record of one of her sons.

[4] Agnes W. Morrow may have died in infancy.

7. James McClurg (1857–1903) immigrated to Australia, and married Nora Rush in 1886. They were the parents of three children who all lived in New South Wales:

    i. Mary McClurg (1888–)
    ii. James McClurg (1890–)
    iii. Alice McClurg (1894–)

    In 1888, following the death of his father Thomas McClurg, James inherited the family home in Killinchy in the Woods on the condition that he come home to Ireland and live there. Apparently, the only thing he had to do to fulfill that condition was to sleep in the house one night, which he did. James then put the house up for auction. Although his sister Christiana and her husband, Thomas Robert Morrow, had been living in the house, they were out-bid by a man from Belfast. It was then that the McClurg home went out of the family.

8. Susanna McClurg (1860-1896) married Andrew Cherry in 1888 in Saintfield, Co. Down. They had one daughter, Mary Wallace Cherry, who was born in 1889. They immigrated to New York City in 1891 and lived with Susanna's sister and brother-in-law, Agnes and John Morrow, before eventually getting their own flat.

    I have some wonderful letters written by Susanna to her sister Christiana, and they show how very homesick Susanna was for Ireland. I can't imagine how difficult the adjustment must have been moving from rural County Down to New York City.

    Susanna only survived five years in New York before succumbing to tuberculosis in 1896. Her husband and daughter later returned to Ireland, where he remarried.

9. Christiana McClurg (1863-1942) was my grandmother. In 1884, she married Thomas Robert Morrow in the Raffrey Presbyterian Church. Thomas Robert was the only child of Robert Morrow and Jane Carse.

    Christiana McClurg and Thomas Robert Morrow had eight children:

i. Jane Morrow, born 1885 in Ballywillin, Co. Down; died 1976 in Winnipeg, Manitoba, Canada; married John Crawford Davie on 31 March 1910 in Winnipeg, Manitoba, Canada (parents of three children).
ii. Thomas Morrow, born 1887 in Ballywillin, Co. Down; died 1972 in Belfast, Ireland; married Emma Matilda Yeates in 1913 in Raffrey, Co. Down (parents of eight children).
iii. Alice Morrow, born 1889 in Ballywillin, Co. Down; died 1944 in Toronto, Ontario, Canada; married Frederick Gaffikin on 26 January 1924 in Toronto, Ontario, Canada (no children).
iv. Margaret Morrow, born 1891 in Ballywillin, Co. Down; died 1962 in Miami, Florida, United States; married Francis Thomas Mason on 1 June 1916 in Campbellford, Ontario, Canada (no children).
v. Maud Watts Gibson Morrow (my mother), born 1894 in Killinchy in the Woods, Co. Down; died 1973 in Toronto, Onatio, Canada; married William White McCormack (my father) in Toronto, Ontario, Canada (parents of five children).
vi. Robert Morrow, born 1896 in Raffrey, Co. Down; died 1917 in France (no children).
vii. Anna Eleanor Kathleen Morrow, born 1903 in Belfast, Ireland; died 1904 in Belfast, Ireland.
viii. Christiana Morrow, born 1905 in Belfast, Ireland; died 1982 in Belfast, Ireland; married Richard Humphreys on 5 October 1926 in Belfast, Ireland (parents of two children).

Christiana and Thomas Robert lived part of their married life in her father's home in Killinchy in the Woods, perhaps caring for him and also raising some of their children. Following the sale of the McClurg home in about 1901, they moved to Ballywillin in the parish of Killyleagh for a period of time while her husband worked in Belfast.

Christiana's husband was a carpenter and worked on the Titanic. His boss was given free passage on the maiden voyage, but he was ill and offered it to my grandfather Thomas Robert.

However, the offer was withdrawn when the boss recovered enough to take the voyage.

My grandparents Thomas Robert Morrow and Christiana McClurg (photo: ca. 1915).

By 1911, Christiana and her husband were living on Farnham Street in Belfast. They later leased property at 63 Ormeau Road, which had two upper levels of living quarters and a store on the street level where Granny (Christiana) sold fruits, vegetables, and baked goods.

Thomas Robert Morrow died in 1925 and Christiana McClurg Morrow died in 1942. They are buried in the Raffrey Presbyterian churchyard.

Hamilton McClurg (ca. 1818–)

Hamilton McClurg has been a very elusive individual. I first learned about him from a letter written in 1892 by Susanna McClurg Cherry (1860–1896), the daughter of my great-grandfather Thomas McClurg (ca. 1814–1888). In the letter, Susanna wrote, "Aunt Catherine, Uncle Hamilton's wife, died."

It took me many years, but I eventually learned the identity of "Aunt

Catherine" from the death record of a woman who died in December 1891 in Brooklyn, New York, and was buried in the Greenwood Cemetery. Her name was Catherine McLeod, and she last resided at the same address in New York as Susanna McClurg Cherry.

As for "Uncle Hamilton", Catherine's husband, I have found a Hamilton McClurg who applied for a land grant in Artemesia, Ontario, Canada, about the same time as Joseph McClurg/McLeod, the brother of my great-grandfather. There is also a Hamilton McCloud/McLeoud listed on both the 1881 and 1891 censuses of Canada and living in Artemesia with the family of John and Jane McKee. His place of birth is shown as Ireland. Jane is the daughter of Joseph McClurg/McLeod, and if Joseph and Hamilton were brothers, then she would be Hamilton's niece.

The 1881 census shows Hamilton as a widow. However, the informant on the census form may not have had the correct information.

Robert McClurg (1821–1908)

I learned about Robert McClurg as a result of a trip I made to Ireland in 2009. During my visit, I attended the Raffrey Presbyterian Church, where I met Ethel McClurg Murdock and her parents, James and Flora McClurg. Ethel had researched her McClurg ancestry back to Robert McClurg and gave me a copy of her family tree. Since all the sons of my great-grandfather Thomas McClurg had immigrated to Australia in the 1800s, I was curious about this present-day McClurg family attending the same church and living in the same area as my ancestors.

When I got back to Canada and reviewed my research notes, I discovered that I had recorded the death of this Robert McClurg. The informant of the death was identified as "M. J. Meharry, niece". I knew that M. J. Meharry was in fact Margaret Jane Meharry, the daughter of Mary Ann McClurg and John Meharry. She was also my great-grandfather's niece. Thus, Robert McClurg was the brother of my great-grandfather Thomas McClurg (ca. 1814–1888).

The baptism of Robert McClurg on 4 June 1821 is registered in the records of the Killyleagh Parish Church of Ireland, and his parents are identified as James McClurg and Ann Morrow. Since Robert is the brother of my Thomas, I now had the names of my great-great-grandparents.

Robert McClurg married Agnes Morrow (ca. 1819–1911) about 1844.

Much of the information I have on Robert McClurg's five children and descendents was provided by Ethel McClurg Murdock.

The children of Robert McClurg and Agnes Morrow were:

1. Jane McClurg (1846–ca.1920) married James Ritchie in 1869 in Raffrey, Co. Down. Their first two children were born in County Down and the rest in Scotland.

    i. Agnes Jane Ferguson Ritchie (1870–)
    ii. William Ritchie (1871–)
    iii. Annie Ritchie (1872–)
    iv. Mary Frances Ritchie (1875–)
    v. Janet Ritchie (1878–)
    vi. Margaret Neilson Ritchie (1880–)

2. Anne McClurg (1849–) was born in Killinchy in the Woods. The 1900 United States census shows that she was living with her husband, Charles E. Day, in Paterson, Passaic, New Jersey. The census also indicates that she had emigrated from Ireland in 1871 and married about five years later. I have wondered why she went to this particular place, and so I plan to research to see if there were relatives that had previously settled there.

    Anne McClurg and Charles E. Day had two children and possibly another child who may have died in infancy.

    i. Annie Janet Day (1878–)
    ii. Minnie Day (1881–)

3. Thomas McClurg (1853–) was baptised on 21 February 1853 in the Killyleagh 1st Presbyterian Church. I have no further information on him.

4. Robert McClurg (1856–1942) was born on 5 September 1856 in Killinchy in the Woods. He married Margaret Anne Bailie in 1898 in Seaforde, Co. Down, and they had eleven children:

i. Robert McClurg (1900–1960)
ii. William McClurg (1902–1982)
iii. Mary Ann McClurg (1904–1992)
iv. Thomas John McClurg (1906–1981)
v. Isabella Jane McClurg (1908–1981)
vi. Margaret Jane Meharry McClurg (1911–1981)
vii. Samuel McClurg (1913–1985)
viii. Ellen McClurg (1914–2006)
ix. Sarah Alexandra McClurg (1915–1936)
x. Hamilton McNeilly McClurg (1917–1989)
xi. James Reid Bailie McClurg (1918–2012); married Emily Flora Stevenson.[5]

5. James McClurg (1864–) was born in Killinchy in the Woods and married Margaret Ann Ellison in 1892 in Saintfield, Co. Down. Their children were:

i. Thomas McClurg (1894–1939)
ii. James McClurg (1895–1962)
iii. Mary Agnes McClurg (1902–1979)

Mary Ann McClurg (ca. 1823–1896)

Mary Ann was born in Killinchy in the Woods. At age 21, in 1844, she married John Meharry, son of John Meharry and Margaret Morrow, in the Killyleagh 1st Presbyterian Church.

I had the photograph shown on the next page for over 40 years. However, it was unidentified. My mother thought it was a photo of a McClurg or a Meharry.

About a year ago, I sent it to a member of the Meharry Family Tree on TribalPages,[6] who passed it on to another Meharry relative, who recognized it immediately. The gentleman was her mother's Uncle John of Ireland—that would be John Meharry—and he is standing with his wife Mary Ann McClurg.

---

[5] Emily was alive in 2013.

[6] TribalPages (www.tribalpages.com/)

Moral of the story? Keep the pictures, even if they aren`t identified.

The identity of the couple in this photo remained a mystery to me for more than forty years. See text for their names (photo: ca. 1883).

Mary Ann and John Meharry were the parents of six children:

1. William Meharry (1845–1886)
2. James Meharry (1847–1874)
3. Thomas Meharry (1851–)
4. Margaret Jane Meharry (1853–)
5. Robert Meharry (1855–1935)
6. Ann Meharry (1858–1941)[7]

---

[7] I am quite sure that Ann (1858–1941), the daughter of Mary Ann McClurg and John

Joseph McClurg/McLeod (1826–1898)

Joseph was baptised in the Killyleagh Parish Church of Ireland on 26 April 1826. He may have been named for an uncle who had immigrated to the United States.

Joseph married Margaret Cunningham in 1849, and that same year the couple left for America. They first stayed briefly in New York State, but at the suggestion of one or more of Margaret's brothers, they travelled on to Ontario, Canada, where they applied for a land grant in the township of Artemisia. Shortly after their arrival in Canada, they began using "McLeod" (also spelled McCloud or McLoud), a surname which has been carried on by their descendants.

Margaret (Cunningham) McLeod died on 19 September 1895 and is buried in the Orange Valley Cemetery, Grey County, Ontario. The tombstone does not record her husband Joseph's death, and family lore suggests that he had returned to Ireland for a visit and died there. So I inquired at the Public Records Office of Northern Ireland (PRONI) and was able to obtain a copy of the inquest into his death He was staying with a Mary Cunningham and helping a neighbour when he died suddenly on 8 July 1898 in Ballyalgan, Co. Down. The inquest identified Mary Cunningham as his sister-in-law.

Joseph McClurg/McLeod and Margaret Cunningham had seven children:

1. James Irving McLeod (1850–1916) married Scottish lassie Christine Ramsey McKenzie in 1876. They were the parents of seven children, all of whom were born in Little Current, Manitoulin, Ontario, except the first child, who was born in Markdale, Grey, Ontario.

    i. Joseph William McLeod (1877–1946)
    ii. James Irving McLeod (1879–1955)
    iii. Margaret Aline McLeod (1881–)

Meharry, is the Ann Meharry who was a good friend as well as first cousin of my grandmother Christiana McClurg Morrow.

iv. Robert Alexander McLeod (1884–)
v. Christabel Jane McLeod (1886–1956)
vi. Jannie Cunningham McLeod (1890–1971)
vii. Emma Rae McLeod (1891–1996)

2. Mary McLeod (1852–) … no information available.

3. Jane McLeod (1853–1937) married John McKee, a native of Co. Antrim, in 1877. They had two known children:

   i. Joseph McKee (ca.1878–)
   ii. May McKee (ca.1885–)

   Jane died on 2 March 1937 in Artemesia, Ontario, Canada.

4. William A. McLeod (1856–1915) married Amelia Emma James in 1879 in Collingwood, Simcoe, Ontario, Canada. Their five children were all born on Manitoulin Island, Ontario.

   i. Mary Amelia McLeod (1880–1967)
   ii. Margaret Jane McLeod (1884–)
   iii. Ida Jane McLeod (1885–1948)
   iv. Emma Charlotte McLeod (1888–)
   v. Helen C. McLeod (1891–)

5. Joseph Edward McLeod (1858–1929) was born on Manitoulin Island, Ontario, Canada, and died 21 December 1929 in Bay City, Michigan, United States.

6. Robert G. McLeod (ca. 1862–1918) married Mary Ann Little in 1889 in Sandfield, Algoma District, Ontario, Canada, and had four known children. Their two oldest children were born in Ontario, and the two youngest were born in North Dakota, United States

   i. John C. McLeod (ca. 1893–)
   ii. James A. McLeod (ca. 1896–)

iii. Robert F. Harman McLeod (ca. 1898–)
iv. William O. McLeod (ca. 1899–)

7. Samuel McLeod (1863–1928) married Harriet Riggin in 1884 in Assiginack, Manitoulin Island, Ontario, Canada. They were the parents of six children, all born in the Algoma district of Ontario:

   i. Ernest N. McLeod (1885–1980)
   ii. Samuel Victor McLeod (1887–1951)
   iii. Eleanor M. McLeod (1889–1954)
   iv. Ethel Harriet McLeod (1892–1967)
   v. Gordon Kerr McLeod (1895–)
   vi. Clifford Ray McLeod (1899–)

William McClurg (ca. 1830–)

William McClurg married Alice Wallace of Simmy Island, Co. Down, on 2 October 1851 in the 1st Killyleagh Presbyterian Church (see "Chapter Sixteen" for details on the Wallace family). He is listed as a mechanic in the marriage registration. Alice is the sister of Agnes Wallace, wife of William's brother Thomas McClurg (ca. 1814–1888). This line of McClurgs needs more research. They may have also immigrated to Canada or the United States.

* * *

McClurg is a fairly common surname in parts of the United States. Oral family history indicates that my grandmother Christiana McClurg Morrow had a great uncle who became the governor of a state in the United States. Research seems to point to Joseph Washington McClurg, the former governor of Missouri. He was born in St. Louis, Missouri in 1818, the son of Joseph McClurg of Ireland and Mary Brotherton. This Joseph McClurg would be about the right age to be a brother of my great-great-grandfather James McClurg who was born about 1782. Many of Joseph's descendents appear in cemetery records in Lebanon, Missouri. I am hoping to someday find documentation to link these families.

CHAPTER SEVEN

Four Generations of Ancestral Roots

The Wilsons of Kilkeel Parish

BY ANDREA PICTON (ENGLAND)

THIS CHAPTER IS A SUMMARY of the research I have carried out on my Kilkeel connections to the Wilson family. Sheila Phillips, late of Ballymartin, Co. Down, was of invaluable help in assisting me in this endeavor.

The earliest ancestor I have identifed from the parish of Kilkeel is my great-great-great grandfather Archibald Wilson (ca. 1796–1878). His son (my-great-great-grandfather) John Wilson (ca. 1825–1873) and grandson (my great-grandfather) William Wilson (1870–1940) were both born in Kilkeel. My grandfather James Hamilton Wilson (1901–1987), although born in Scotland, spent time in Kilkeel as a child and as an adult, and it was a place that he held very close to his heart all through his life.

Great-Great-Great-Grandfather Archibald Wilson (ca. 1796–1878)

Archibald Wilson was born about 1796; this being an estimated date from his will and death certificate as there appears to be no record of his birth or baptism. He was a farmer and married Isabella Kernaghan in Clough

A view of Aughrim Hill, Kilkeel, Co. Down (photo: 2012).

Presbyterian Church, Loughinisland, Co. Down, on 27 January 1824.[1]

From the available records, Archibald Wilson and Isabella Kernaghan had at least seven children:

- John Wilson (ca.1825–1873), my great-great-grandfather
- James Wilson (ca. 1829–1884)
- Thomas Wilson (ca. 1830–1880)
- Margaret Wilson (ca. 1837–1901)
- Annabella Wilson (1840–1907)
- Mary Wilson (1841–1914)
- Jane Wilson (1842–)

All of the children were presumably born in the Kilkeel area since the baptism of the youngest daughter, Jane Wilson, states that her father was a resident of Ballinran, Kilkeel.

Sometime between 1856 and 1861, Archibald moved from Ballinran to Aughrim, also in the parish of Kilkeel. In 1863, he was leasing over 90 acres of land from the trustees of the Kilmorey Estate.[2]

Archibald Wilson died on 16 January 1878 in Aughrim. He was predeceased by his eldest son, my great-great-grandfather John Wilson, so the second eldest son James was the chief benefactor in Archibald's will.

> In the name of God Amen. The twenty fifth day of March eighteen hundred and seventy five. I Archibald Wilson of Aughrim farmer being sick and weak of body but of perfect mind and memory … give and bequeath to my son James Wilson all my lands and tenements by him freely to be possessed and enjoyed after my death …
>
> – Will of Archibald Wilson (ca. 1796–1878)[3]

The land in Aughrim remains in the family to this day.

---

[1] Sheila Phillips kindly obtained a poorly typed transcription of the church record from the General Register Office in Roscommon, Ireland.

[2] AskAboutIreland, "Griffith's Valuation," database and images (www.askaboutireland.ie/griffith-valuation/index.xml).

[3] Public Record Office of Northern Ireland, "Will Calendars," database and images (http://www.proni.gov.uk).

Great-Great-Grandfather John Wilson (ca. 1825–1873)

Archibald Wilson's eldest son John had left the family farm in Kilkeel to seek employment in Liverpool, England, the hometown of his future wife, Susana Fogg.[4]

Susana was born in Liverpool on 29 May 1837.[5] Her mother, Catherine (nee Twist), was a boarding-house keeper in Liverpool, having been widowed when Susana's father, James Fogg, died on 30 May 1841. It is very possible that John Wilson, who was employed as a dockyard labourer, met Susana whilst lodging at this boarding house.

John later returned to Ireland where he and Susana were married on 18 June 1856 in the Mourne Presbyterian Church, Kilkeel, Co. Down. They had four children:

- Archibald Wilson (1856–1926)
- Isabella Wilson (1861–)
- Thomas Wilson (ca.1867–)
- William Wilson (1870–1940), my great-grandfather

The first child was born around the same time that John and Susana were married in Ireland as his birth was registered in Liverpool between April and June 1856. It seems that the couple may have gone back to Kilkeel to marry in order to conceal Susana's pregnancy.

In 1861, John and Susana were living on Emma Anne Street in Liverpool with Susana's mother, Catherine, when their second child Isabella was born. By the time my great-grandfather William was born in 1870, John and Susana were back in Ireland and residing in Kilkeel. They may have returned to Ireland for support from John's family after Susana's mother died in England of bronchitis on 5 January 1865; or perhaps Johns' own health was deteriorating as he also died of bronchitis on 12 February 1873 in Aughrim, Kilkeel.

After her husband's death, Susana stayed in Ireland and remarried on

[4] Christened "Susana", but the name varies between this and "Susan" on subsequent records.

[5] FamilySearch, "England Births and Christenings, 1538-1975," database (familysearch.org).

18 May 1874 in the Mourne Presbyterian Church, Kilkeel. Her second husband was John Hagan, a labourer from Drummond, and they had two known children, Annie and Margaret (known as Maggie). Susana later died in 1912.

Archibald Wilson (1856–1926)

Archibald, the eldest child of John Wilson and Susana Fogg, was born in 1856 in Liverpool, Lancashire, England. He married Janet Hamilton, daughter of James Hamilton and Isabella McMeekin, on 1 April 1880 in Anniesland, Renfrewshire, Scotland.

In 1891, Archibald was employed as an ironstone miner and residing in Redtown, Renfrewshire, Scotland. By this time, he and Janet had five children: Isabella (10 years), Susanna (8 years), John (5 years), Janet (3 years), and James (9 months).

Ten years later, in 1901, Archibald was still working as a miner, but he was living in Bellshill, Lanarkshire, with his children Susan and John. Meanwhile, his wife, Janet, was residing in Aughrim, Kilkeel with her children Janet (13 years), James (10 years), Archie (7 years), Thomas (5 years) and Maggie (2 years). She was farming land leased from the Kilmorey Estate that Archibald had inherited from his uncle James Wilson in 1884.

> Aughrim 5th February 84. I James Wilson being weak of mind and body but perfect in mind and memory do make this my last Will and testament ... I give and bequeath to my nephew Archibald Wilson all my lands and housed cattle and chattels of all kinds freely to be enjoyed by him.
>
> – Will of James Wilson (1829-1884)[6]

By 1911, the family were reunited and farming for a living at Aughrim. They now had another daughter named Sarah who was 8 years old. Later that year, Archibald purchased the Aughrim farm from the Kilmorey Estate on 2 December 1911.

[6] Public Record Office of Northern Ireland, "Will Calendars," database and images (http://www.proni.gov.uk).

Archibald Wilson died on 15 March 1926, and his wife, Janet, died in 1949. After Archibald died, his son John managed the Aughrim Farm.

John Wilson was born on 15 July 1885 in Aughrim. He married Sarah Mitchell and they lived in Bellshill, Lanarkshire, for a while before immigrating to Australia in 1914. They later returned to Kilkeel where John took over the running of the farm in Aughrim.

John Wilson, the son of Archibald Wilson (1856–1926) and Janet Hamilton (photo: ca. 1900).

John Wilson died on 24 November 1976 in Aughrim, Kilkeel. There are still members of the Wilson family in and around Kilkeel today.

Isabella Wilson (1861–)

Isabella, the second eldest child of John Wilson and Susana Fogg, was born on 8 December, 1861 in Liverpool, England. I have found no further mention of her in any records, so she may have died in childhood.

Thomas Wilson (ca. 1867–)

Thomas, the third child of John Wilson and Susana Fogg, was probably born in England. I have very little information about him until he married Jemima Boyd on 4 August 1909 in the Mourne Presbyterian Church. In 1911, he and Jemima were living in Bellshill, Lanarkshire. Thomas was a coal miner and they had one daughter, Mary.

Great-Grandfather William Wilson (1870–1940)

William Wilson, the youngest child of John Wilson and Susana Fogg, was born on 24 April 1870 in Kilkeel, Co. Down. He married Mary Hamilton[7] on 16 July 1891 in Anniesland, Renfrewshire, Scotland.

William and Mary remained in Scotland where he worked as a miner. They later settled in the town of Bellshill, Lanarkshire, Scotland, and had a large family. The couple remained in Bellshill where William died from myocarditis on 5 January 1940 and Mary followed on 3 September 1941.

The children of William Wilson and Mary Hamilton were:

- Isabella ("Bella") Wilson, born 7 June 1892 in Jordanhill, Renfrewshire, Scotland; died 1974 in Bellshill, Bellshill, Lanarkshire, Scotland; married James Dickie on 26 December 1913 in The Manse, Bellshill, Lanarkshire, Scotland.
- Susannah ("Anna") Wilson, born 30 June 1894 in Coatbridge, Old Monkland, Lanarkshire, Scotland; died 17 October 1978 in Bradford,

[7] Sister of Janet Hamilton and wife of Archibald Wilson (1856-1926).

The family of my great-grandfather William Wilson in about 1912. Back row (left to right): my grandfather James Hamilton Wilson (1901–1987), Mary Wilson (1896–1918), Isabella Wilson (1892–1974), and Susannah Wilson (1894–1978). Front row (left to right): Archibald Wilson (1905–), William Wilson (1870–1940), Rebecca Hamilton Wilson (1907–1987), John Wilson (1899–1973), William Wilson (1903–), Thomas Wilson (1911–1963), and Mary (Hamilton) Wilson (1869–1941).

My great-grandfather William Wilson (seated centre) in the Salvation Army band with his sons (left to right) James Hamilton Wilson, William Wilson and Thomas Wilson. The gentleman on the far right is James Dickie (photo: ca. 1920).

McKean, Pennsylvania, United States; married Robert Gault on 28 April 1916 in Bellshill, Lanarkshire, Scotland.

- Mary Wilson, born 27 February 1896 in Anniesland, Renfrewshire, Scotland; died 2 November 1918 in Glasgow, Scotland; married William Paton on 14 September 1917 in The Manse, Bellshill, Lanarkshire, Scotland.
- John ("Jackie") Wilson, born 30 December 1899 in Clydebank, Dumbarton, Scotland; died in 1973 in Bellshill, Lanarkshire, Scotland; married Elizabeth Eccles on 3 March 1922 in The Manse, Bellshill, Lanarkshire, Scotland.
- James ("Jim") Hamilton Wilson, my grandfather (see next section)
- William ("Willie") Wilson, born 12 July 1903 in Coatbridge, Lanarkshire, Scotland; married Jeannie Martin Buchanan on 13 April 1923 in Bellshill, Lanarkshire, Scotland.
- Janet Hamilton Wilson, born 12 July 1903 in Coatbridge, Lanarkshire, Scotland; died 22 March 1905 in Bellshill, Lanarkshire, Scotland.
- Archibald ("Archie") Wilson, born 29 May 1905 in Bellshill, Lanarkshire, Scotland; married Mary Mcleod Moore on 3 June 1927 in Bellshill, Lanarkshire, Scotland.
- Rebecca ("Becca") Hamilton Wilson, born 7 July 1907 in Bellshill, Lanarkshire, Scotland; died in 1987 in Bellshill, Lanarkshire, Scotland; married Thomas Gemmell on 29 August 1930 in Bellshill, Lanarkshire, Scotland.
- Thomas ("Tommy") Wilson, born 10 March 1911 in Bellshill, Lanarkshire, Scotland; died 12 March 1963 in Ontario, Canada; married Grace Pate Grant 15 July 1932 at Bellshill Baptist Church, Bellshill, Lanarkshire, Scotland.

In addition to the above children, family historians know that William and Mary had one other daughter, named Margaret or Maggie, who died in childhood.

Whilst researching the children of Tommy Wilson and his sister Becca, I came across a pitiable record. They both lost a child to whooping cough in the early hours of the morning on 4 February 1939. I asked one of Tommy's sons about this and he told me the family story was that Tommy was on his way to register his daughter's death when he met his brother-in-law Thomas Gemmell (Becca's husband) and regrettably discovered that he had suffered the same loss during the night. The men went together to register their daughters' deaths, and hence they appear in the register side by side.

Grandfather James ("Jim") Hamilton Wilson (1901–1987)

My grandfather Jim was born on 14 April 1901 in Coatbridge, Lanarkshire, Scotland, and married Edith Wilson on 30 September 1930 in the Salvation Army Hall, Burnley, Lancashire, England.

My grandfather had very fond memories of his family in Kilkeel as he spent time on the Aughrim farm convalescing from an illness when he was a young man. At the time, the farm was being managed by his aunt and uncle, Janet Hamilton (his mother's sister) and Archibald Wilson (his father's brother)

The nearby Mourne Mountains must have seemed idyllic to my grandfather after the industrial environment of his home back in Scotland. In the mid-19th century, his hometown of Coatridge was described as follows:

> There is no worse place out of hell than that neighbourhood. At night the groups of blast furnaces on all sides might be imagined to be blazing volcanoes at most of which smelting is continued on Sundays and weekdays, day and night, without intermission. From the town comes a continual row of heavy machinery: this and the pounding of many steam hammers seemed to make even the very ground vibrate under ones feet. Fire, smoke and soot with the roar and rattle of machinery are its leading characteristics; the flames of its furnaces cast on the midnight sky a glow as if of some vast conflagration. Dense clouds of black smoke roll over it incessantly and impart to all buildings a peculiarly dingy aspect. A coat of black dust overlies everything.
>
> – Robert Baird, 1845[8]

After his marriage to Edith Wilson, the couple travelled all over the United Kingdom with his work. They were fortunate to spend more time

[8] Peter Drummond and James Smith, *Coatbridge: Three Centuries of Change* (Monkland Library Services, 1982).

in Ireland in the 1960s before retiring to Burnley, England, where Jim died in 1987.

* * *

Whilst it is interesting to learn about who my ancestors were, it is also important to me to understand a little about their lives in a historical context.

From my research, I have discovered that the Wilsons and extended family, for decades and across generations, travelled between County Down and the West coast of Scotland. This was not unusual as the Irish had been immigrating to Scotland in reasonable numbers from as early as the 1820s to seek employment during the agricultural season—the small fare for a deck passage from Ireland to Greenock made an attractive proposition. In the early years, the work was mainly seasonal, and there were few permanent settlements. However, the Great Famine of 1845–1852 and the employment opportunities created by the industrial revolution during this time, changed this behaviour as large numbers of Irish chose to make Scotland their new home.

The Irish immigrants tended to disembark and settle around the west coast of Scotland. Poverty and ill health prevented most families from travelling far from their point of arrival, and whilst the Irish also journeyed to the east coast, the industrial areas in the west witnessed the largest concentration of migrants. In 1851, for example, the Irish population in Coatbridge (where many of my grandfather's generation were born) was 35.8%.[9]

This life, whilst tough, possibly provided the means by which my great-great-grandfather's son Archibald Wilson (1856–1926) finally purchased the Aughrim farm in County Down in 1911; a property that has meant so much to generations of the Wilson family, both past and present.

[9] Education Scotland: *Irish emigration to Scotland in the 19th and 20th centuries* (www.educationscotland.gov.uk/higherscottishhistory/migrationandempire/experienceofimmigrants/irish.asp : accessed 2 Oct 2013).

CHAPTER EIGHT

My Ancestors

The Family of S.J. Stewart (1931-2007)

BY ALISON ALDERSEA (AUSTRALIA)

IN CHAPTER FOUR, MY DAD Samuel J. Stewart wrote about his recollections of working in the Harland and Wolff shipyards. The following fills in some more of our Stewart family story, very much centred on County Down and the shipyards for four generations. It also reflects the ever present theme of Ireland—emigration.

Dad's father (my grandfather), Sammy Stewart, was also a shipyard worker and was employed as a driller for Harland and Wolff. He was born in 1908, and he followed his father (my great-grandfather), Samuel Stewart, a holder-on, into the yard.

Sammy was a very clever and talented man, known for inventing some machines and methods in the yard when a new solution was needed. He started as a driller but was soon made a foreman.[1] Towards the end of his career, he was put in charge of the construction of the Goliath crane that was completed in 1969. He often talked of the stress it caused him, especially when the wind blew the crane around. As his son (my father)

[1] Foremen in the shipyards were known as "hats" because they wore bowler hats instead of the everyday caps that the ordinary workers wore.

Grandfather Samuel Stewart (right) with his brother John (photo: ca. 1912).

was to do years later, he died of lung cancer in 1972, possibly the result of his years of asbestos exposure in the shipyard.

The first Stewart in my family to work in the shipyards was my great-great-grandfather John Stewart. He was born in 1859 and later worked in one of the Belfast yards as a caulker.[2] John, like so many people at that time, had a tragic life, although he lived a long time. His wife, Ellen Gregory, was from Newtownards. Her mother's maiden name was McNeilly and the family owned quite a few houses there. Ellen died of a brain aneurism at just 34 years of age, leaving John with five young children. Only two of these children went on to have children of their own. One of these was their eldest son, Samuel, my great-grandfather.

Another son was James Stewart, a blacksmith. He had immigrated to Canada in 1911 and subsequently disappeared off the face of the earth—or so it seemed at the time.

His father, John Stewart, travelled to Canada to look for him, but to no avail. Quite a few family myths grew up around this strange disappearance. One was that he disappeared in an earthquake, maybe even the San Francisco earthquake, although that was in 1906. The best story was that he became the father to James ("Jimmy") Stewart, the famous American actor, who did happen to look a lot like members of our Stewart family, especially my dad.[3] Unfortunately, the real story is much sadder.

It turns out that James Stewart immigrated to British Columbia, Canada. His brother David was with him at Camp Courtney in British Columbia in 1911. We know this from a letter written to his father saying

[2] A caulker makes seams tight in metal.

[3] The actor Jimmy Stewart was born on 20 May 1908 in Indiana, Pennsylvania.

David was doing well. David returned to Belfast soon after and died in 1916 of tuberculosis at the age of 24 years. It seems that James had contracted syphilis in Canada and died in July 1913. He was only 28 years old. Maybe his father did find out what had happened to him but didn't tell the family. We will never know.

In addition to their three sons (James, David and Samuel), John and Ellen had two other children: Nellie, who had no children of her own, and Rowena Stewart, who married her cousin Thomas McDowell. Thomas was the son of Robert McDowell and Elizabeth Morrow Stewart, the sister of my great-great-grandfather John Stewart. Elizabeth had been born in Comber, Co. Down around 1864.

Great-great-grandparents John Stewart and Ellen Gregory with their children (left to right) Samuel, James and Rowena (photo: ca. 1888).

The parents of John and Elizabeth Morrow Stewart were Samuel Stewart and Margaret Bowman. There were three other children of this marriage: Agnes Stewart, who married Hugh Drain; Margaret Stewart, who married David McBride; and Samuel Stewart, who married Mary Jane Kaine.

The earliest Stewart I have definite records for is a James Stewart. He was a farmer and had been named as the father of the groom on the marriage certificate of Samuel Stewart and Margaret Bowman. They were married on 13 May 1853 in the Second Presbyterian Church, Comber, Co. Down. Margaret's father was Samuel Bowman, a labourer. This is where the paper trail ends. There are scores of Bowmans and Stewarts in Comber, often with the same Christian names repeated in each generation, so untangling the thread is nigh on impossible.

DNA testing of our Y chromosome (passed along the male line, father to son) is typically representative of ancient inhabitants of the Orkney Islands—Pict, Celt and Viking. Our Stewart Y- DNA is R1b1a2 (M269), a typical north Atlantic type. It seems to be particularly prevalent among

Stewarts from Perthshire, Scotland, so our ancestors may have passed through there and then came to Ireland sometime after (or before) the Plantation of Ulster in the 17th century.

Now our family has branches throughout the world; two of Dad's brothers are still in Northern Ireland, a sister lives in England, while Dad and his brother John came to Australia. Various cousins live in the U.S. and other parts of the world.

We are a typical County Down family and have carried our proud heritage throughout the world.

Me with my Stewart grandparents in Belfast (photo: 1960).

CHAPTER NINE

Two Hundred Years of Family History

The Livingstons of County Down

BY SHELLEY ANDRE (CANADA)

THE LIVINGSTON SURNAME IS AN ancient name, existing before the twelfth century and originating from the surroundings of West Lothian, south-west of Edinburgh. It is derived from a Saxon named Leving who held lands in West Lothian and titled his grant "Leving's Toun". In time, Leving's descendants assumed the name of "Livingston". Members of this family were prominent in Scottish history between the years of 1300 to 1715 and held several peerages, notably the earldoms of Callender, Linlithgow, and Newburgh.

The Livingstons of County Down belong to the Livingstons of Callendar House at Falkirk, who held this seat from the fourteenth century. From the Callendar branch descended such notables as Sir James Livingston, who was created Lord Livingston in 1458; Alexander (5th Lord) Livingston, who was made guardian of the young Mary Queen of Scots in 1543, and again in 1548 when she remained in France during her betrothal to the Dauphin; the 7th Lord Alexander Livingston, who was made 1st Earl of Linlithgow in 1600; and Reverend John Livingston (1603-1672), a renowned minister of the Church of Scotland during the days of the covenanting persecutions who came to Ireland in 1630.

Our story begins with my great-great-great-great-grandfather Samuel Livingston, a farmer in Gransha, Dromara, Co. Down. Although unproven at this time, past generations of this Livingston family have for centuries recounted legends and narratives that Samuel descended from the covenanting hero Reverend John Livingston.

Samuel Livingston
ca. 1740–1796
Great-Great-Great-Great-Grandfather

Farmland that was once leased by Samuel Livingston (ca. 1740–1796) in Gransha, Co. Down.

Samuel Livingston of Gransha leased a corn mill and farmlands from the Right Honorable Arthur Hill-Trevor, 1st Viscount Dungannon. Through his lease, dated 2 December 1762, Samuel received exclusive use of the waters of the Gransha Lough for the running of his corn mill. He also leased four acres and sixteen perches of land from Richard Magenis of Waringstown in the townland of Finnis, Co. Down.

In about 1860, Samuel married Ann Massey and together they raised a large family of eight known children who were all baptized at the First Dromara Presbyterian Church.

- John Livingston, born 1762.
- Robert Livingston, born 1763.
- Samuel Livingston (I), born 13 June 1766;[1] died before 1779.
- James Livingston, born 4 October 1768.
- Joseph Livingston, born 23 June 1771.
- Mary Livingston born 29 October 1773.

[1] Samuel Livingston's birth and baptism are the first church records to be found for this family as no records from the First Presbyterian Dromara Church prior to 1763 have survived.

- Ann Livingston, born 7 November 1776.
- Samuel Livingston (II), born 17 May 1779.

Following Samuel's death in 1796, the heirs to his sizable farms, corn mill, kiln, and houses were his youngest son, Samuel Livingston (II), his eldest grandson, Reverend Samuel Livingston of Portaferry, and Isabella Speers, daughter of David Speers. Isabella might be a granddaughter of Samuel, but this needs further research to confirm.

Site of the former corn mill operated by Samuel Livingston of Gransha in the 18th century.

John Livingston (1762–)

John, who was the first child of Samuel Livingston (ca. 1740–1796). married Sarah Martin in Dromara, Co. Down. Their children were: Samuel Livingston, born 7 December 1784; John Livingston, born 17 April 1786; Joseph Livingston, born 16 June 1790; James Livingston, born 22 August 1792; and Ann Livingston, born 25 May 1795.

Samuel Livingston (1784–1864)

The eldest son of John Livingston (1762-) was a pupil at Kilmore Academy in Rademon, about eleven miles east of Dromara. The *Belfast News Letter* dated 30 June 1797 gives Public Examination results for the 22nd and 23rd of June when "Sam Livingston of Drumara" obtained second class honours in Latin. The Academy, operated by the Reverend Moses Neilson of Kilmore, is said to have been 'impressed' with their young scholar.

Samuel later graduated from the University of Glasgow in 1806 with a Master of Arts degree and became a licensed minister of the Irish Presbyterian Church in 1809. He then moved to Portaferry, a busy seaport at the southern tip of the beautiful Strangford Lough, where he ran a school in the Square and had a reputation for being a fine teacher.

On 2 May 1811, Reverend Livingston married Elizabeth Dalzell of Marlfield, Newtownards, Co. Down and they had ten children: Jonas, James, Ann Jane, Rachel, Eliza, Isabella, William John, Robert, Susan, and Samuel.

The year 1833 marked the end of Reverend Livingston's teaching days in Portaferry. The family moved across 'the river', as the Strangford Lough is still called, to the picturesque village of Strangford where the reverend opened a school for local children. This school was held in the extremely large house known as Isle O'Valla, which had once been a Charter School.[2] He taught Latin, Greek, and French in addition to mathematics, geography, use of globes, arithmetic, writing, and elocution to day pupils and boarders. After he retired, Reverend Samuel Livingston moved to Belfast where he died on 1 February 1864 at the age of 80 years old.

Robert Livingston (1863–)

Robert, the second child of Samuel Livingston (ca. 1740–1796), was farming in Moybrick in the Parish of Dromara by 1789. He married Margaret Patterson and they had six children: Samuel Livingston, born 4 October 1787; Mary Livingston, born 4 February 1793; John Livingston, born 13 February 1796; Isabella Livingston, born 3 December 1797; Margaret Livingston, born 16 May 1801; and Joseph Livingston, born 1 January 1806.

James Livingston (1768–)

James, the fourth child of Samuel Livingston (ca. 1740–1796), married Jane Hill and they had six children: Joseph Livingston, born 25 January 1785; Margaret Livingston, born 28 December 1786; Samuel Livingston, born 23 April 1789; William Livingston, born 23 December 1790; Elizabeth Livingston, born 3 May 1793; and James Livingston, born 5 September 1797.

[2] A school established by the Charter Society (founded in 1733) to provide a Protestant education to poor Catholics in Ireland.

Joseph Livingston

1771–1832

Great-Great-Great-Grandfather

Joseph Livingston, the fifth son of Samuel Livingston (ca. 1740-1796), was born on 23 June 1771. He was baptized the following day at the First Dromara Presbyterian Church.

Joseph was a tanner by trade and known to be a merchant farmer as well. In 1797, he leased twenty acres of land from Lord Dungannon in Gransha. At about the year 1792, Joseph married Margaret McFadden, daughter of John and Mary McFadden, from the townland of Skeogh in the Parish of Dromore. Margaret's father was a farmer in this area of Co. Down. His only son, Dr. John McFadden, was the surgeon for the town of Dromore until his untimely death in 1820.

Joseph and Margaret (McFadden) Livingston made their home in the Parish of Dromore. The following children were born from their union.

- Samuel Livingston, born 1794; died 11 March 1873.
- John Livingston, born 1798; died January 1834.
- Joseph Livingston, born 1800; died 27 August 1854.
- Hertford Livingston, born 1806; died 13 March 1860.
- Mary Livingston, born 1809; died 24 April 1861.
- Margaret Livingston, born 1810; died 22 April 1897.
- Ann Livingston, born 1812; died 6 August 1882.

In July 1812, Joseph received land that was transferred to him by Margaret's mother, Mary McFadden. This was done according to the will of his late father-in-law, John McFadden.

Joseph fell ill and died on 14 September 1832 at the age of 59 years.

> On the 14th inst. At Dromore, in the 59th year of his age, Mr. Joseph Livingston, tanner, after a short illness, borne with fortitude and pious resignation. In him was united a powerful degree of activity, both of body and mind. His loss will be long and deeply lamented by a sorrowing family, and regretted by numerous circle of friends and acquaintances.
>
> – *Belfast Newsletter*, 21 September 1832

Joseph's wife, Margaret, remained in Dromore where she lived with her daughters Mary and Ann until her death on 7 September 1840. She was buried next to her husband in the Dromore churchyard.

> On the 17th ult. at Dromore, in the 73d year of her age. Margaret, relict of the late Joseph Livingston. In prosperity, a pattern of meekness—in adversity, of patience—and through all chequered scenes of life, full of faith, hope, and charity.
>
> – *Belfast Newsletter*, 2 October 1840

Samuel Livingston (1794–1873)

The eldest child of Joseph Livingston (1771-1832) was born in Dromore, Co. Down, and named after his paternal grandfather, Samuel Livingston (ca. 1740–1796) of Gransha. He later inherited farming property from his maternal grandfather, John McFadden.

In the year 1828, Samuel married Rachel Frackelton of Lisnasure, Parish of Magheralin, Co. Down. Rachel was born in 1787 to Andrew Frackelton and Mary Stannus.

Samuel and Rachel Livingston had two children—John and Mary Anne—who both died in infancy. Rachel died on 24 December 1860 in Dromore, Co. Down.

Samuel never remarried and lived the remainder of his life in the town of Dromore in a house on Meeting Street. He died on 11 March 1873 in Dromore and is buried in the Livingston family plot in the Dromore churchyard.

> LIVINGSTON–March 11, Mr. Samuel Livingston, of Dromore, County Down, in the 80th year of his age. The funeral will take place this (Friday) afternoon, at two o'clock, in the Cathedral Churchyard of Dromore, from his late residence in Meeting Street.
>
> – *Belfast Newsletter*, 14 March 1873

John Livingston (1798–1834)

John, the second child of Joseph Livingston (1771-1832), immigrated to Upper Canada in the year 1820 and settled in the town of York, today known as Toronto. He was a tanner, following in his father's footsteps.

In January 1834, John became suddenly ill. He succumbed to the illness a few days later, leaving a young widow and three small children.

Joseph Livingston (1800–1854)

The third child of Joseph Livingston (1771-1832) was a business partner with his brother Hertford. In 1835, they were co- proprietors of the Banbridge Hotel and Coach Offices in the town of Banbridge, Co. Down.

Joseph died in Belfast on 27 August 1854.

Mary Livingston (1809–1861)

Mary, the eldest daughter of Joseph Livingston (1771-1832), was born in Dromore, Co. Down. She was named after her maternal grandmother, Mary McFadden.

When Mary became of age, she left Dromore for Belfast, where she met a Scottish Highlander named Thomas Frazer. Thomas, who first set out as a linen draper, eventually acquired the Imperial Hotel in Belfast, turning it into the leading hotel in the north of Ireland at that time.

In 1842, Thomas Frazer and Mary Livingston were wed. Soon after, two sons were born to the couple—Hugh Frazer and Joseph Frazer.

Thomas and Mary enjoyed a few prosperous years together with the management of the Imperial Hotel until the sudden death of Thomas on 27 February 1849. Left to raise two young boys, and with the immense task of managing the hotel, Mary married a few years later in 1851 to Dr. Charles Hurst. Dr. Hurst, giving up his profession, assumed the responsibility of managing the Imperial Hotel.

Ad for the Imperial Hotel in Belfast, 1885 [Wikimedia Commons].

Mary became ill in April of 1861 and died shortly afterwards.

> April 24–Mary, wife of Dr. Hurst, Belfast. Her remains will be removed from Ashfield, Ballynafeigh, for interment in Dromore

Churchyard, on Saturday, the 27th inst., at 10 o'clock A.M.
– *Belfast Newsletter*, 25 April 1861

Her two sons, Hugh and Joseph Frazer, were left in the care of their step-father, Dr. Hurst, and their aunt Ann (Livingston) Dalzell, Mary's sister. They assumed the name of their step-father (their family name became Frazer-Hurst) and both were sent to private schools in Belfast for their education.

Joseph Frazer-Hurst (1845–1902)

Mary's eldest son Joseph eventually entered Queen's University College in Belfast to study for the Presbyterian Ministry. Once a minister, he took the name of Reverend Joseph Livingston Frazer-Hurst. He married Sara Smythe, daughter of James Alexander Smythe, on 10 May 1878 in Maghera, Co. Down. After his marriage, Joseph held a few pulpits in Ireland. He then ministered in Dunedin, New Zealand, at the Caversham Presbyterian Church from the years 1882 to 1888. He and Sara then returned to Ireland in 1888 to the townland of Fermoy in the Parish of Magheralin where he preached for twelve years until his death in 1902.

Hugh Frazer-Hurst (1847 –1913)

Hugh Frazier-Hurst and Maria Smythe.

Mary's other son chose the profession of medicine and studied in Dereham, Norfolk, England. While still a medical student, Hugh married Maria Smythe.[3] He eventually qualified to continue his studies in Edinburgh, Scotland, where he assisted in various practices. Hugh then moved his growing family to Walker-On-Tyne, a suburb of Newcastle in England, where he had a prosperous medical practice and was well respected in

[3] also see "Chapter Fourteen" for more on Hugh Frazier-Hurst and Maria Smyth.

the community. He died in Edinburgh, Scotland in 1913.

Margaret Livingston (1810–1897)

The second eldest daughter of Joseph Livingston (1771-1832) married William Egan, and they left County Down to establish themselves in County Monaghan where two children were born—a son they named Francis, and a daughter they named Margaret. Sometime between the years 1845 and 1848, William and Margaret immigrated to Canada and settled in a small community in Ontario on the shores of Georgian Bay called Owen Sound. There, four daughters were born: Fanny, Elizabeth, Clara, and Mary Ann.

William died in 1864, leaving Margaret to raise their family by herself. Margaret died at the age of 87 years on 22 April 1897 and is buried in the Greenwood Cemetery in Owen Sound, Ontario.

Ann Livingston (1812–1882)

Ann, the youngest daughter of Joseph Livingston (1771-1832), married Captain Samuel Dalzell, but was widowed very early into her marriage.

After the death of her sister Mary (Livingston) Hurst in 1861, Ann moved into the home of Mary's second husband, Dr. Charles Hurst, and two sons, Joseph and Hugh Frazer-Hurst, to help with the household duties. Once Ann's two nephews were off to university, she moved into several residences in Belfast. She also held several properties in the Parish of Dromore, including residences on Pound Street, Meeting Street, Brewery Lane, and a farm in the townland of Drumbroneth, Dromore, Co. Down.

Ann died on 6 August 1882 in Belfast. Her funeral was held in the town of Dromore where she is buried alongside her parents and siblingsThe executors of Ann Dalzell's will were her two nephews Hugh and Joseph Frazer-Hurst. Ann's estate was equally divided amongst Hugh, Joseph, and several of her nieces.

Hertford Livingston

1806–1860

Great-Great-Great-Grandfather

Hertford Livingston, the fourth son of Joseph Livingston (1771-1832), chose to make his living in the purchasing and selling of real estate throughout the north of Ireland. In the 1830s, he was proprietor of several prime real estate properties such as the Banbridge Hotel and Coach Offices in Banbridge, Co. Down, and the Dublin Hotel on Ann Street in Belfast.

The year 1836 initiated many changes in Hertford's life. He placed the Dublin Hotel in Belfast on the market for sale, and his partner, Margaret Sullivan, gave birth to a daughter on the first day of May. The child was named Margaret and was baptized at the St. Anne's Cathedral in Belfast. Shortly afterwards, Margaret Sullivan disappeared. It is not clear if she abandoned Hertford and their daughter, or if she died unexpectedly.

On 19 April 1838, Hertford eloped with a young girl named Belinda Burrowes from Ballyvicknacally, Dromore, Co. Down, and they married at the St. Anne's Cathedral in Belfast. The marriage created quite a scandal in Belfast as well as in Dromore. Belinda, the daughter of a prominent family in the Parish of Dromore,[4] was only fifteen years of age at the time, and her family greatly objected to the marriage. They insisted that Hertford be prosecuted as the law allowed. He was brought before a magistrate in Belfast, convicted of abduction, and sentenced to serve three months in prison for his crime.

> Mr. Hertford Livingston, of Belfast was arraigned... for the abduction of Belinda Burrows [sic], otherwise Livingston, of Dromore, and marrying her, she being under the age of eighteen years, against the will and consent of her natural parent and

[4] Belinda Burrowes was the daughter of Alexander Saunderson Burrowes and Mary Napier from the townland of Ballyvicknacally, Co. Down. Originating from Co. Cavan, the Burrowes of Stadone House, Co. Cavan held the position of High Sheriff in the area as early as 1728. Belinda Burrowes' paternal grandparents were the Reverend Francis Burrowes, who was appointed schoolmaster of Dromore in 1802, and Belinda Stothard, the daughter of Sir Coslett Stothard, Knight Bachelor of Dromore. Coslett Stothard was knighted on 1 August 1787 at Dromore by the Lord Lieutenant of Ireland who was George Nugent-Temple-Greenville, 1st Marques of Buckingham.

> guardians. Verdict—Guilty of unlawfully, but not fraudulently, taking away.
>
> His Lordship said that ... he would lose no time in making a representation of it to his Excellency the Lord Lieutenant, for a mitigation of the punishment, and he had no doubt of having it considerably lessened. In the meantime the sentence of the court was, that he be imprisoned for three months.
>
> – *Freeman's Journal*, 27 July 1838

Once Hertford was released from prison, he left Belfast with Belinda and his two year-old daughter Margaret. They headed south and divided their time between the City of Dublin and the townland of Naas, Co. Kildare, never to return again to the north of Ireland.

After relocating, Belinda gave birth to the following children:[5]

- Mary Ann Livingston, born 1842.
- Elizabeth Lucinda Livingston, born 3 November 1846; died 3 February 1934.
- Alexander Francis Livingston,[6] born 1855; died 1856.
- Frances Anne Livingston, born 1858; died March 1928.
- Belinda Livingston, born 11 August 1860.

Hertford and Belinda supported their family from earnings on the sale of Hertford's various properties as well as revenue from rent on property that Belinda inherited from her father in County Cavan.

One of Hertford's earliest transactions was in 1841 when he sold a hotel he owned in Blaris, Lisburn, Co. Down, to his brother-in-law Thomas Frazer.[7] *The Digger*, a newspaper of the time, reported:

> Thomas Frazer, the proprietor of the Shakespeare Hotel advertised his business informing "noblemen and gentlemen" who intended

[5] Prior to the birth of Mary Ann in 1842, Belinda had given birth to other children who all died at a young age.

[6] Alexander Francis Livingston was born in Ballysax, Co Kildare, and named after his mother's father and grandfather. He died one year later at the military hospital in Curragh Camp, Co. Kildare.

[7] Husband of Mary Livingston (1809–1861).

> to visit the Maze racecourse, that he would have a pavilion erected on the ground, formerly occupied by his brother-in-law Hertford Livingston. Thomas claimed that the accommodation would be "in all respects superior to any hitherto offered on the Race Course. No expense shall be spared in procuring Viands of the best quality, and supplying them at very moderate charges."
>
> – *The Digger*, 1841

The property Belinda inherited in County Cavan had been passed down from many generations and was located in the townland of Killyfanna, Parish of Annagh, Co. Cavan. The land was of excellent quality, mostly heavy clay, and gave superior wheat crops. The tenants were respectable and industrious. There was excellent shooting on this property and in the neighbourhood. The lakes that adjoined the property abounded in the season with duck, teal, and snipe. They also afforded excellent trout and pike fishing. The neighborhood was most peaceable. Belinda and Hertford retained this property until 1853, when financial difficulties forced them to sell.

Hertford Livingstone died on 13 March 1860 at the age of 54 years. His sudden and unexpected death was a devastating event for his family. As shown from the inscription on his headstone in the graveyard at St. Paul's Church in Ballysax, Co. Kildare, Hertford was much loved by his wife Belinda and daughters Margaret, Mary Ann, Elizabeth Lucinda, Frances Anne, and Belinda.

> Here lieth the remains of Hertford Livingston Who departed this life 13th March 1860 Aged 54 years To the inexpressible sorrow Of his wife and family who Deeply deplore the loss of The best of fathers and Fondest of husbands May he rest in peace till The resurrection of Christ Amen.
>
> – Headston Inscription

Following her husband's death, Belinda (Burrowes) Livingston married Henry William Marjoram in 1863 in the City of Dublin. She died on 20 July 1880 in Dublin.

Margaret Livingston (1836–)

Margaret, the eldest child of Herttford Livingston (1806-1860), was born on 1 May 1836 to Margaret Sullivan who Hertford had a relationship with prior to his marriage to Belinda Burrowes. His daughter's first husband was Christopher Clarke, a steward from Cabra Castle, Kingscourt, Co. Cavan. They married at St. Peter's Church in Dublin on 6 April 1859 and had one daughter, also named Margaret, who was born at Curragh, Co. Kildare, on 24 July 1864.

Margaret's second marriage was to Joseph Hill on 4 December 1874 at St. Thomas Church in Dublin.

Mary Ann Livingston (1842–)

Mary Ann was the first surviving child of Hertford Livingston (1806-1860) in his marriage to Belinda Burrowes. She was born in Dublin and married James Covington Wright at the age of 15 years. The marriage took place with parental consent at St. Thomas's Church in Dublin on 27 January 1857.

The only known child born to James and Mary Ann was a son in 1866 who they named Hertford.

James Wright died a few years after the birth of his son, and Mary Ann, who was living in Belfast by 1870, met her future second husband, a Scotsman and jeweler by the name of John Dick. They married at St. Anne's Cathedral in Belfast on 25 February 1871 and afterwards left Ireland for England. The couple first settled in Birmingham, Warwickshire, and then in Newcastle, Upon-Tyne, where John established a prominent jewelry business. They had six children: John, Susan, Mary Ann, Margaret, William, and Francis.

Elizabeth Lucinda Livingston (1846–1934)

The third daughter of Hertford Livingston (1806-1860) was my great-grandmother, and she also married at the young age of 15 years.

Not far from Naas, Co. Kildare, where the Livingston family lived, was situated Curragh Camp, an army base and military college for the Irish Army. Throughout the early 1860s, a German named Frederick Charles

Stoeckel was the bandmaster of the 29th Regiment stationed at the camp. Playing horn, Frederick performed with the Classical Harmonists' Society in Belfast and throughout Ireland. The public concerts were praised for their finest ensembles.

Frederick also gave private music lessons to families from the surrounding area, and Elizabeth Lucinda Livingston was one of his students. Shortly after Hertford's unexpected death in 1860, a relationship developed between his daughter Elizabeth and Frederick beyond what normally exists amongst a teacher and student. They eloped on 6 May 1861 and were married at the Ballysax Church in Naas, Co. Kildare.

Fifteern-year old Elizabeth began her new life as a military wife, traveling with her husband to his various postings throughout the United Kingdom and beyond. In 1862, while stationed at Aldershot, Hampshire in England, Elizabeth gave birth to a daughter who they named Emily Belinda Stoeckel. In 1865, at the Newry Barracks in Newry, Co. Armagh, Elizabeth gave birth to a son named after his father, Frederick Charles Stoeckel. This child only survived ten days.

In 1871, Frederick was posted in the West Indies where a second son was born in Jamaica and named after him. One year later, Frederick Stoeckel was reassigned to the St. Ann's Garrison in Barbados where he died on 30 March 1872.

Elizabeth Stoeckel, a young widow with two young children, eventually returned to Ireland where she sought the support of her aging aunt Ann (Livingston) Dalzell in Belfast. After the death of her aunt in 1882, Elizabeth was introduced to a widower from Dumbarton, Scotland, named William Kennedy Sloan[8] through her cousin Dr. Hugh Frazer-Hurst. William Kennedy was the uncle of Dr. Hugh-Frazier's wife, Maria Frazer-Hurst (Smythe), and he had traveled to Ireland for the introduction to Elizabeth as well as to visit his family living in the townland of Ballyrush, Comber, Co. Down. A year later, on 19 September 1883, Elizabeth and William were married at May Street Church in Belfast.

> SLOAN–STOECKEL. September 19, at May Street Presbyterian Church, Belfast by the Rev. R.J. Lynd, B.A.,W.K. Sloan, Esq., J.P., Shamrock Bank, Dumbarton, to Lucinda Elizabeth Stoeckel,

[8] also see "Chapter Fourteen" for more details on William Kennedy Sloan.

third daughter of the late Hertford Livingston, Esq, Belfast.
– *Belfast Newsletter*, September 1883

Elizabeth returned to Dumbarton, Scotland, with her new husband and daughter Emily Belinda. Emily settled in Edinburgh where, in 1889, she married a young doctor by the name of Allen Cuthbertson Sym. Elizabeth's son Fred Stoeckel Jr. remained in Ireland as he was attending a naval academy.

Elizabeth Lucinda Livingston (left) with her son David Livingston Sloan and daughter Emily Belinda in Calgary, Alberta, Canada (photo: ca. 1930).

Elizabeth and William Kennedy Sloan resided at Shamrock Bank in Dumbarton. During their marriage, four sons were born but only two survived. William died of pneumonia and heart failure on 22 October 1904 at his residence in Dumbarton, Scotland.

In 1908, Elizabeth Lucinda remarried for the third time to a man 20 years her junior by the name of William Gould. They were wed in Edinburgh and soon afterwards went to live in Belfast, Ireland. After a few years in Belfast, William Gould decided to immigrate in 1912 to Calgary, a booming new city in the western province of Alberta, Canada. He was a builder and took advantage of this fact to seek better employment in Canada.

The following year, in 1913, Elizabeth, along with her son David Livingston Sloan and his wife, joined William in Calgary. Elizabeth remained in Calgary with her son David until her death on 3 February 1934.

Frances Anne Livingston (1858–1928)

Frances Anne, the fourth daughter of Hertford Livingston (1806-1860), was born in Ballysax, Co. Kildare. She went on to marry John Kelly, a house painter and the son of James Kelly, on 26 February 1881 at St. Mark's Church of Ireland in Dublin. Shortly before the birth of their first child John in 1882, Frances Ann and John Kelly converted to the Roman Catholic faith. They later had two other known sons named Michael and Joseph.

John Kelly died just before the taking of the 1901 census. Frances Ann and her youngest son, Joseph, were forced to seek lodging in a boarding house, while her eldest son, John, sought work as a painter in the City of Dublin and surrounding area. By 1911, Frances Ann and her two sons were once again living together.

Frances Ann developed bronchitis in March of 1928 and shortly afterwards succumbed to the illness.

Belinda Livingston (1860–)

The youngest child of Hertford Livingston (1806-1860) was born in Ballysax, Co. Kildare, just five months after the sudden death of her father. Belinda and her sister Frances Anne were raised in the home of their mother and their step-father, Henry William Marjoram.

In 1882, the year after her sister Frances Anne's marriage to John Kelly, Belinda married his brother James Kelly. James and Belinda left Ireland to work in England.

Epilogue

For centuries, the Livingston families of Dromara and Dromore, Co. Down, have prospered in the area—large tenant farmers, merchants, land and property owners, doctors, ministers, and teachers. Today, these families have now all but vanished. What remains are the tales and accounts passed down from generation to generation. Many of the descendants of these brave, hardworking characters of the past are consumed with passion to uncover the remaining mysteries surrounding their origins. What is left to discover are two generational gaps that would tie Samuel Livingston of Gransha (1740-1796) with his ancestor, the Reverend John Livingston (1603-1672).

In time, with persistence and steadfastness to our goals, it is hopeful that newfound materials and evidence will be uncovered and the lingering brickwalls will be at last torn down. Oh, what joy that day will bring!

Bibliography

Douglas Frazer-Hurst, The Bridge of Life (Belfast, Ireland: William Mullan & Son, 1962).

Public Record Office of Northern Ireland (PRONI), "Mary McFadden, Skeogh, Co. Down, Widow," Articles of Agreement (3 July 1812), PRONI Reference: D682/23.

Public Record Office of Northern Ireland (PRONI), "Robert Hawkens Magill of Gillhall, Co. Down," Lease for lives (1739), PRONI Reference: D1046/3.

Public Record Office of Northern Ireland (PRONI), "John McFadden of Skeagh, Co. Down. Will," (29 July 1788), PRONI Reference: D1046/14.

Public Record Office of Northern Ireland (PRONI), "John McFadden, Copy of Will" (22 September 1811), PRONI Reference: D1046/32.

Public Record Office of Northern Ireland (PRONI), "John McFadden of Dromore, Co. Down," Copy Will (31 July 1820), PRONI Reference:

D1046/371.

Public Record Office of Northern Ireland (PRONI), "Lease of Farm at Finnis, Iveagh, Co. Down," (1794), PRONI Reference: D3914/1/E/1.

Public Record Office of Northern Ireland (PRONI), "1st Dromara Presbyterian Church Co. Down," Baptisms (1763-1806), PRONI Reference: T1447/1.

Public Record Office of Northern Ireland (PRONI), "Bundle of c.70 documents relating to the estate of the late Anne Dalzell, Dromore, Co. Down," (1854-1898), PRONI Reference: D2167/8/5.

Adair.ca Website (www.adair.ca).

Alberta Genealogical Society (abgensoc.ca).

Ancestry.ca (assorted records), database and images (www.ancestry.ca).

Bob Murray, Root & Branch Irish Family Research. Belfast, Ireland (www.youririsheyes.com).

Bruce and Grey Branch of The Ontario Genealogical Society (www.brucegrey.ogs.on.ca).

FamilySearch (assorted records), database and images (familysearch.org).

Findmypast (assorted records), database and images (findmypast.com).

FreeBMD (birth, marriage, death index), database (www.freebmd.org.uk).

General Register Office for England and Wales (www.gro.gov.uk/gro/content).

Irish Genealogy, "Church Records", database (www.irishgenealogy.ie/en).

Library and Archives Canada, "Genealogy and Family History", database (www.collectionscanada.gc.ca/index-e.html).

Manitoba Genealogical Society (www.mbgenealogy.com).

Manitoba Vital Statistics Agency, "Genealogy Searches for Unrestricted Records" (vitalstats.gov.mb.ca).

National Archives of Ireland, "Census of Ireland 1901/1911", database and images (www.census.nationalarchives.ie).

Robert Sewell's Genealogy Site, "Livingston of Callendar" (www.robertsewell.ca/livingston.html).

RootsIreland.ie (birth, death, marriage, gravestone transcriptions), database (www.rootsireland.ie).

Ros Davies' Co. Down, Northern Ireland Family History Research Site (freepages.

genealogy.rootsweb.ancestry.com/~rosdavies).

Scotlands People (birth, marriage, death records), database and images (www.scotlandspeople.gov.uk).

CHAPTER TEN

Researching Emily

The Shaw Family of Belfast

BY LYNETTE NUNN (AUSTRALIA)

EMILY ELIZABETH BEAVAN (NÉE SHAW) is my great-great-grandmother.

Oral tradition said we had an authoress in the family, and once I started researching my family, I soon discovered it was Emily. She was born in Belfast, Ireland, about 1818.

As well as being a wife, mother, and teacher, Emily was also an author of novels and poems; and she kept an album, rather like the autograph album of my day, in which she drew and wrote some of her poems and short stories. I discovered this album in the belongings of a fourth cousin I met through the course of my research. He was also descended from Emily. Amongst Emily's own writings, there are also poetry contributions from a few others, including her husband, and keepsakes like pieces of lacework, dried flowers, and all kinds of other fascinating things. The album was begun in 1835 in Belfast and travelled with her wherever she went until she passed away in Sydney, Australia in 1897. It has remained in the family ever since and became an integral part of my research.

The story that follows is one of a merry dance all over the world in search of clues about Emily's family and the identity of her parents.

First Stop—Australia

My story starts with scrolling through the Victorian BMD microfiche indexes in search of the birth certificate for Emily's daughter and my great-grandmother Amy Bastable (née Beavan). The entry in the indexes took a bit of finding because I was a real novice then, and unbeknownst to me, Amy had been registered without a name. As a consequence, the indexes had recorded her as "F Beavan". It wasn't until later, when I noticed a "M Beavan" with the same parents that I thought I was looking for, that the penny dropped, and I realised "F" was for female and "M" was for male!

Amy's birth certificate showed she was born in 1856 in Kilmore, Victoria, Australia, and stated that her parents' full names were Frederick Williams Cadwalleder Beavan and Emily Elizabeth Shaw. The certificate also gave me the extra information that they had been married in Saint John, New Brunswick, Canada.

Knowing that Amy had lived most of her life in Sydney, Australia, I searched through the New South Wales (NSW) indexes for Emily's death, and I discovered that Emily had died in Sydney. By purchasing her death certificate from the NSW Registry of Births, Deaths and Marriages in Sydney,[1] I found that her eldest son, Alfred Beavan, was the informant. He stated that Emily's father was Samuel Shaw, Master Mariner, and that her mother was Isabella Pringle.

Onward to New Brunswick, Canada

Through extremely generous and kind archivists at the University of New Brunswick and fellow genealogists in Canada, I was able to find a marriage record for Emily Shaw and Frederick Beavan. According to a book that was written by B. Wood-Holt (1986),[2] the marriage took place on 19 June 1838 in Norton, Kings County, New Brunswick. However, I also found an announcement of the marriage in the *Belfast Newsletter*

[1] Registry of Births Deaths & Marriages, New South Wales (www.bdm.nsw.gov.au/).

[2] B. Wood-Holt, *Early marriage records of New Brunswick: Saint John City and County from the British conquest to 1839* (St. John , New Brunswick: Holland House, 1986).

which was dated some six months later and with a slightly different date for the marriage:

> June 20, at Norton, near St. John's N.B. Surgeon Bevan to Emily Elizabeth Shaw, eldest daughter of Mr. Samuel Shaw, late of Belfast.
>
> – *Belfast Newsletter*, 1 January 1839

With the help I received in Canada, I was able to piece together quite a long story of Emily's life in that country. This included one period that she wrote about in a book about life in the "the backwoods of New Brunswick" at Long Creek where she lived with her husband and growing family for seven years. Journals and newspapers of the time also carried her stories and poems, which gave me a unique insight into small windows of her life and her contemporaries. Her stories and poems were often based on her own experiences or those of people or events she knew, even if they were somewhat embellished for the sake of a good story. Militia lists and other people's diaries and memoirs, much to my surprise, also held snippets of information about her husband, Frederick.

As well as Emily's own teaching career, I found some details about the lives of some possible siblings: Frances, Pringle, and Samuel Shaw. Friends had managed to find at the National Archives in Ottawa their petitions for a licence to teach. From these petitions, I was able to obtain various details about their religion, places of birth, and education levels, as well as estimate how long they had been in New Brunswick. They were teachers in the same area of New Brunswick and appeared to be connected to Emily because her husband provided references for some of their petitions. I sailed along quite happily for a couple of years finding all sorts of wonderful things about Emily, her husband and, in particular, her brother Pringle Shaw.

Next Stop—Ontario, Canada

Pringle Shaw was a teacher, writer, and a very community-spirited person who made small appearances in newspapers and is mentioned in local histories in the area around Kettleby, a small community in King Township,

Ontario, that I learned about by using Google to search the Internet for his name. An unusual name is always a bonus in family history research!

Ancestry.com has recently added merchant navy records to their online databases. From these, I discovered that Pringle had returned to Ireland where he was trying his hand as a sailor from 1843 until 1845 when he was paid off in Quebec. He then apparently went to the United States as he authored a book, published about 1850, that describes his travels through California during the gold rush. He next turns up in the 1851 Ontario (Canada West) census as a school teacher once again.

At one stage, I joined an Irish Yahoo group on the Internet when they were using a chat room to get to know each other. I was chatting one afternoon to a lady from Canada and, as you often do, I asked where she lived in Canada. What a moment of serendipity it was when she replied that she came from Tilbury—the same township in Essex County, Ontario, that Pringle had finally settled in! On her bookshelf was a local history of this township, and it was to be a very late night while she sent me transcribed excerpts and photos from the book about Pringle, his wife, family and especially his eldest son, William Shaw, who had been a Mayor of the township. The next week she was out taking photos of their headstones for me and managed to get me a copy of the book for my library as well. This family was fast becoming a family historian's dream.

Conflicting Information

Then a setback in my research quickly dissipated the euphoria. I had sent for and received the registration of the death of Pringle in Tilbury, Ontario, which was dated 1 March 1915. The registration had been made by Pringle's son William Shaw. William had stated, in agreement with Emily's death registration, and as I expected, that Pringle's father was Samuel Shaw, Master Mariner. The pinch, however, was reading his statement that said Pringle's mother's name was Isabel Adelaide McMoran and not Isabella Pringle as Emily's son had stated on her death certificate!

This very unexpected development was especially perplexing as it had always seemed to me that Pringle had been named with his mother's maiden name—the name given on Emily's death certificate. The use of a mother's maiden name as a forename was something I had seen quite a few times before, and I had thought it was a perfectly logical scenario. What now? Could there be an error on Pringle's certificate? Perhaps Samuel had married two Isabellas. How was I ever going to solve such a conundrum, especially in those reputed difficult and missing Irish records that I heard so much about and was rather reluctant to go near?

Time went on and I continued to research by following Emily and the other "siblings", although I was always never quite sure I was on the right track. However, I felt that if I researched sideways, I just might uncover more evidence one way or the other.

The Search Resumes in Ireland

So it was that my research eventually took me to Ireland in search of Emily's parents. Little did I know that, despite my reservations, I would end up learning so much more about her life and that of her family.

My first success with Irish research came about as a result of a very kind and generous fellow family historian who lives in Belfast. He had discovered the obituaries for Samuel and Isabella Shaw in the *Belfast Newsletter*. I found that they had both died in their eighties and were buried in the same grave at the Clifton Street Cemetery by searching the burial registers and cemetery records which I found were online.[3]

After writing to the General Register Office (GRO),[4] I obtained the death registration certificates for Samuel and Isabella Shaw. The informant was identified as "O'Connell Shaw" on both death registrations, and Isabella had been residing with him at the time of her death. I had not come across this name before and suspecting he was probably a son, one of the things I set out to do then was find out who he was and whether records about his life would help.

Eventually, the opportunity arose to take a trip to Ireland to see if I could unlock the secret of my Shaw family in that difficult arena of Irish research.

It was on a visit to the Linen Hall Library in Belfast, where there are card indexes of the *Belfast Newsletter*, that I discovered the marriage of

[3] Clifton Street Cemetery (www.cliftonstreetcemetery.com).

[4] General Register Office, Government Offices, Roscommon (www.welfare.ie/en/Pages/General-Register-Office.aspx).

Samuel Shaw and Isabella McMorran at St George's Chapel in Belfast on 20 September 1817; and to be sure, as one should always do, I checked the original newspaper and later the parish registers on film through a local Family History Centre[5] and found it to be correct. To my disappointment, however, this information had confirmed that the parents on Pringle's death registration were correct and therefore added still more weight to my ever increasing doubt about Emily's connection to Pringle and the other Shaw family members.

One thing I was quite certain about, however, was that if Emily and Pringle were brother and sister, they could not have had different mothers. Various sources had narrowed Emily's birth year to about 1818, while Pringle had given a birth date of 2 January 1825 in the 1901 Canada census.[6] As Emily was older than Pringle, there was no way her father could have married a second time after she was born to an Isabella Pringle when he had married Isabella McMorran in 1817. So that put paid to that theory.

Normally, I would have decided that they were from a different family and I was probably on the wrong track, but there was something nagging in my mind. For one thing, Pringle had written a poem in Emily's album, suggesting there had to be some sort of connection. It seemed unlikely they could be cousins as their fathers had the same name and occupations. I felt there just had to be a logical explanation somewhere, and I set out to find it, starting with O'Connell Shaw, the informant on Samuel and Isabella's death registration.

A visit with the friendly staff at the General Registrar Office for Northern Ireland (GRONI) while I was in Belfast gave me a clue that O'Connell had passed away before 1922 as he wasn't on their computerised indexes that started in that year. Armed with this knowledge and by using the Public Record Office of Northern Ireland (PRONI) Will Calendar indexes,[7] I was very fortunate to find a copy of O'Connell's will which

[5] Family History Center operated by The Church of Jesus Christ of Latter-day Saints (LDS).

[6] Ancestry.com, "1901 Census of Canada," database and images (www.ancestry.com).

[7] Public Record Office of Northern Ireland, "Will Calendars," database and images (www.proni.gov.uk).

gave me his death date of 5 June 1918. If you have never seen an Irish will from this time, it can be an amazing resource full of information about parents, children, siblings etc. Once again, using the information from the will, the *Belfast Newsletter* came to the rescue with a death notice that announced his burial was to take place at Dundonald Cemetery in Belfast:

> SHAW—June 5, 1918 at his residence, Woodlea, Shandon Park, Knock O'Connell Shaw (late of Belfast Harbour Office). Funeral (private) to Dundonald Cemetery to-day (Friday), at 11 a.m. No flowers
>
> – *Belfast Newsletter*, 7 June 1918

Clues from the Crypt

Back home in Australia, I wrote to Dundonald Cemetery to confirm the burial information for O'Connell Shaw. I learnt from them that buried in the same grave as O'Connell were his sisters Matilda Shaw and Adelaide Shaw, and one of his nieces, Maude Wilson. Three of his children and a sister-in-law, Emily Shaw, were buried in the adjoining grave.

The identity of his sister-in-law in the grave was confirmed by her death certificate that I subsequently sent for from the GRO in Ireland. This Emily Shaw was another person I had not heard of before. I knew that she couldn't be my great-great-grandmother as she was married and had died in Sydney. From the certificate, I learnt that this Emily was the widow of Thomas Shaw, a Captain, and that she was born about 1857 and therefore probably belonged to the same generation as O'Connell. Most importantly, I learnt from this record that O'Connell had a brother named Thomas.

Following Up on Old Research

Determined to leave no stone unturned, and because I am very curious by nature, I then decided to follow someone who I suspected was one of O'Connell's children to see where that might lead. Her name was Edith, and I was fairly certain she was another daughter as other newspaper research had led to the *Brooklyn Eagle* (New York) with a legal notice regarding an estate. The notice listed, in addition to other apparent relatives of the deceased, the sons and daughters already known to me as those of O'Connell Shaw. Amongst the list of those particular children was an Edith Sibley. This indicated to me that if Edith was a daughter of O'Connell, then she had probably married someone with the surname Sibley. So, using the Cheshire parish registers at FamilySearch,[8] I discovered an Edith Shaw who had been married to Osbert Carden Sibley in 1906 in Cheshire, England!

Armed with another irresistible unusual first name of Osbert, I was able to find his birth registration in the GRO indexes at FreeBMD[9] and his baptism in the Cheshire parish registers index at FamilySearch, revealing that his father was Septimus Sibley. Always curious, I searched their names using Google and found out they were surgeons and that Osbert's father was quite famous. So I decided to check *The Times* newspaper (London) and some of the 19th century Gale newspaper databases which are available online through my National Library of Australia membership, as I thought there might be something newsy about it since they were obviously "society".

The newspaper search came up with a description of Edith Shaw's wedding in the *Liverpool Mercury* (29 September 1894)—what she wore, the bridesmaids, and so on—and they mentioned that the bride was the niece and adopted daughter of Thomas Shaw, who gave her away. The guests included O'Connell Shaw, Miss Isabel Shaw, and Miss Susie Shaw. Researching Isabel and Susie I discovered that they were the daughters of William McNiece Shaw and his wife, Mary. Was he another brother of O'Connell?

A search of the Irish civil registration indexes[10] enabled me to order Edith's birth registration and this confirmed that her father was O'Connell Shaw, even though it wasn't mentioned in the newspaper article. Therefore, because Thomas was mentioned as uncle as well as adopted father in the newspaper, Thomas and O'Connell must be brothers.

I wondered ... Was this Thomas Shaw, who was the uncle and adopted

[8] FamilySearch, "England, Cheshire Parish Registers, 1538-2000," database (familysearch.org).

[9] FreeBMD (birth, marriage, death index), database (www.freebmd.org.uk).

[10] FamilySearch, "Ireland, Civil Registration Indexes, 1845-1958," database, (familysearch.org).

father of Edith, also the husband of Emily Shaw buried at Dundonald Cemetery? So I decided to check FamilySearch again and found a marriage of Thomas Shaw and Emily Connor in Lancashire in 1872.[11] Using this information, I was able to get the references from the civil registration indexes at FreeBMD and order a certificate from the GRO in England which confirmed it was the right entry by his father's name, Samuel Shaw. The witnesses were William McNeice Shaw and Mary Brown. Through using the various England and Wales censuses, it subsequently turned out that both Thomas and William were Master Mariners and lived in the Liverpool area from at least 1871.

Tying Things Together

When I was in Ireland, I had also taken the opportunity in Dublin to check the 1911 Irish census which showed O'Connell, a widower, living with his sister Adelaide and two daughters, Ada and Sara Campbell Shaw. Both the 1901 census and the 1911 census were available at that time if you visited the National Archives in Dublin and knew the address. I only had an idea of the 1911 address, and this census gave me their places of birth and the presence of a hitherto unknown niece, Maude Wilson. I have since located them in the 1901 census as the census for both years are now online at the National Archives of Ireland website.[12]

Interestingly, the census said Maude Wilson had been born in Hong Kong in 1866. This sure was a family of travellers! As Maude had also been buried in one of the plots in Dundonald Cemetery, I sent for her death certificate from the GRO. Her death certificate revealed she was the daughter of Thomas Wilson, and the abstract of his will from PRONI revealed his wife's name was Maria and that he was a Master Mariner who had died at sea in 1867. FamilySearch[13] confirmed that Maria Caroline Shaw married Thomas Wilson in 1856 in Belfast, and the details were confirmed by using the Ireland civil registration indexes available at FamilySearch[14] and purchasing a certificate from the GRO.

[11] FamilySearch, "England Marriages, 1538–1973," database (familysearch.org).
[12] The National Archives of Ireland, "Census of Ireland 1901/1911," database and images (www.census.nationalarchives.ie/).
[13] FamilySearch, "Ireland Marriages, 1619-1898," database, (familysearch.org).
[14] FamilySearch, "Ireland, Civil Registration Indexes, 1845-1958," database (familysearch.

The certificate also revealed that one of the witnesses at Maria's marriage was William Shaw—the same name recorded as a witness in the marriage of Thomas Shaw and Emily Connor. This gave me evidence of a familial relationship between Maria, Thomas, and William.

Another name that was of particular interest to me was Matilda Shaw as I had found her signature in my great-great-grandmother Emily's album. A Matilda Shaw was also buried in the same grave as O'Connell Shaw at Dundonald but had died prior to him. Therefore, she was not listed as a sibling in his will, unlike his sister Adelaide who was still alive at the time. Using the Irish Family History Foundation website,[15] I discovered that Matilda Ann Shaw was baptised in St Anne's Church, Belfast, on 26 January 1828, the daughter of Samuel Shaw and Isabella McMurran.

I now had two children born to Samuel Shaw—Matilda in Belfast and Pringle in Canada—with a mother named Isabella McMorran/McMurran, and another, my great-great-grandmother Emily, with a mother named Isabella Pringle. I also had a record of the marriage of Samuel Shaw to Isabella McMorran; confirmation that Samuel was the father's name of both Maria and Thomas Shaw; and proof that Thomas was a brother to Maria. Moreover, I am fairly certain Thomas was also a brother to William Shaw.

Further research on O'Connell himself also proved to be rewarding. While the Public Record Office of Northern Ireland (PRONI) indexes, FamilySearch, and his will obtained from PRONI gave me O'Connell's children's names, it was a search at ScotlandPeople[16] that confirmed to me the identity of his parents. I had no particular reason to look in Scotland, except that I couldn't find anything in Ireland, and I know there are sometimes close links between Ireland and Scotland. The records showed his marriage to Margaret Trimble on 27 September 1867 in Glasgow and revealed the names of his parents as Samuel Shaw and Isabella Shaw (nee McMoran)—the same people whose death records identified O'Connell as the informant. I now had full parental confirmation for three children.

It seems that family members followed certain career choices with the men being seafarers, sometimes working later on for the Belfast Harbour

---

org).

[15] Irish Family History Foundation (www.rootsireland.ie/).

[16] ScotlandsPeople (www.scotlandspeople.gov.uk).

Commission, and/or teaching. The women all seemed to choose teaching. According to the 1911 census of Belfast, Adelaide Shaw, the previously mentioned sister of O'Connell, was a teacher; and O'Connell, like his father when he retired from the sea, had worked for the Harbour Commissioners.

Once again, I searched the indexes of British newspapers through the Gale online databases, and I was fortunate to find an article in the *Belfast Newsletter* about Adelaide's career when she retired from teaching in 1892. The dream family returns!

As can be seen, newspapers would have to be one of my favourite areas of research, no matter what country I am researching in. They are an invaluable resource for finding out something about the lives of your family. Sometimes you have to be creative with your search terms, but the rewards can be plenty.

Thinking a little laterally ... *Who is Isabella Pringle?*

I have never found a marriage of a Samuel Shaw and Isabella Pringle. I did, however, locate an interesting reference to a marriage of William McMorran and Eliza Pringle on 11 December 1785 in Saul Parish, Downpatrick, Co. Down, on the International Genealogical Index (IGI) database at FamilySearch.[17] Downpatrick is not far from Belfast, and this marriage would fit with the birth year of Samuel Shaw's wife, Isabella Adelaide McMorran which would be about 1797 according to information on her death certificate and burial record. Although this is twelve years after the marriage of William McMorran and Eliza Pringle, I thought they could very well be her parents.

I decided to follow up this lead by checking the source, which is a transcript by the Reverend Edward Rea, when I was researching at PRONI on a second trip to Belfast. I found yet one more little piece of evidence that my hunch was correct. The transcript notes that William McMorran was of Belfast, while Eliza Pringle was of Downpatrick. Isabella was a native of Belfast according to her burial record, although on a Canadian census, her son Pringle stated she was born in Scotland. So perhaps she

[17] FamilySearch, "International Genealogical Index (IGI)", database (familysearch.org).

was actually born in Scotland but spent most of her life in Belfast, and hence was considered a native of Belfast. It is certainly possible that William and Eliza could have lived in Belfast after their marriage and also that they may just as easily have lived in Scotland as well for some of the time. Directories do show a William McMorran in Belfast in the early 1800s. I cannot be totally certain that these are Isabella's parents as I have yet to discover her baptism. However, there seems to be some kind of link to Scotland in the family since Isabella's son O'Connell had gone there just to be married and then returned with his wife to live in Belfast. If William and Eliza are Isabella's parents, it seemed to me to be a feasible explanation that Pringle was actually named after his maternal grandmother rather than his mother.

Seeking more evidence, I then decided to recheck the Clifton Street Cemetery burial registry , searching by grave number as it is not indexed, to see who else might be buried in the grave of Samuel and Isabella Shaw. Lo and behold, I found the burial of Elizabeth McMorran on 15 February 1843 who was entered in the record as

> … relict of the late William McMorran, Great Patrick St. Born at and came from Downpatrick. One daughter in Belfast and one in America.

Also, there was an Eliza Moran, daughter of E. Moran, Patrick Street, buried in 1847 at the age of 52 years and so born about 1795. They are both buried in the same grave as Samuel and Isabella which, after further research, appears to have been purchased as a McMorran burial plot. Isabella was quite likely the daughter "in America" as research into her husband, Samuel Shaw, shows she must have been back in Belfast by the end of 1844 and so, in 1843, was probably still in Canada, which is sometimes referred to as America. Eliza, daughter of E. Moran, would be the "One daughter in Belfast".

In the alphabetical section of *Martin's Belfast Directory for 1841-2*[18] is an entry that reads: "McMorran, teacher of needlework, 18 Tomb Street."

My great-great-grandmother Emily Shaw lived on Tomb Street before the family went to live in Canada. I know this from one of the stories she

---

[18] Available online at PRONI (http://www.proni.gov.uk).

wrote and also because her father, Samuel Shaw, is recorded as living there in the Belfast directories for the years 1831-32 and 1835-36 online at PRONI. *Henderson's New Belfast Directory and Northern Repository for 1843-44* has the entry, "Mrs McMorran, teacher, seminary 64 Great Patrick St."

I think these listings all relate to Eliza Pringle, wife of William McMorran, who died in 1843.

Conclusion

My theory has taken many years to formulate. An examination and research of all the possible avenues that I can think of in a wide and sometimes obscure variety of resources in archives, record offices, libraries, historical societies. and on the internet has brought me to my conclusion. I have researched sideways, not only backwards and forwards, and by doing this I have discovered a huge amount of information about this family and their lives. I have constantly reviewed, revisited, and reassessed my research whenever something new came to light. The evidence I have uncovered seems to me to overwhelmingly tie them all in together.

The names Elizabeth, Isabella, Adelaide, and William are all names used throughout the family, especially Emily's family; and combined with all the other evidence, I believe that there is an error and it is on Emily's death registration. I am now certain that her mother's name was in fact Isabella Adelaide McMorran and that William McMorran and Eliza Pringle/McMorran are Emily's grandparents.

Perhaps the explanation for error lies in the fact that death is a very stressful time for relatives of the deceased and the informant on a death certificate is not always fully aware of all the facts when giving the information. It is possible that either informant on the two death certificates in my case could have been mistaken. As it turns out, however, it appears to be the informant on Emily's death certificate, her son Alfred Beavan, who was confused. Isabella Pringle did not exist. I guess I was lucky her son did make that error because otherwise I probably would not have found out half of what I know about them or even that some of them ever existed.

I do consider myself incredibly fortunate to have been able to build up a very good picture of Emily and her family. The search, however, does still continue, especially for the baptism of Emily and the rest of her siblings which will hopefully provide a maiden surname to prove once and for all who her parents were, or perhaps it may yet turn into another conundrum! Only time will tell.

Lyn Nunn
45 Scott St
Deagon Qld
Australia 4017
genielynau@yahoo.com

Appendix

The Family of Samuel Shaw & Isabella Adelaide McMorran

Emily's father, Samuel Shaw, was a Master Mariner and various records show that he and the family travelled back and forth between Belfast, Ireland, and Saint John, New Brunswick, Canada, throughout their lives.

Samuel Shaw was born about 1789 in Killyleagh, Co. Down, Ireland, and died on 3 November 1869 in Belfast, Ireland. He married Isabella McMorran, daughter of William McMorran and Eliza Pringle, on 20 September 1817 at St George's Chapel in Belfast. Isabella was born about 1797 and died on 11 September 1878 in Belfast. The children of Samuel and Isabella are:

- Emily Elizabeth Shaw, born ca. 1818 in Belfast, Ireland; died 6 August 1897 in Sydney, New South Wales, Australia; married Frederick Williams Cadwalleder Beavan on 9 June 1838 in Norton, King Co., New Brunswick.
- Frances Shaw (a probable daughter), born ca. 1819 in Sligo, Ireland(?); died 18 May 1898 in New Brunswick, Canada; married James Thompson on 2 March 1842 in Queens County, New Brunswick. [see Note]
- Samuel Shaw (a probable son), born ca. 1821 in Belfast, Ireland(?); died before 1918. [see Note]
- Pringle Shaw, born 2 January 1825 in Belfast, Ireland; died 1 March 1915 in Tilbury Centre, Kent, Ontario, Canada; married Sarah Ashton in ca. 1862; next married Ellen Eales in ca. 1879.
- Matilda Ann Shaw, baptized 26 January 1828 in Belfast, Ireland; died 17 February 1906 in Belfast Ireland; did not marry.
- William McNiece Shaw, born 27 December 1831 in Belfast, Ireland; died 25 August 1897 in Egremont, Cheshire, England; married Mary [surname unknown] in ca. 1861.
- Maria Caroline Shaw, born ca. 1831 in Belfast, Ireland(?); died before 1918; married Thomas Wilson on 21 October 1856 in Belfast, Ireland.

- Thomas Wilkie Shaw, born 16 January 1832 in Belfast, Ireland; died 30 October 1917 in Liscard, Lancashire, England; married Emily M. Connor on 20 February 1872 in Walton on the Hill, Lancashire, England.
- O'Connell Shaw, born ca. 1837 in New Brunswick; died 5 June 1918 in Belfast, Ireland; married Margaret Trimble on 27 September 1867 at St Mary's Episcopal Cathedral in Glasgow, Scotland.
- Adelaide Shaw, born ca.1838 in New Brunswick; died 14 December 1925 in Belfast, Ireland; did not marry.

Note:

It is believed that Samuel and Isabella were the parents of Frances Shaw and Samuel Shaw who were teachers at the same time and in the same area of New Brunswick as Emily and Pringle. Further research is needed to positively confirm these probable siblings. Descendants of Frances say that, according to oral tradition, her father was Samuel and her mother had the maiden name of Irwin. Perhaps, however, this is another case like Emily where the mother has been misidentified. Frances was also said to have been born in Sligo. However, no records have yielded any information on her birth or parents, so this link remains a little tenuous. Very little information has been found about the younger Samuel except for his teacher's licence in New Brunswick and a link back to a Belfast address used by Samuel and Isabella and another used by their son William McNiece Shaw.

* * *

One other male child was buried as an infant at sea in about the year 1836 or 1837. Emily described him in the prologue to a very touching poem about him in her album:

> … he was a child remarkable for infantile intelligence and extreme beauty—the deep lustre of his clear blue eyes, beautiful curls of his sunny hair waving over his lovely forehead always brought to my mind the forms of those bright thousands who sing the holy song before the eternal throne in the blest place where I hope once

more to meet him. A few days after leaving Ireland his spirit took its flight and his body was committed to the deep waves of the Atlantic there to repose till the mighty voice that shakes Heaven and Earth shall say: Give up thy dead thou Sea.

– Emily Elizabeth Shaw [undated]

CHAPTER ELEVEN

The Search For My Ancestors

Finding McMullan Roots in Downpatrick, County Down

BY TOM W. MCMILLAN (UNITED STATES)

THIS IS A STORY ABOUT how I worked my McMillan family's roots back to Downpatrick in the parish of Down. The story is not complete, but I have accumulated considerable information to share, starting with the life of my great-grandfather William John McMillan Sr.

Some of what follows is working backwards, as that's mostly how my family information was found. I began with my great-grandpa's death record and little by little was able to get back to Ireland with my research.

Great-Grandfather William John McMillan Sr.

My branch of the McMillan family was disconnected from our origins in Ireland. My grandfather William John McMillan Jr. and grandmother Michaelena ("Lena") Schmidt/Smith lived in Minnesota and relocated to Oregon about 1904. Grandpa died twenty years prior to my birth and there was little family lore on the McMillan family handed down.

In 2009, I found information left by my grandmother Lena where she had recorded the deaths of her parents and siblings in a prayer book.

Using this information on the Schmidt family, I started searching at the Minnesota Historical Society website.[1] I found they held death records for all four of my paternal great-grandparents. I ordered these records in the hope that they would give me more information about my McMillan roots. It was the death record I found of my great-grandpa William John McMillan Sr. that started me on my quest to find my family roots.

It's good to keep an open mind, as I've found some records and/or parts of records aren't always correct. Since receiving William John McMillan's death certificate, I have found the following pieces of information on the certificate are incorrect: date of birth, given name of father, place of birth for mother, and possibly place of birth for father.

Census records show William John's mother was born in Ireland, and all but one census show his father born in Ireland (another census has him born in Scotland). I spent considerable time searching for a David McMillan as shown on the certificate, but it turned out that was not his father's given name (I later learned it was John).

I found an obituary for my great-grandfather William John McMillan Sr. in a newspaper from St. Paul, Minnesota, which reads in part:

> William J McMillan, veteran Great Northern railroad conductor, and believed to have been the oldest Shriner[2] in the United States, died suddenly Wednesday … He was 88 years old.
>
> Mr McMillan … came to St Paul 43 years ago and until his retirement eleven years ago had been a conductor on that road. He was born in Toronto, Ont.
>
> He became acquainted with Thomas A. Edison when the latter was telegraph operator for the Great Western at Kingston, Ont and is said to be the first man to have taken a telegraphic order from the electrical wizard.
>
> Mr McMillan was president and founder of the Great Northern Veterans Association, composed of employees of the railroad who have been 25 years or more in its service …
>
> –*The Pioneer Press,* 2 January 1930

[1] Minnesota Historical Society (www.mnhs.org).

[2] Shriners International is a charitable organization founded in 1872 that evolved from Freemasonry.

Later research revealed that William John McMillan was actually 82 years old at his death (perhaps someone wanted him to be known as the oldest Shriner), and he was not born in Toronto.

As mentioned in his obituary, William John was a founding president of the Veterans' Association of the Great Northern Railway. To the right is an early photo of him from a book about the proceedings of the group.[3]

William John McMillan - President, Veterans' Association of the Great Northern Railway (photo: ca. 1913; see text for source).

His obituary also indicated he was acquainted with Thomas Edison during his years in Ontario. Other than the obituary, however, we have no proof that Edison and William John knew each other. Nonetheless, the fact that it's mentioned in the obituary does give weight to it possibly being true.

In 1869, William John was in Fergus, Ontario, where his son W. J. McMillan Jr. was born. According to his son's birth record, and to family lore, William John McMillan Sr. was a sailor for a large passenger vessel on the Great Lakes. It is said that his wife objected to the roughness of sailors and his absence from home, so William John sought a different line of work. I later learned he was recorded as a carpenter on the 1871 Canada census, which turned out to be difficult work since it involved digging cellars for homes.

Sometime in the early 1870s, William John went to work as a conductor for the railroad out of Palmerston, Wellington County, Ontario.

James J. Hill, known as "The Empire Builder" for having built the railroad from the Great Lakes to the Pacific Coast in the United States, recruited men from the Wellington County area for his railroad in Minnesota. William John hired on and went to Breckenridge, Minnesota,

[3] *Veterans Association of the Great Northern Railway, 1908-1914*, Proceedings of the Veterans Association of the Great Northern Railway (1913).

in 1879. The family joined him there in 1880, and all emigrated to St Paul, Minnesota, about 1887. I have found a number of newspaper articles[4] that describe William John planning birthday events to honor his employer and friend James J. Hill, who presided for many years over the Great Northern Railroad.

James Jerome Hill was born in Eramosa, Wellington County, Ontario, near Fergus and left for Minnesota in the mid-1850s, likely before W. J. McMillan's arrival in Wellington County. James, his wife Mary Mehegan, and William John were all of Irish ancestry, their parents having been born in Ireland. So Irish roots may have sparked the friendship between William John and James. Interestingly, many of the men James Hill hired to work on the railroad were also Irish or of Irish descent.

James J. Hill was a controversial man. I have read a good deal about him, studied his life, and have grown to admire him in many ways. While he was not Catholic, a priest married him and his wife, Mary; and he was always very generous and supportive of the Catholic Church. He supported a number of charitable causes and was a good family man, although his work kept him away from family a lot.

The following are a couple of accounts from books about the association between James Hill and William John McMillan:

> When Conductor McMillan sold his farm in the valley for ten thousand dollars, he asked Mr. Hill what he should do with the money. "Buy Northern Securities," was the answer. He did so and saw them jump one-third.
>
> –Elbert Hubbard, 1909[5]

> To this time belongs the interesting recollection of Mr. W. J. McMillan, who was at the time of Mr. Hill's death a conductor on the Great Northern Railway, grown old in the service, the head of the Veteran Employees' Association, and one of Mr. Hill's most devoted men. Mr. McMillan said that he first met Mr. Hill when he was taking a party of guests over the road. The latter addressed

---

[4] GenealogyBank (www.genealogybank.com).

[5] Elbert Hubbard, "James J. Hill." In *Little Journeys to the Homes of Great Businessmen* (New York & Chicago: Wm. H. Wise & Co., 1916), 399-435.

> him with that unfailing friendliness that he always showed to his men, especially when they had been long with him, and asked him if he had not been a railroad conductor before and where he had worked. "Yes," said Mr. McMillan, "on the Great Western of Canada." "Then," said Mr. Hill, "you must have been in Guelph." Then he asked him if he remembered a little grocery store near the track, and said that was where he earned his first money.
>
> After four weeks' work his Scotch employer, on Saturday night, put his hand on his shoulder and said, "James, ye hae done right weel. If ye keep on, ye'll mak' your way in the world." Then he handed him an envelope. The boy hastened home to give the four dollars it contained, his pay for his first month of hard work, to his mother. "I never felt so rich," he said. "I never expect to feel so rich again in my life, as when I looked at those four dollars and whenI handed them over to my mother."
>
> –Joseph Gilpin Pyle, 1917[6]

As noted previously, William John McMillan Sr. was instrumental in starting the Veterans Association of the Great Northern Railway and served as president of that organization for many years. The Association was organized on 23 February 1913. A meeting was held at the newly opened Glacier Park on 16 September 1913 to honor James J. Hill's birthday and to have a formal meeting of the members of the Association.

Overleaf is a photo from the Veterans Association book about that meeting and shows William John McMillan, President, with the other officers in attendance.

From a family book written by his granddaughter Annie Laurie Baker, we get a personal glimpse of William John ("Grandpa") McMillan:

> Grandpa made the tower in his bedroom his office for conducting the business of the Association. Many widows came to see him seeking financial help. I recall when I was visiting there at age eleven he got all dressed up in his morning suit, with tails, took his high hat and gold headed cane and boarded the street car and

[6] Joseph Gilpin Pyle, *The Life of James J. Hill* (Garden City, New York: Doubleday Page & Company, 1917), Volume 1.

My great-grandfather William John McMillan (fourth from the left) with other officers of the Veterans Association, Great Northern Railway, at Minot, North Dakota (photo: 1913; see text for source).

> went off to have lunch with Mrs James J Hill. His purpose was to .request a grant from her to help the widows. He was a dramatic story teller, and I remember his account of the visit that night at dinner. He said "She looked at me with tears in her eyes and said 'Willie, I can't have our people in want.' She gave him $10,000 which he parceled out in $15 amounts."
>
> –Annie Laurie Baker, 1991[7]

Ontario Family Roots

When I realized from researching my great-grandpa that there was an Ontario connection for the family, I searched the 1871 Canada census and found him recorded as Wm. John "McMillen" (age 23, born in Quebec) along with his wife, "Annie" (age 29, born in Scotland), and two sons, Matthew (age 4) and William John (age 2), both born in Ontario. His brother David "McMillen" was also with the family, and he was recorded as born about 1853 in Ontario and working as a harness maker. After this census, six more children were born in Ontario by 1880. A ninth child was born in Minnesota after 1880.

I found an 1867 marriage record for William John Sr. and Anderson Todd (transcribed below), which gave me the names of William John's parents—John McMullin and Margaret Orr:

Marriage Transcription—William McMullin, age 20, born Montreal. Quebec Canada, residing in Nichol Township, son of John McMullin and Margaret Orr, married Miss A. Todd, age 25, born in Scotland, residing in Nichol Township, daughter of Matthew Todd and Helen Drummond, on 23 Mar 1867 in Wellington County, Ontario.[8]

Knowing the names of William John's parents, I was able to find his baptismal record:

[7] Annie Laurie Baker, *Grenville and Annie McMillan Baker Family with notes on William John McMillan and Anderson "Annie" Todd* (publisher unknown, 1991).

[8] Ancestry.com, "Ontario, Canada, Marriages, 1801-1928," database and images (www.ancestry.com).

Baptismal Transcription—William John, son of John McMullian, of Quebec, and of Margaret his wife, her maiden name Orr, was born on this twenty fourth of August and was baptized on the Seventh day of November in the year of our Lord, One thousand eight hundred and forty Seven. By me John Cornwall, Assist Curate. [Witnessed by] John McMullian, Margaret McMullian [her mark], Patrick White [his mark], Jane Leeson.[9]

The baptism took place at The Holy Trinity Cathedral (Anglican) located in Quebec City, Quebec. Other records (1851 marriage and 1861 census) showed William John born at Montreal. Perhaps he was, but it seems odd to backtrack to Quebec City for the baptism.

The spelling of "McMullian" on the baptismal record is unusual. Could those signing the record have felt obliged to sign as the curator wrote the name? And it is curious that Margaret is shown signing with her mark. She had made a sampler on which was stitched the year (1833) and her age (10 years), so I believe she was literate and had signed this record. It does appear possible Margaret just signed "Margaret M" and the curator completed her signature, as that part appears similar to what he wrote in the body of the record. Or, perhaps the mark should have been for Jane.

The timing between the birth on 24 August and the baptism on 7 November also seems odd, although perhaps not unusual. I did find one interesting possibility for the delay.

A John McMullen was arrested for damaging hotel property in Quebec City. He was tried, convicted, and had to pay a fine or serve 60 days in jail. This John McMullen was from Ireland, 5 feet 9 inches tall, and 24 years old when jailed on 6 September 1847. His initial release date would have been 6 November 1847. However, he was pardoned and released from custody on 6 October 1847 after serving 30 days.[10]

Perhaps Margaret made early arrangements to have William John baptized on 7 November 1847 because she was thinking her husband wouldn't be available for the ceremony until after his original release date of 6 November. Speculative, but possible.

---

[9] Ancestry.com, "Quebec, Vital and Church Records (Drouin Collection), 1621-1967," database and images (www.ancestry.com).

[10] Bibliothèque et Archives nationales du Québec (www.banq.qc.ca).

John McMullan and Margaret Orr in Quebec and Ontario

Based on Irish marriage and birth records I later found, I know my great-great-grandparents John and Margaret (Orr) McMullan arrived in Quebec from Ireland with their first son, Arthur, sometime between 1845 and 1847. While the name in Ireland may have been McMullan, in Canada I have found it mostly spelt as McMullen.

I did not find a John McMullen (or any McMullen) in the 1847 diretory for Quebec City.[11] However, I believe I found him listed as John McMullen in *The Montreal Directory* for the years 1848, 1849 and 1850.[12] The 1848 directory lists him as a laborer on Colborne near Gabriel Street; the 1849 directory as a laborer on the corner of Durham and Lorchester streets; and the 1850 directory as a shoemaker at 15 St. Mary Street (a John Hall had previously occupied 15 St Mary Street as a shoemaker in 1848 and 1849). I did not find John McMullen in the 1851 or later directories in Montreal.

I found my great-great-grandmother Margaret and her two sons Arthur and William John McMullen Sr. (my great-grandfather) on the 1851 census of Canada East (Quebec) living in Montreal. For that year, they were with a Johnston family that included a pensioner and tailors in the family. Margaret is recorded as married, but her husband John is not shown on the census.

I don't know what happened to my great-great-grandfather John McMullen after 1850. One possibility is that he left the Montreal area in search of more opportunity for his shoe trade.

I found there was a shoemaker's strike and rebellion at Montreal in 1849.[13] Apparently, shoemakers were upset with the mechanization of shoemaking in Montreal, and some individuals destroyed equipment in a shoemaking enterprise. A few were arrested, but I've found no mention of any involvement by John McMullen. Perhaps John left the area, since

[11] Internet Archive, *The Quebec Directory and City and Commercial Register, 1847-8* (Montreal: Printed at the Canada Gazette Office, 1847), database and images (archive.org/).

[12] Bibliothèque et Archives nationales du Québec *Annuaires Lovell de Montréal et sa banlieue (1842-1999)*, database and images (www.banq.qc.ca).

[13] Eric Tucker, "That Indefinite Area of Toleration: Criminal Conspiracy and Trade Unions in Ontario," *Labour / Le Travail.* 27 (1991): 15-54.

mechanization of the trade in Montreal would have made it hard for an individual to compete as a shoemaker.

I have found other shoemakers with the name John McMullen, although I've been able to eliminate most. Of course, he could have changed occupations.

Another possibility is that John died prior to 1861. There were many John McMullens from Ireland, but I don't have a definitive death entry. I have been in contact with Mount Royal Cemetery in Montreal and there is one John McMullen buried there in 1852, but that John died in 1846 and was later moved to the Mount Royal location. They also have a John McMullen buried in 1857 in an unmarked grave, but I believe his family had left the area prior to that year.

Then there is the possibility that John and his wife went separate ways because, by the time of the 1861 Canada (West) census, Margaret had remarried. Her new husband was John Hinds, and they lived in Toronto, Ontario. This census showed Margaret was born in County Antrim, Ireland. Their children on the census were recorded as Arthur Hinds, William John Hinds, and David Hinds. The first two boys were actually the sons of John McMullen. I can't be absolutely sure of David's parentage.

On this census, Arthur was shown as age 14 and born in Downpatrick, Ireland; William John as age 12, born at Montreal, Quebec; and David as age 7, born at Kingston, Ontario. Actually, Arthur and William John, according to their birth records, would have been one or two years older than recorded on the census. I have no birth record for David, so can only assume he was born about 1854. There was a James Hinds and Elizabeth Hinds also listed on the census, but they were John Hinds' children by his first marriage.

The 1861 census is the last I can be sure of Arthur McMullen's whereabouts. Family lore says he served in the United States Civil War, but we have no proof. I also don't know what happened to David after the 1871 census when he was with William John and family at Fergus, Wellington County, Ontario.

I searched the early city directories for Toronto at the Toronto Public Library website[14] and found John Hinds listed as a tinsmith and parasol

[14] Toronto Public Library (www.torontopubliclibrary.ca).

maker for several years in the early 1860s.

The 1864-65 Toronto directory also shows "Mrs Margaret Hinds (widow John), broker, second-hand, 82 Church Street".

Margaret married for a third time in 1865 to Matthew Todd (the record shows "Dodd" which is wrong) and a transcript is shown below:

Marriage Transcription—Mathew Dodd [sic], age 56, born Scotland, residing in Fergus, son of Robert and Isabella married Margaret Hinds, age 39, born in Ireland, residing in Toronto, daughter of David and Catherine, on 24 May 1865 in York County. (Toronto).[15]

This record is where I found the names of Margaret's parents—David [Orr] and Catherine.

Matthew Todd was actually born in England in 1802, not Scotland. He is the father of Anderson Todd who married William John McMillan, my great-grandfather and son of Matthew's second wife Margaret. Matthew's first wife died in 1863 at Fergus, Ontario, where he and Margaret lived until Matthew's death in February of 1878.

In October 1878, Margaret married for a fourth time to Andrew Gartley in Fergus, Ontario. They remained in Fergus through the 1881 and 1891 Canada censuses, and Andrew died there in June of 1892.

On the 1901 Canada census, Margaret Gartley is recorded as widowed and still living in Fergus with James Hinds, her stepson from her marriage to John Hinds.

While I'm aware Margaret was married four times, family lore indicates she may have been married seven times. I may be missing marriages prior to the 1861 census when she is shown married to John Hinds. I don't have a marriage record for Margaret and John, which could reveal her surname if a record were to be found.

An archivist at the Wellington County Museum and Archives,[16] from records they hold, told me Margaret Gartley was admitted to the House of Industry and Refuge in Wellington County in 1902. The Refuge was located where the Museum and Archives is located today. Margaret's

[15] Ancestry.com, "Ontario, Canada, Marriages, 1801-1928," database and images (www.ancestry.com).

[16] Wellington County Museum and Archives, Guelph, Ontario, Canada.

death record[17] shows she died there on 16 October 1910. It is a mystery as to where she is buried.

John McMullan and Margaret Orr of Downpatrick, Co. Down

From the 1861 census, I know Arthur McMullan, the son of my great-great-grandparents, was born in Downpatrick, Co. Down, Ireland. At FamilySearch, I found an indexed record for Arthur McMullan showing he was baptized on 18 April 1845 in Downpatrick and born to John McMullan and Margaret.[18]

Sheila Phillips[19] found the original baptism record for me at the Public Records Office of Northern Ireland (PRONI) in Belfast. The record is very dark, but I was able to make it out. The information is the same as on the indexed record and further shows his birth as 8 March 1845. James Ford/Forde, a Church of Ireland Minister at Downpatrick,[20] baptized him. The original record also indicated Arthur's father John McMullan was a shoemaker.

At FamilySearch, I found a marriage for John McMullan and Margaret Orr that showed they married on 2 May 1845 at Downpatrick.[21] I later received the same information from Sheila Phillips who sent me a record she found at PRONI that had marriages indexed from 1844 and 1845.

However, I later found another record at FamilySearch which showed that John and Margaret had actually married a year earlier, in 1844, at Downpatrick Parish Church of Ireland[22] (this record gave Margaret Orr's year of birth as 1823). At Ancestry.com,[23] I also found a transcription for John McMullan marrying Margaret Orr at Saul Parish in Downpatrick in 1844.

---

[17] Ancestry.com , "Ontario, Canada, Deaths, 1869-1938 and Deaths Overseas, 1939-1947," database and images (www.ancestry.com).

[18] FamilySearch , "Ireland Births and Baptisms, 1620-1881," database, (https://familysearch.org).

[19] Sheila Phillips (1951-2012), late of Ballymartin, Co. Down, Northern Ireland.

[20] RRos Davies' Co. Down, Northern Ireland Family History Research Site (freepages.genealogy.rootsweb.ancestry.com/~rosdavies).

[21] FamilySearch , "Ireland Marriages, 1619-1898," database (familysearch.org).

[22] FamilySearch, "International Genealogical Index (IGI)," database (https://familysearch.org).

[23] Ancestry.com, "Irish Records Extraction Database," database (www.ancestry.com).

A very kind person from Fiona's County Down Genealogy Group[24] acquired a marriage record for me from PRONI.[25] This record appears to be written by one person (so possibly a handwritten transcription) and is on a Downpatrick Cathedral form. Here's my transcription of it:

Marriage Transcription—John McMullen of Down Parish and Margt Orr of Down Parish were married in this Cathedral by license with consent of parents this second day of May in the year one thousand eight hundred and forty four, by me Jas Milligan. This Marriage was solemnized between us John McMullen, Margt Orr. In the presence of Daniel Hurst, Wm George Hurst.

Ros Davies' website indicates that a William George Hurst was a shoemaker in Downpatrick in 1852. I have found a family tree at the RootsWeb website[26] for William George Hurst showing that he and his family emigrated to Australia where he owned a hotel or inn.

My understanding is that "consent of parents" was required for anyone younger than 21 years old at the time of marriage. In John and Margaret's case, this meant that one or both had been born in 1823 or later.

John's date of birth is still a mystery, but the one marriage record I found showed that Margaret was indeed born in 1823. Moreover, I have seen a sampler she made that shows she was 10 years old in 1833. The only record of the day on which she was born comes from the 1901 Canada census which recorded her birth as 7 December 1825. Other records also show Margaret born during this period.

Family lore relates that John was the second son of a well-off family and fell in love with Margaret Orr while a student at a college where she was a maid. Margaret was said to have been very beautiful, with auburn hair and yellow-brown eyes. I've heard that, when John and Margaret married, his family disowned him since she was a commoner. In reality, I have found a great deal of family lore has proven false. But who knows, it may be true.

---

[24] Fiona's County Down Genealogy Group at Yahoo!Groups (groups.yahoo.com/neo/groups/CountyDownGenealogy/info).

[25] Public Record Office of Northern Ireland (PRONI), "Parish of Downpatrick, Diocese Down, Co. Down," Marriages, 1837-44, microfilm, PRONI Reference: MIC1/39/1.

[26] Ancestry.com, "WorldConnect Project" (www.rootsweb.ancestry.com).

A friend found another reference to John and Margaret's marriage at PRONI.[27] This source indicated that John lived on Bridge Street in Downpatrick at the time of the marriage and shows Margaret was a servant with the surname Orr. It also has a John McMullan, shoemaker, who lived on Bridge Street and died on 10 June 1848 at the age of 81 years.

This same source gives the death of a Susan (Galway) on 5 December 1846. She was a 60-year old widow of Arthur McMullan, a pensioner, and she had lived on Bridge Street when she died. John and Margaret named their first son Arthur, so perhaps this Arthur and Susan McMullan are John's parents.

Another reference at PRONI[28] shows a James McMullan who lived on Bridge Street in Downpatrick in 1843. It also has a Susan McMullan who that year was living in the townland of Demesne of Down, Downpatrick. Perhaps she is the same Susan who died at Bridge Street in 1846.

The Search for McMullan & Orr Roots in County Down Continues

This is the extent of the information I have for my great-great-grandparents John McMullan and Margaret Orr.

I have searched extensively for further details, but other solid information escapes me for the moment. I don't give up easily and will continue my search.

From census and marriage records, it seems likely Margaret Orr was born in County Antrim to a David Orr and Catherine. I know nothing more about her parents.

John and Margaret's third son appears to have been named after Margaret's father, David Orr. This would seem to vary from the usual naming pattern some used at the time in Ireland. For that pattern, as I understand it, the first son is named after the paternal grandfather of the child, and the second son is usually named after the maternal grandfather. If John and Margaret used this naming pattern for their first son, then

[27] Public Record Office of Northern Ireland (PRONI), "A. Pilson, Downpatrick. A register of marriages (1727-1862) and obituary (1693-1862) of persons in Downpatrick and neighbourhood. Transcribed from the original by R.W. Blackwood 1933," microfilm, PRONI Reference: T1711/3.

[28] Public Record Office of Northern Ireland (PRONI), "Grand Jury Cess applotment of Parish of Down Summer Assizes," 1843, microfilm, PRONI Reference: T684/11.

John's father would be Arthur McMullan. I'm still curious who William John, their second son, was named after. One possibility is that he was named after both his father John and William George Hurst who was a witness at the marriage of John and Margaret Orr.

I have spent a great deal of time collecting British military records at Findmypast.com[29] for McMullans/McMullens in Downpatrick and in County Down. I have found well over a hundred men with similar surnames who served between the late 1700s and about 1845.

One that stood out for me was Arthur McMullen who was born in Downpatrick in 1780 and was shown as a "cordwainer" (shoemaker) on the military records. He served in the 11th Foot Regiment from 1808 until he was discharged with disability in 1815.

Another was a John McMullen who was born in Downpatrick in 1775 and worked as a tailor. He also served in the 11th Foot Regiment from 1807 to 1815, then served with two other regiments before being discharged in 1821.

In addition, there was a James McMullen, a laborer with Downpatrick roots, who served in the 11th Foot Regiment from 1808 until 1819 when he was discharged with disability. James was born about 1791.

It seems possible that these three McMullens are the same persons mentioned earlier who lived on Bridge Street in Downpatrick during the 1840s. John may have become a shoemaker after his military service or taken over the shoemaking operation after Arthur died.

Ros Davies' website shows an Arthur McMullan of Downpatrick who died on 1 February 1830 at age 52 and is buried at the Downpatrick Church of Ireland graveyard. Perhaps he was the husband of Susan Galway who died in 1846. There is an inscription of his gravestone published in Clark (1983),[30] but apparently the gravestone was lost during later improvements to the cemetery.

I have noted other Arthur McMullans listed at Ros Davies' website with children born in the 1700s and baptized at the Downpatrick Cathedral.

I came into contact with a person at the RootsChat.com website[31]

---

[29] Findmypast.com (www.findmypast.com).

[30] R.S.J. Clarke, *Gravestone Inscriptions County Down.* (Belfast: Ulster Historical Foundation), Volume 19.

[31] RootsChat.com (http://www.rootschat.com).

who shared a connection with the McMullans and had Church of Ireland roots in Downpatrick. This person provided me with contact information for a McMullan family who are still living in County Down. So far, we have not determined a common ancestry.

At the close of 2012, I had a male Y-DNA 37 marker test done at FamilyTreeDNA[32]and had several fairly close matches. One who matched me closely had worked his ancestry back to Coleraine, Co. Londonderry, Ireland, in the 1820s. Another person I tested closely with had worked his ancestry back to the Campbeltown area of Argyll, Scotland, in the 1700s. A third person who matched closely had a McMullen ancestor that married in 1854 at Ahoghill, Co. Antrim, Ireland.

I am hopeful that other McMullan/McMullens with known ancestry in Downpatrick or County Down will have their DNA tested.

If anyone feels they might have common McMillan or Orr ancestry, or may know more about the families I mentioned, please do get in touch with me. My contact information is: email – tomwdcraftr@yahoo.com; mailing address – Tom McMillan; 3820 Addy Street; Washougal, WA 98671; USA.

[32] FamilyTreeDNA (http://www.familytreedna.com).

Appendix

McMillan Family Poem

It's time to reflect on the history we share,
I'll recount a bit how our family did fare.

Dad's Gladstone birth must have started a fest,
He was a tailor who could sing with the best.

He was a noted fly fisher who could hit the right spot,
Many fish struck his fly and fought, with most being caught.

Grandpa McMillan was a big man you see,
His strength was astounding, and smart men would flee.

He went to Alaska, the railroad to build,
A steam shovel he used, and buckets he filled.

Alaskan winters were too cold to dig rock,
So Grandpa did work at an Alaskan Cigar shop.

Seems cigars were a family tradition you see,
But, perhaps that trait has now stopped with me.

Great Grandpa was born at Canada in eighteen forty seven,
Years later he set out on his own, when just eleven.

At Fergus, Ontario he married Anderson Todd,
Her dad was a farrier, so horse's he shod.

Great Grandpa became a conductor, for the railway in time,
Very good at his job, said the best on the line.

James Hill, his employer and he were friends, both Irish descent,
William John and James Hill did travel together, on the railroad

they went.

The Veteran's group for the railway Great Grandpa did start,
Great Northern men could retire when they and their work did depart.

Great Great Grandpa John McMullan could have been Irish born,
We know he married at Downpatrick, but life in Ireland became a concern.

John was a shoemaker, but the trade wasn't sought in such times of strife,
John, Margaret, and Arthur left others behind, and headed for Canada to start a new life.

John was in Quebec, on directories we've seen,
His trade as a shoemaker, perhaps competition too keen.

He may have left town, a new opportunity for his trade to create,
Sadly, we don't know, our Great Great Grandpa John's fate.

But, who before John is in our direct line,
Finding the "who" would really be fine.

I have found an Arthur McMullen, Downpatrick born,
A shoemaker, in 1808 the British military he joined.

Arthur could be the name of John's father,
With the Irish naming pattern that name could matter.

As long as I'm able I'll seek our family beginnings,
The joy of the hunt is making a find, to feel like we're winning!!!

CHAPTER TWELVE

Working Backwards and Sideways

Finding the Hunsdale Family

BY BRENDA ANDERSON (CANADA)

THIS STORY IS ABOUT OUR Hunsdale connections and my husband's great-grandfather Hans Hunsdale. He was a sailor and worked his way up to sea captain on a steam paddle wheeler. By the end of my research, I found that he had two wives and ten children. His part of this family history story has been the most interesting to research of all the family.

My husband is the immigrant from Belfast and, at the age of 65, my mother-in-law also immigrated to Canada to join her sons here. Shortly after I started working on genealogy, she decided she would like to know about her family. And so began the quest to find the Cameron family and the yet to be discovered Hunsdales, her maternal family.

My mother-in-law knew some things about her father William Cameron, but remembered very little about her own mother's family as she was only two when her mother died, and all the relatives she had had contact with were known by their married names. She thought she knew her mother's maiden name, but wasn't sure.

Within a couple of weeks, however, she had found her own birth certificate and was able to tell us her mother's name—Mary Elizabeth Hunsdale. So where, I wondered, do I start when researching an Irish family?

At this time, I only had dialup Internet access and there were only a few resources available on-line. We had Raymond's County Down Website,[1] the FamilySearch site,[2] and a few pay-for-view websites. The FamilySearch site was able to provide us with Mary Elizabeth's birth in 1868 in Kilmood, Co. Down. But here I was, sitting with my husband and my mother-in-law, both from Northern Ireland, and they have no idea where Kilmood is. It's not on a map that we can find. I later learned that more information might be available by visiting a Family History Center run by The Church of Jesus Christ of Latter-day Saints (LDS). There was one about five miles from my house, and so I started there.

Mary Elizabeth Hunsdale and her husband William Cameron in Belfast (photo: ca. 1890).

First, I found that I had to order a microfilm with the birth indexes on it and then wait for it to come in. That took about a month. The births were listed with a year (1868) and volume number (1). So then I needed to order the next film that was for this specific part of the birth registrations—and then wait another month before I finally received it.

It was a long search through all the births of that year as it was divided by Registrars' districts. When you don't know where to look, you start at the beginning and work through it alphabetically. Finally, I found that the Kilmood area was listed under Newtownards. The family certainly knew where that was! And there on the film were Mary Elizabeth's parents listed as Hans Hunsdale and Annie Vincent. "Annie" was a common name in the family. But "Hans"? It was never used again for any of the following generations. So where do I go from here?

[1] Raymond's County Down Website (www.raymondscountydownwebsite.com).
[2] FamilySearch (familysearch.org/).

Finding the Great-Grandparents

The next document I went searching for was the marriage of Hans and Annie to see if I could find when they were married. I did manage to find information at the Ulster Historical Foundation website (now known as AncestryIreland.com)[3] for a price. It was a transcribed version rather than a copy of the actual registration page. I later ordered the marriage record on microfilm from the local Family History Center so I could have an actual copy of the marriage. A transcription of the record is shown below:

Marriage Transcription—Hans Hunsdale, age 21 years, bachelor, sailor, Tullynakill, Parish of Tullynakill, son of John Hunsdale, fisherman; married Annie Vincent, age 21 years, spinster, Castle Espie, Parish of Tullynakill, daughter of John Vincent, sailor; witnesses: Hans Shaw and Jane Vincent; Registrar's Office, Town of Newtowards, District of Newtownards; 7 May 1861.

After reading the information, I noted that both fathers were named John. I wondered about this and questioned it, but it has since been proven that both were named John by using the Griffith's Valuation Revision Books available through the Public Record Office of Northern Ireland (PRONI).[4]

It is interesting when you actually get to read a full document and not just the little piece they give you before you buy it. It lists more places, such as Tullynakill and Castle Espie, that again the family has never heard of. However, finding that both the bride and groom could write their name was a bonus. I also find it interesting that they were married in the Registrar's Office rather than the local church. Maybe the parents didn't want them to get married.

So where do I go next?

I decided to see what information there was on Hans himself. No record of his birth or baptism can be found on the Internet. If I calculate his age from his marriage certificate, then he could have been born in about 1840, well before civil registration. So there would be no birth certificate

[3] Ulster Historical Foundation (www.ancestryireland.com).
[4] Public Record Office of Northern Ireland, PRONI (http://www.proni.gov.uk).

and I would need to find a church baptism for him.

I have since found a year of 1842 as a possible birth year for Hans from his ship's master papers. After many years of searching, however, I still have no exact birth or baptismal information for either Hans or his wife Annie. There are lots of Hunsdales or variants on several of the websites that I have checked. Perhaps if I went back and looked at some of those websites I would find some clues of where else to look for Hans himself. This has been my brick wall, and a big one to get through.

In June of 2007, on a visit to Ireland, my husband and I drove to the area where Hans and Annie lived. Both of their addresses were townland roads—just one road, really, which follows the coast of the Strangford Lough. When you travel north on Tullynakill Road and come to a stop sign, the road becomes Castle Espie Road. So I guess that Hans and Annie must have lived fairly close to each other.

While searching for Hans, I noted others with the same last name or the variants. What this search basically came down to was a one name study on this family from County Down. While there were many different versions of the last name, and they have spread out around the world, they all seem to be connected. So far we have Hunsdale, Hansdale, Huntsdale, and Huntsdal. It seems to be dependant on how the name was spoken and how the person hearing it spelt it.

Finding the Great-Great-Grandparents

My first glimmer of hope of finding more on Hans' family came from the FamilySearch site, which listed several Hunsdales being baptized as early as 1828 in the First Presbyterian Church in Killinchy, Co. Down (located near the lower part of the Strangford Lough). I made a note of all these names and tried to piece them together. Several families started to emerge from all these names. Now to pin down how some of these families were related to Hans.

Finally, I was on high speed Internet and able to spend more time on the web. I visited all the RootsWeb pages[5] using the names, locations, and whatever else I could find to post messages about this family. Eventually, I was contacted by another researcher and we put together

[5] RootsWeb (www.rootsweb.ancestry.com).

what we had found so far. She later made a visit to PRONI and was able to find the baptismal records for one of her family in the parish records of Ardmillian, Co. Down which is located on Tullynakill Road. Now we were getting somewhere.

It was not possible to photocopy any of the records at PRONI; you were only able to write everything down and hope you could read your own writing later. As she transcribed the information, she forwarded some of what she had found. We were able to find that her relative and John Hunsdale, who is Hans' father, were cousins. Moreover, some of the children of a John Hunsdale and Martha Middleton were listed in the parish records, and through this we were able to confirm the marriage of John and Martha. We had found their marriage a while ago on the FamilySearch site and now the Tullynakill parish records gave us further proof.

John Hunsdale and Martha Middleton were married on 23 March 1833 in Killinchy, Co. Down. John had been baptized in 1812 and Martha in 1816, both in the Killinchy Presbyterian Church. John's father was listed as another John, but no mother was listed.

We do know from these records that Hans had eight siblings—seven brothers and one sister — who were all baptized in Tullynakill.

- John Hunsdale, born 28 October 1839; baptized 10 November 1839.
- William Hunsdale, baptized 8 September 1842.
- Agnes Hunsdale, baptized 26 September 1845.
- Frew Hunsdale, born 12 September 1848; baptized 8 October 1848.
- Alexander Hunsdale, born 28 January 1850; baptized 23 February 1850.
- Arthur Thomas Farrell Hunsdale, baptized 28 September 1853.
- David Hunsdale, baptized 6 July 1856.
- Stewart Hunsdale, born 16 February 1859; baptized May 10, 1859.

I have found nothing further on the two eldest sons, John or William. However, I have been able to follow and connect with the families of three of the siblings—Agnes, Frew and Arthur— and I am able to confirm from their marriages that their father was John Hunsdale. David and Stewart died in their late teens according to the parish records.

From the Tullynakill parish records, we know that, when Hans' brother Frew was born in 1848, his father John's occupation was sexton of Tullynakill Parish Church. By 23 February 1850, when his brother Alexander was born, his father's occupation had changed to fisherman.

There is mention of John Hunsdale in the registers of Tullynakill Church in 1845 and 1846, and again in 1860, indicating that he was a witness to several marriages. From 1848 to the 1860s, there are also various references to John and his church activities from the church parish notes which shows he might have been the sexton for the church in Tullynakill for at least twelve years. His responsibilities as sexton would have included opening the church for Sunday worship, weddings, and funerals. His duties may have also included digging graves and, on occasion, being recruited to act as a witness at weddings, as we have already seen. The job of sexton may have been a second job to supplement his fishing and provide a second income. In 1834, the sexton was John Middleton, who may have been John's father-in-law. He was paid £1–10–0 for work carried out over a nine-month period, which suggests that John Hunsdale would have been paid for his work as well.

Confirmation that I had the correct family was recently found on PRONI's website using the Valuation Revision Books. Starting with the parish of Tullynakill (1866-1879), I found that Annie's father, John Vincent, leased property in the townland of Ballydrain, parish of Tullynakill, and that his name has been crossed out and the property was transferred to Hans Hunsdale in 1871. It was a house and garden of 0 acres, 1 roods, 0 perches, equivalent to a quarter of an acre. I am wondering if they used this as a base when Hans was not at sea, or if they used it as a family home all the time.

As I was still trying to piece at least three generations of this family together when information wasn't as easily available on the Internet as it is now, I started by using three websites (Emerald Ancestors,[6] FamilySearch, and the Ulster Historical Foundation). I searched for anyone who had one of the last names I was looking for and copied all the birth and marriage information, as these were the only two records where it is possible to find a parent's name. I was able to identify several families in this way by finding the fathers' names on the children's birth or marriage certificates.

[6] Emerald Ancestors (www.emeraldancestors.com).

Going Sideways to Find More on Hans and His Other Children

I had now gone back four generations from Mary Elizabeth, but what about going sideways? Who were the siblings of Mary Elizabeth Hunsdale and the children of Hans Hunsdale? There had to be more of them out there.

Although I had found a couple of names that could be a sibling of Mary Elizabeth on the FamilySearch site, I hadn't pursued this avenue due to the cost of ordering certificates with the Canadian dollar. Then I found a new resource where I could order copies of the page of registrations from The Church of Latter Day Saints in Utah at a very cheap price. Armed with the volume number, page number, year, and film number, I ordered birth certificates for two more of the children that I knew about—Jane and Agnes. At least I thought they were mine. Their records, transcribed below, show that they were born in different places.

Birth Transcription—Jane Vincent Hunsdale, female, born 19 October 1865, Castle Espie; father: Hans Hunsdale, sailor, Castle Espie; mother: Annie Hunsdale (nee Vincent); informant: Hans Hunsdale, father, Castle Espie; registered 21 October 1865, District of Kilmood, Union of Newtownards, County of Down.[7]

Birth Transcription—Agnes Hunsdale, female, born 14 January 1871, Ballydrain; father: Hans Hunsdale, sailor, Ballydrain; mother: Annie Hunsdale (nee Vincent); informant: Susanna McMede, Ballymartin; registered 14 February 1871.[8]

I could find no information for Hans' eldest child, Annie, other than an approximate age which I received from her family that I connected with a few years later. I had known about Annie and Annie's daughter Jane because they were the only two relatives that my mother-in-law had spent time with.

So I had found the names of Jane Vincent (the middle name fits with her mother's maiden name) and Agnes. Since they were not born in the

[7] FamilySearch, "Quarterly returns of births in Ireland, 1864-1955, with index to births, 1864-1921," FHL film no. 101130, volume 16, page 11, entry no. 300.

[8] ibid. FHL film no. 255810, volume 1, page 962, entry no. 117.

same place, it was difficult to know if I was going in the right direction. But the parents' names matched, so it had to be them. Sadly, I also found later that Jane had died in 1880 at the age of 25 and Agnes died in 1889 at the age of 18.

I eventually found two more children. Hans, who was born in 1873, I found when I located the grave of his mother, Annie Vincent, and what would have been two of his nieces. They are all buried in the same grave in the Belfast City Cemetery. He died on 14 January 1894 in Belfast, Ireland, when he was 19 years of age. I located the last son, John, who was born 14 May 1877 in Ballymacarrett, Co. Down, when I was searching for the marriages of other family members.

The next record I found was the death of Annie, the wife of Hans. She was only 43 years of age at the time of her death and had left behind four children aged 17, 14, 12, and 8 years. Her eldest daughter was married and the next two daughters were working outside of the family. I found the death of Annie by going through civil registration deaths at my local Family History Centre and then ordering the certificate from GRONI (General Registers Office of Northern Ireland) in Belfast.

Death Transcription—Annie Hunsdale, female, age 43, married, 1 Wolff Street, died 25 February 1885; wife of Hans Hunsdale, sailor; cause of death: consumption, 12 months, no medical attention; informant: Hugh Vincent, brother, 5 Enteral Street, present at death; registered 27 February 1885 in the District of Belfast Urban No. 11.[9]

As you can see, there isn't as much information on Irish death certificates as you may get in some other countries. However, it did give me confirmation that I had the right family.

It didn't take Hans long to remarry after the death of his wife Annie. It was a surprise for me when I went looking on the Ulster Historical Foundation website for a marriage for his son Hans. It was only after ordering the certificate from GRONI that I found it was Hans Sr. who married Mary Ann Long on 24 December 1885 in Belfast.

[9] General Registers Office of Northern Ireland, original death certificate, 1st quarter, volume 1; book 18, entry no. 135.

Marriage Transcription—Hans Hunsdale, full age, widower, sea captain, Belfast, son of John Hunsdale, sailor; married Mary Ann Long, full age, spinster, Belfast, daughter of John Long, carpenter; witnesses: John McMorran and Eliza Jane Long; Elmwood Presbyterian Church, Belfast, Co. Antrim; 24 December 1885.

The Next Family

Once again, it was time to put more family names into place, and I found more that didn't make sense. There were two girls, Jane and Agnes, who were born after the death of Han's first wife, Annie. So they may belong to Hans and his second wife, Mary Ann; but why, I wondered, would someone name their children from a second marriage after the deceased children from the first marriage? However, after further research, I found they were definitely the children of Hans and Mary Ann.

- John Hunsdale, born 1886 in Newtownards.
- Jane Hunsdale, born 1888 in Belfast; married George Dixon in February 1911.
- Alexander Hunsdale, born in 1892 in Belfast; married Lizzie Woods in 1918.
- James Hunsdale, born August 5, 1894 in Belfast; married Mary Ann Rea on 26 October 1918.
- Agnes Long Hunsdale, born 28 June 1897 in Belfast; married John Topping on 13 April 1919.

As another Remembrance Day rolled around, and military records became available, I was checking out names on the National Archives (United Kingdom) website.[10] I was searching the World War I records for anyone who was about the right age. I found a death for a James Hunsdale, who I was able to confirm was indeed the son of Hans and Mary Ann Hunsdale.

According to his service record, Stoker 1st Class James Hunsdale (Service No. SS112672) joined the Royal Navy on 13 August 1912. The 17 year-old was listed as five feet four inches with black hair bown hair and

[10] National Archives, UK (www.nationalarchives.gov.uk/).

a dark complexion. It was nice to see physical information about him, and I am able to imagine what he looked like.

During his time in the Royal Navy, James served on the following ships:

Pembroke	03 August 1912 – 13 December 1912
Vangaard	14 December 1912 – 10 July 1915
Pembroke	14 July 1915 – 20 August 1915
General Wolfe	11 September 1915 – 4 November 1918

Sadly, James Hunsdale died of pneumonia on 4 November 1918 in Kent, England, just seven days before the war ended and only nine days afer his marriage to Mary Ann Rea. So it was on to the Commonwealth War Graves Commission (CWGC)[11] to see if I could find grave information for him. I found him listed in Naval Grave Reference 5-249.

> In Memory of Stoker 1st Class James Hunsdale, SS/112672, HMS General Wolfe, Royal Navy who died on 04 November, 1918. Remembered with honour. Gillingham (Woodlands) Cemetery.
> – CWGC

I am always honored to read about our relatives who participated in the war.

Now to Find More About the Sea Captain

Hans Hunsdale's occupation throughout my searches had been listed as a sailor and then a sea captain. The question was, how could I find out about his seafaring career?

In 2008, after posting a message to the IRL-Belfast-City mailing list at RootsWeb and asking how to find out about what type of sea captain Hans was, I received a reply from a fellow member of the list. He had found some information on the Glenravel website.[12]

[11] Commonwealth War Graves Commission (www.cwgc.org).
[12] Glenravel Local History Project (www.glenravel.com).

> I have turned up some interesting info about Capt. Hans Hunsdale for you.... He was the Captain of the Bangor steamer 'Erin' which seems to have ploughed the route from Bangor to Belfast and was licensed to carry up to 515 passengers.
>
> – Gary, 9 January 2008

Wow, what great information to receive! I had helped this fellow researcher and he returned the favor. Thank goodness for all the RootsWeb mailing lists.

I then found information on the *Erin* on another County Down website and wrote to Ros Davies,[13] the owner of the site, and was able to obtain a picture of the *Erin* which, in fact, is an old fashion steam paddle wheeler. It was a two-funnel vessel which was capable of going from Belfast to Bangor in forty minutes. It was operated by Moore Bros.

I visited our local library looking for a copy of *Lloyd's Captains' Registrar* that a RootsWeb Belfast mailing list member had suggested I try. I understood that Hans should be listed if he was indeed a captain. Unfortunately, they did not have a copy, but the Toronto Reference Library did. This was about an hour's journey away, but something I could do. When I was able to check the *Captains' Registrar,* there was no record for Hans listed. So I went back home to try and find out more.

A few months later, a notification came through from the RootsWeb County Down mailing list to tell us about an offer to check out the newspapers on the Gale website[14] for free. What a day that was!! I found twenty-seven newspaper articles that listed Captain Hans Hunsdale. They all confirmed that Hans was a sea captain and that he worked on the steamers between Bangor and Belfast, and between Larne and Belfast. Although I found these articles quite a few years ago, they are now available at the pay site of British Newspaper Archives.[15]

Although they are too long and numerous to put into this story, I found some of them very interesting. Amongst the articles, there was one about a testimonial for Captain Hunsdale that was held at a hotel

---

[13] Ros Davies' Co. Down, Northern Ireland Family History Research Site (freepages.genealogy.rootsweb.ancestry.com/~rosdavies).

[14] Gale Cengage Learning (gale.cengage.co.uk).

[15] British Newspaper Archives (www.britishnewspaperarchive.co.uk).

in Bangor. It went on to describe how he was a wonderful captain and a valuable employee, and that he was honoured by his crew with a gold watch. The article was lovely to read and I felt I was becoming to know Hans better.

> PRESENTATION TO CAPTAIN HUNSDALE. On Friday, Captain Hunsdale of the Erin, was presented with a testimonial as a mark of esteem by the crew and a number of friends. This presentation took place in the Abercorn Hotel, Bangor, immediately after the arrival of the boat leaving Belfast at twelve o'clock.... Miss Johnston, proprietress of the hotel, presented Captain Hunsdale with a handsome watch-guard with a compass and seal bearing the inscription, "Presented to Captain Hunsdale by the crew of the Erin, 29th August, 1894".... Mr. W. James Brown, mate of the Erin, said he was glad to have an opportunity of doing honour to Captain Hunsdale, who was one of the most careful navigators he had ever sailed with, and his experience of river and deep-sea sailing was not limited.
>
> – *Belfast Newsletter*, 1884

This new information was extremely interesting for me considering the fact that, prior to 2007, I didn't even know that he was a ship's captain.

In 1885, there was an article in the *Belfast Newsletter* titled "Fatal Accident in the Lough. A Yawl Run Down By A Steamer". Well this certainly caught my attention. Hans was the captain of the steamer, and one of the men on the yawl was killed during the incident. This was obviously a serious accident, and the same story was also reported again in the *Belfast Times* in August of 2009 ("Lough death probed"). So, even 100 years later, it was something of importance for the Strangford Lough area. The article also mentions the ship's mate was Arthur Hunsdale. I take this to be Han's brother, but I can't prove this for sure.

There were other interesting articles in 1886, 1887, and 1888, which included articles about the Bangor steamers, a school outing, the Bangor Season, the Ward School in Bangor, and my favourite, the Police Intelligence Report covering a court case about intoxicated passengers and the crew of the Erin.

In 1890, there were four articles in the months of July and August concerning a collision between two Belfast steamers. The event showed up in the *Belfast Times*, the *Freeman's Journal* of Dublin, the *Morning Post* of London, and the *Dundee Advertiser* of Angus, Scotland. It seems that the captains of the two rival steamer companies were racing towards the town dock to see who could arrive first. Not a good idea. Both captains were arrested and charged, and the case was taken to court. Who knew a relative could be written about so much.

What a surprise to see more articles about Hans for the year 1891. Most articles were from the *Belfast Newsletter*. The first one was an appeal by Hans and his employer of the court case the year before. The next article was about another collision, this time between the steamer *Erin* and a steamer from Ayr, Scotland, named the *Alisa*. Captain Hunsdale was arrested again. This article was listed under the title "Dublin Law Reports". The collision was taken to the Board of Trade for an inquiry. A full report is given on who said what in court and, in the end, Captain Hunsdale was saved jail time as the judge heard such good things about him. However, he was fined five pounds towards court costs.

Hans had quite an eventful career, and I really enjoyed learning about him in all the newspaper articles.

In the fall of 2012, I found information on Hans at Ancestry.com[16] which came from the London National Maritime Museum. To my surprise, I learned that Hans had become a first mate in 1873. Unfortunately, there was no information as to which ships he had sailed on.

Also on Ancestry.com, I found a certificate showing that Hans became a sea master in 1879. It didn't take long for him to move from mate to master.

When PRONI offered the Belfast Street Directories as a new online feature, I was able to compile a list of addresses for Hans from the directories and also the addresses from various family certificates [see overleaf].

This gave me a good picture of where the family lived over a 20-year time frame. Sometime around 1877, Hans made the move from the shores of Strangford Lough into Belfast. He then moved house several times over the years. I do wonder why they moved around so much. Was it because he couldn't afford some locations, or because he wasn't sailing during the

[16] Ancestry.com "Masters and Mates Certificates, 1850-1927," database and images (www.ancestry.com).

off season, or because the family was growing? I can only specualte.

1877	Hunsdale, Hans – Seaman	10 Wolfe Street
1880	Hunsdale, Hans – Seaman	16 Rotterdam Street
1881	[marriage of daughter Annie]	12 Wolfe Street
1885	[death of wife Annie]	1 Wolfe Street
1887	Hunsdale, Hans – Sailor	7 Garfield Terrace
1889	[death of daughter Agnes]	31 Madrid Street
1890	Hunsdale, H. – Sea Captain	31 Madrid Street
1892	Hunsdale, H. – Sea Captain	64 Paxton Street
1894	[death of son Hans Jr.]	64 Paxton Street
1895	Hunsdale, H. – Sea Captain	4 Mount Street
1896	Hunsdale, H. – Sea Captain	4 Mount Street

After months of searching, I finally ordered a possible death certificate for Hans Hunsdale from GRONI in Belfast.

Death Transcription—Hans Hunsdale, male, age 44 years, married, storekeeper, 15 Crawford Street, died 9 December 1898; cause: congestion of lungs, 7 days certified; informant: Elisa Jane Long, sister-in-law, 10 Crawford Street, present at death; registered 9 December 1898 in the District of Belfast No. 6; book 53, entry no. 67.

I had looked at this registration several times, but the age of 44 years was wrong, as he was actually 58 years old, and the occupation was that of storekeeper, not a sailor or sea captain as I would have expected. However, I couldn't find any other death that would fit. I wondered if perhaps this was the right man after all.

The certificate did reveal one clue, which was the name of the informant Eliza Jane Long, who was also a witness at Hans' second marriage to Mary Ann Long. To prove this was the right person, I looked for any records that I could find from the time of death and onwards to see if I could find Mary Ann as a widow. I was able to find her living at 31 Dunvegan Street, Belfast in the 1907 directory.

This had to be our man. His sister-in-law Eliza Jane just hadn't known his age, and he may have been doing work as a storekeeper while his ship was in the dock for the winter months.

I have been able to find what we believe is Hans' burial in the Tullynakill Cemetery with his parents, John and Martha. Unfortunately, all the metal plaque says is "The Burying Ground of Hunsdale." There is a working plan for this graveyard, but all it says is that there are three plots with the name "Hunsdale".

* * *

My one regret, with all the researching I have done and all the connections I have made, is that no one has a picture of Hans Hunsdale. I really would have liked to know what he looked like. Although I have a picture of his daughter Mary Elizabeth with her husband William Cameron, there is no way of knowing if she looks anything like her mother or her father.

I would like to thank all those who are researching the Hunsdale family for their help and hope we can find further information in the years to come.

CHAPTER THIRTEEN

A Native Son of County Down

George McLorn (1887–1933)

BY DEBORAH SCANDURRA FEHRINGER (UNITED STATES)

Although he died twenty five years before I was born, I've often pondered the life of my mother's father, a farmer's son from Taghnabrick, County Down.

George McLorn was born in 1887, the fourth of five children of George McLorn Sr. and his wife, Elizabeth Armour. Their small family farm was located on the Ballynahinch Road just south of Lisburn and was surrounded by other farmlands leased or owned by McLorn relatives. In accordance with Irish custom of the times, the family farm would be inherited by the oldest son upon the deaths of the parents. Being a second-born son, I can only imagine the difficult position George found himself in when faced with the question of how to earn his own living.

The path that George's future would take was greatly influenced by County Down native Sir Robert Hart. Hart, who was from the neighboring townland of Ravernet, had left the area in 1854 to work in China. Decades later, he had returned to his homeland as an accomplished businessman and diplomat. At local Masonic lodges and churches, he spread the word about the opportunities to be had overseas, and many fellow Ulstermen took up his call. James Armour, a brother of George's mother and a contemporary of Hart's, was one such person who had already gone out to China for work. When James Armour and his wife died at the turn of the century, their children were sent to live in Taghnabrick with my grandfather's family. Tales of exotic lands told by these China-raised cousins, along with the precarious economic and social climate in Ireland at the time, must have been enough influence for young George McLorn to make up his mind.

George McLorn Sr. (standing) and Elizabeth Armour (seated middle) with their children (left to right) James, Sarah Jane, George (my grandfather) and Caroline (photo: ca. 1888).

In 1905, George boarded the steamship *Palawan* in London and headed for China. Accompanying him were Dan and John McLorn, two first cousins on his father's side who, like George, were hoping to find their futures on the other side of the world. The adventures for this trio had just begun.

George immediately started work with the Chinese Maritime Customs Service in the city of Canton, while Dan and John, after short stints with Customs, went to work with the Chinese Postal Service. Robert Hart is credited with having been one of the most significant forces behind the establishment of these two institutions' infrastructures which he staffed with many of his own countrymen. George's job in the early years, first as a "Watcher" and later as a "Tidewaiter", required him to travel to Chinese port cities where he was responsible for monitoring cargo-carrying vessels as they entered the ports. His work took him to the port cities of Shanghai, Tientsin, Amoy, Hankow, and others.[1] This new life must have been quite an eye opener for a single young man from the green fields of County Down!

A true fraternity existed among the young men employed by the Customs Service, and throughout the years, they engaged in all kinds of social and sporting activities together including shooting, football, golf, billiards, tennis, and racewalking. At six foot one in height, George was recognized as an all-around athlete and was a force to reckon with on the Customs athletic teams. The 19 November 1912 issue of *The China Press* dedicated a full page to the results of the International Walking Competition in Shanghai. The headline reads "Irish Team Wins the International Walk" and shows a photo of the victors in shirts with shamrocks pinned on. The caption lists the Irish team members of "P.J. Dunne, Phillips, Scanlan, J. Sullivan, T. Dunne, and G. McLorn." George placed first for his team and second place overall in the 16 mile racewalk with a time of 2 hours, 30 minutes and 30 seconds—7 seconds behind the winner. It was one of many medals he received in his sporting career.

Around 1910, George met Florence Mann Clifton, known as "Jimmie", a British subject who had been born in China. After a courtship carried out through letters and group outings, they were married on 14 April 1914 at the Cathedral of St. John in Victoria, Hong Kong. Afterward, the bridal

[1] For this essay, city names are written as they were at the time these events took place (1905–1945). Modern use of the Pinyan Romanization of Chinese words has changed the spelling of most places. Tientsin is now written as Tianjan, Peking is Beijing, Shanghai (no change), Hankow is Hankou, Amoy is Xiamen and Canton is Guangzhou.

party celebrated with tiffin[2] at the Hongkong Hotel. In 1916, their first child, George Frederick Clifton McLorn, was born in Tientsin, followed by a second child two years later—my mother, Patricia Sybil McLorn.

My grandfather George McLorn standing with his prizes from the 1912 International racewalking competition in Shanghai. Note the shamrock proudly displayed on his jersey.

[2] Colonial English/Indian word meaning a light lunch.

While their countrymen at home may have been struggling, life in China was relatively easy for the young McLorn family. They lived in the international concession in the cities of Tientsin and Shanghai, mingling with British, Americans, French, and others who had made China their home. Their days were a pleasant mix of work and play, highlighted by activities that went along with their memberships in various civic and social clubs. As time went on, George's career required less travel and afforded more family time. As Chief Appraiser of the Shanghai Customs office, he was now pulled to work in a rickshaw each morning.

Every seven years, George was entitled to a one-year "home leave" through the Customs Service, and in 1927, his family traveled to Ireland for one such visit. Sybil and George, now 9 and 11 years old, were enrolled in the Friends School in Lisburn, and my mother recalled it as the happiest of times. The official Friends School photograph of 1928 shows the teachers, staff, and students in front of the ivy-covered institution—the younger children cross-legged in the front row and the older students standing in the back. George must have been proud of his son who clearly followed in his father's footsteps as the 14 May 1928 issue of the *Northern Whig and Belfast Post* ran a photo of him winning the Friends School 100 yard dash. His mother, Jimmie, wrote on the newspaper clipping "George came in first in every race he was in."

Meanwhile, in other parts of China, George's cousins were also faring well. Dan McLorn had moved into a senior position with the Postal Service and was also involved in early dealings of the Hong Kong and Shanghai Bank in Asia. In 1919, he received the "Insignia of the Order of the Excellent Crop Class II" from the King of England in recognition of British officials' valuable service in China. He later married American writer Olive Gilbreath, and they continued to travel and work in various Chinese cities.

Dan's brother John McLorn had also established himself away from home. His early tutoring in Mandarin at Queens University in Belfast had proven advantageous as he was chosen to set up a branch of the Chinese Postal System in Urumchi, Chinese Turkestan;[3] a mysterious and untamed outpost in northwest China that was more Russian than Chinese. At age 40, he married F. Dorothea Raitt, a British subject who

[3] Today known as Urumqi, Xinjiang.

had been born and raised in St. Petersburg, Russia. They were later posted to the city of Tientsin where he and his wife had three children.

My grandfather's time in China was to come to an early end. During a particularly hot and humid summer in August of 1933, George McLorn was felled by heatstroke and died at the Country Hospital in Shanghai. At the age of 46, he left behind a widow and two teenage children who, within ten years, would themselves be forced to leave China because of the ravages of World War II.

Although this son of County Down was no longer alive, George McLorn's story would be incomplete without mentioning the fate of his family during the ensuing war years. The Japanese, who had been fighting with China for decades, formally declared war in December 1941. George's daughter Sybil, now married, had been able to secure a berth on what would be one of the last ships allowed to leave Shanghai. In November 1941, she left for the United States with one steamer trunk in her possession. Expecting to reunite with her husband after he settled their personal business and booked passage, she believed they would ride out the war in another location and return to China when the climate improved. That, however, would never be. Any foreign residents who had not made plans to leave China by this time were now, essentially, locked in the country.

Within a year of war being declared, bank accounts were frozen and private possessions, including cars, houses, and investments, were being confiscated by the Japanese. Foreigners lived on rationed food and were forced to succumb to a life that was both difficult and dangerous. By the end of 1942, all foreigners in China were ordered to report to civilian internment camps. Former neighbors, friends, and colleagues would spend the next three years living together in barrack-like housing in communal, sub-par conditions. Camp records show thousands of internees claiming British and Irish nationality. In the camps, food and heat were scarce, and for the sick and elderly, it was a particularly difficult time. For others whom the Japanese deemed "suspicious," this period was downright brutal, and stories of torture and cruelty are well documented. Sybil's British-born husband experienced this brutality first hand.

After the death of George McLorn in 1933, his wife Jimmie had taken a job with the British Consulate. This move would prove fortuitous, as employment with the consulate would accord her a privileged status during the war years. Instead of being sent to a camp, consulate workers were expected to continue working at their jobs. And although Jimmie was confined—first to the consulate building and later to a local hotel with other employees— she was spared the privations of camp life that many of her friends and family had to endure. Less than a year later, she became part of a well-publicized prisoner of war exchange and was able to get to England where she spent the next decade.

In the meantime, George's other relatives in China continued to serve out the war years in internment camps. Dan McLorn and his wife, Olive, were held at the Chapei camp in Shanghai, while John McLorn and his family of five were interned in a former school at the Weihsien Civilian Assembly Centre outside of Tientsin. Each of their stories of internment is worthy of its own telling.

The end of the war in 1945 also marked the end of the glory days in China for foreigners. I'm grateful my grandfather never knew of the hardships his family suffered after he was gone, but I can't help but believe he thought they would all return to his Irish homeland for good someday. Alas, that was not to be, and the descendants of this one man from County Down were soon to call other lands their home. His wife, Jimmie, and daughter Sybil would permanently settle in the United States, while son George and his wife, Jean, would make the land of South Africa their own. Once released from the camps, George's cousin Dan settled in his wife's homeland of Missouri in America. His cousin John and family would put down roots in Canada, joining other siblings who had emigrated there from County Down some years earlier.

I found the following poem amongst my Grandma Jimmie's possessions when she died. Written in my grandfather's small flowing script, I like to think George McLorn, a native son of County Down, took comfort in these words when away from the land of his birth. It seems his homeland was never far from his thoughts.

The Glens of Antrim

It's, oh, to be on the Antrim hills
When an April morn is dawning!
And the sheen of green and gold's on the grass
And the mist's o'er the vale like an awning.

And, it's, oh, to hear the corncrake's cry
And the cuckoo's call and the lark on high.
I'd give the half of my life, would I
For the Antrim hills in the morning.

And, it's oh, to lie in the trembling grass,
And be drunk on the scent of the clover!
And hear the wings of the night that pass,
And the "peet-weet-weet" of the plover!
In what other place can an Irish heart lie,
But in Irish turf, 'neath an Irish sky.
I made a vow with myself, did I,
To be there when my life is over.

(Author unknown)

* * *

Written in memory of George McLorn and dedicated to those who have left their homelands for the unknown.

Deborah Scandurra Fehringer
New York, 2014

CHAPTER FOURTEEN

A Story of Two Brothers

The Sloan(e)s of Ballyrush, County Down

BY JO-ANNE MICHELLE SUNBEAM (NEW ZEALAND)

ROBERT SLOAN AND ELIZABETH KENNEDY are my great-great-great-grandparents. I first became interested in them thirty years ago when my mother and I wrote to the Irish Family History Foundation[1] to see if we could find where their son (my great-great-grandfather) James Kennedy Sloane was born. Since he gave different information for the registration of his marriage and on the birth certificates of his children, we did not know whether he was born in Belfast, or Comber, or somewhere else in County Down. Also, depending on which certificate we looked at, his age varied by about five years either way. Without a townland or a date of birth, our search for James seemed hopeless.

In 2009, I decided to submit a letter to the *Down Recorder* newspaper. Shortly afterwards, I had a reply back from a Mrs. Isobel McFerran to say that she had a Bible with all the names of Robert and Elizabeth Sloan's children in it, and that they were from Ballyrush in the parish of Comber. The birth year of 1824 in the Bible for "James Sloan" was the

[1] Irish Family History Foundation. Main St., Newbridge, Co. Kildare, Northern Ireland.

same as shown on the death certificate I had for my great-great-grandfather James Kennedy Sloane who died on 24 June 1897 in New South Wales, Australia.

At long last, I had discovered where my ancestors once lived in County Down. I contacted Shelley, a cousin in Manitoba, Canada, and together we started on our journey to bring to life the Sloans of Ballyrush in the early 19th century. We found the first historical record of the Sloan family appearing in Ballyrush, Co. Down, in 1818 when my great-great-great-grandfather Robert Sloan was a tenant of the Right Honourable Earl Londonderry. He paid a yearly rent of 19 pounds, 2 shillings and 15 pence.

In 1834, Robert Sloan was recorded in the Tithe Applotment Books for Ballyrush, Co. Down. In 1837, the *Belfast Newsletter* (via the *Down Recorder*) reported that the skull and other remains of a human were found on the farm of Robert Sloan of Ballyrush near the Ballygowan Bridge.

> John George, a road contractor, and his labourers were … cutting through a hillock, on the lands of Robert Sloan, of Ballyrush, near Ballygowan Bridge, [when] they came into contact with a round lump, twenty inches below the surface of the ground, which they discovered to be the skull of a human being. On searching further, they found the arm bones stretched along the ribs, and also the leg and thigh bones. From the appearance of the whole frame, the person must have been, when alive, about 5 feet 10 inches. -Down R
>
> – *Belfast Newsletter,* 19 May 1837

In 1840, Robert Sloan, along with several other men, leased some land for the Ballygowan Presbyterian Meetinghouse.[2]

> The Rt Hon. Price Blackwood of Ballyleidy, Co. Down … and William Kerr of Magherascouse, William Duff of Ravara, Hugh

[2] Public Record Office of Northern Ireland (PRONI), "Draft Lease of a piece of Ground in the Townland of Ballygowan," 1840, microfilm, PRONI Reference: D1071/A/H/2/95.

Garrett of Tullygirvan, James Steward of Ballygowan, and Robert Sloan of Ballyrush, farmers, Co. Down, Trustees of Ballygowan Meetinghouse. Draft Lease of a piece of Ground in the Townland of Ballygowan whereon a Meetinghouse has been built.

The old Sloan farmhouse in Ballyrush, Co. Down (photo: 2012).

It is not known when Robert Sloan was born, nor when he met his wife, Elizabeth Kennedy; but we assume they were married around 1806 or 1807, just prior to the birth of their first child in 1808.

Robert and Elizabeth were the parents of nine children (see Appendix). The eldest son, Robert, took over the family farms in Ballyrush after his father died. While the rest of their siblings remained in Ireland, the two youngest, my great-great grandfather James Kennedy Sloane and his brother William Kennedy Sloan, left their homeland to begin a new life. This is their story.

Immigration of James Kennedy Sloane to "Down Under"

James Kennedy Sloane was born on 8 November 1824 in the townland of Ballyrush, parish of Comber, Co. Down. According to his death certificate, he immigrated to Victoria, Australia, about 1853. Nothing is known of his early days, but in later years he always used an "e" on his last name.

No actual record of James' arrival in Australia has yet been found, but shortly after arriving, he settled in the Heathcote District of Victoria and became a hotel keeper and miner. In 1856, he married Mary Horsburgh in Heathcote. Mary was the daughter of Thomas Horsburgh and Mary May Scott Thomson and was born on 13 December 1838 in Melrose, Roxburgh, Scotland. On the marriage certificate, James put his birthplace as Belfast and his age five years younger than he actually was, probably because Mary was only 17 years old when they married.

James and Mary quickly had two children (William and Alice) in Heathcote and then moved to Wattle Creek in New South Wales, another mining town. There, a second son (Francis Robert) was born to them. As the gold declined in Wattle Creek, the new strikes in Otago, New Zealand, must have beckoned them since they left New South Wales, Australia, and moved to New Zealand where their youngest child (Francis Robert) died in 1863.

The Sloane family then moved up to Hokitika on the West Coast of the South Island of New Zealand following the gold rushes. Another child (Emily Jane) was born in Hokitika in 1866, and then the family moved to Westport, Buller. They stayed there until 1870 or 1871, where two more children (Albert Alfred Kennedy and Louisa Adeline) were born.

James had became Inspector of Mines in Westport, and it was a relatively stable time for the family. However, there was some controversy over the stability of the rail lines in a mining area, and James ended up once again following the gold to the new discoveries in the Lyell. This was a most inhospitable area of Buller, with rugged mountains and copious sandflies that would have deterred anyone—let alone a young family—from making their home there.

Nonetheless, the family braved the inhospitable conditions and settled in the Lyell district where James certainly made a name for himself. He was chairman of the school board, he built a large and imposing hotel called the "Alhambra" and, apart from losing their second daughter in 1870, life appeared good. James, a well educated man, had quite a bit of money for a while in this part of his life. Whether it came from gold mining or was family money is not known.

The following newspaper article describes James's intention to run for political office and gives us an idea of what sort of man he was.

> Mr J.K. Sloan, of Lyell, has signified his intention of contesting the election for the Central Buller, and is going to visit the various parts of the district to expound his political opinions, and, to quote his address "place his candidature entirely at the disposal of his brother electors, boasting of no qualification beyond a plain, unvarnished, candid style of expression, combined with sincerity and singleness of purpose." Mr Sloan was always celebrated for his "plain, unvarnished, candid style of expression," but a little varnish is occasionally requisite in a Council.
>
> – *Grey River Argus*, 19 November 1873

James actually withdrew from the election prior to voting, although he appeared to have good support from his fellow men.

Three more children were born to James and Mary between 1872 and 1875 (Bailie Gordon, Emma Jane, and Norman). Following the birth of their last child, Mary's health began to decline, and she died in 1877. She is buried in a little cemetery on the side of a hill in Lyell which the bush has now reclaimed.

After Mary died, so too, it seemed, did the fortunes of James. Once again, the gold started to peter out, mostly due to the inaccessibility of gold in this mountainous area and new strikes being found in areas north of Lyell. James was left with a huge hotel to run and very little money coming in. He tried to sell it by having an Art Union raffle set up, but there were no willing takers for it. The hotel was eventually sold to a man named Antonio Accolini, and it later burnt down in the 1890s.

About 1883 or 1884, James returned alone to Heathcote, Victoria, Australia. By this time his older children were independent and living on their own. However, for some unknown reason, James had left behind his two youngest children (Emma, aged 10 years; and Norman, aged 9 years) in New Zealand to be taken care of by the state.

James died at the age of 72 years on 24 June 1897 of miner's phthisis[3] at the Rookwood Asylum for destitute men and women and was buried in the Presbyterian part of the Rookwood Cemetery in Sydney, New South Wales, Australia. It is not known if any of his seven surviving children knew where he was or were even aware of his death.

---

[3] A chronic disease of the lungs caused by the inhalation of quartz dust.

The following are the children of James Kennedy Sloane and Mary Horsburgh:

1. William James Sloane was born in 1858 in Heathcote, Victoria, Australia, and died on 22 October 1920 in the city of Nelson, New Zealand.

   William married Aurelia Constance Leech in 1887. She was the daughter of William Haydon Lawley Leech and Pauline Constance Augarde. At the time, William was a miner and carpenter in Reefton, a small town in the Buller where he remained until the family moved to Nelson in 1907.

   William and Aurelia had seven children, but just three of these survived infancy—Louisa Constance Sloane, Alfred Kennedy Sloane and Montague ("Monty") Haydon Sloane. They adopted a small boy born in 1915 and named Nelson Sloane who supposedly was the child of their youngest son Montague. By this time, "Monty" had gone overseas to fight in World War 1.

2. Alice Mary Sloane was born in 1859 in Heathcote, Victoria, Australia, and died on 8 September 1952 in Christchurch, New Zealand.

   Alice married John Armstrong in Gibbstown, Lyell, in 1878. He was a Catholic, while Alice was raised as a Presbyterian. As a result, Alice's family had nothing to do with her again. It has only been recently that contact has been made with this side of the family.

   Alice and John had four children—Emily Mary Armstrong, Alice Maude Armstrong, Louisa Lorraine Olive Armstrong and Alfred Cecil Armstrong. John later deserted Alice, and she sued for divorce. Following the divorce, Alice married George Hamilton Woods.

3. Francis Robert Sloane was born on 10 July 1861 in Wattle Creek, Victoria, Australia, and died in 1863 in East Taieri, Otago, New Zealand.

4. Emily Jane Sloane was born on 18 March 1866 in Hokitika, West Coast, New Zealand, and died in 1870 in Lyell, West Coast, New Zealand.

5. Albert Alfred Kennedy Sloane was born in 1868 in Westport, Buller, West Coast, New Zealand, and died in 1919 in Wellington, New Zealand.

"Bertie," as he was known, worked around the Buller District for a few years—mining and doing engineering. He married Alma Oxnam, daughter of a local Buller farmer, on 7 August 1897 in Nelson.

Bertie and Alma had three children—Alma Isabella Sloane, Albert Alfred Sloane and Bailie Gordon Sloane. Alma became sick and was institutionalised for many years. Bertie looked after their children, but he died suddenly at the age of 49 years.

6. Louisa Adeline Sloane was born in 1870 in Westport, Buller, New Zealand, and died on 5 December 1956 in Auckland, New Zealand..

After her father left the family about 1883 and returned to New South Wales, Loiusa found work at the age of 14 as a maid for a local family. She later married Frederick Simmonds on 31 October 3 1900 in Wellington, New Zealand. They had two daughters—Rimu Simmonds and Ngaire Simmonds.

7. Bailie Gordon Sloane was born in 1872 in The Lyell, Buller, West Coast, New Zealand, and died on 7 July 1938 in Christchurch, New Zealand.

Bailie was the only child of James Kennedy Sloane to have a real affinity for The Lyell District. He remained in the area for many years after his father left for New South Wales, visiting even when he lived in Christchurch. He married Susan Rodden in 1899 and had three children—Mary Sloane, Bailie Gordon Sloane and Catherine Isobel Sloane. His occupation on the marriage certificate was listed as miner.

8. Emma Jane Sloane was born in 1874 in The Lyell, Buller, West Coast, New Zealand, and died on 27 May 1907 in Christchurch New Zealand.

   After her father left for New South Wales, Emma was placed in the hands of the authorities and sent to the Burnham Industrial School in Canterbury, New Zealand. This was a facility for orphaned children under the age of 15 years. Afterwards, she was sent with her younger brother Norman to live with a family on a farm in Woodend, Canterbury. There, she learned to look after a house and attended school.

   Emma married Ernest Edward Brook in Christchurch in 1900 and they had three children—Ernest Alfred Brook, Cecil Albert Brook and Lionel Brook.

9. Norman Sloane was born on 10 January 1875 in Lyell, Buller, West Coast, New Zealand, and died on 5 August 1917 in Wellington, New Zealand.

   Norman was also placed in the Burnham Industrial School after his father left the family. He went with his older sister Emma to a farm in Woodend where he completed his schooling and learned farming as a trade.

   In 1915, Norman married Ellenor Amelia Barham in Wellington, and in 1916, a son Norman Collison Sloane was born to the couple. Sadly, Ellenor and Norman Jr. were left without a husband and a father when Norman Sr. died unexpectedly a year later at the age of 42.

Immigration of William Kennedy Sloan to Scotland

William Kennedy Sloan, the youngest child of Robert Sloane and Elizabeth Kennedy, was born on 4 December 1826 in Ballyrush, Co. Down. William left Ireland for Scotland about the year 1850 and settled in Dumbarton, a town and burgh on the north bank of the River Clyde in the West-Central

A portrait of William Kennedy Sloan.

Lowlands of Scotland.

The next year, William is found to be a draper's assistant and apprentice. Having chosen his career path, he found himself ready to marry and start his own family. On 22 July 1852, William and a Scottish lass named Jane Smith Harris were wed in Glasgow. During the next twenty-three years, fourteen children were born to the couple (see Appendix).

William Kennedy Sloan and his family made their home in Cardoss, Dumbarton, on an estate named "Shamrockbank". He was a prominent figure in Dumbarton as a draper and a ship furnisher in the area. He also served as a magistrate for the town.

Entrance gate to Shamrockbank estate in Dumbarton, Scotland, the home of William Kennedy Sloan (photo: 2011).

A few years after the birth of her last two children (twin girls), William's wife developed an inflammation of the lungs. Weakened from many years of childbirth, and despite the hopes and prayers of William and her children, Jane did not survive this infection. On 3 November 1880, she passed away.

With several young and motherless children still remaining at home, William probably contemplated the idea of remarrying. It so happened that his niece Maria (Smyth) Frazer-Hurst was acquainted with a widow in Belfast, Ireland. Her name was Elizabeth Lucinda (Livingston) Stoeckel (see "Chapter Nine" for more details), a sophisticated and cultured Irish lady who was a first cousin of Maria's husband, Dr. Hugh Frazer-Hurst. She appeared to be a perfect match.

William Kennedy Sloan traveled to Belfast, Ireland, to be introduced to Elizabeth and they married shortly afterward on 19 September 19 1883.

> SLOAN—STOECKEL September 19, at May Street Presbyterian Church, Belfast, by the Rev. R.J. Lynd, B.A., W.K. Sloan, Esq., J.P., Shamrock Bank, Dumbarton, to Lucinda Elizabeth Stoeckel, third daughter of the late Hertford Livingston, Esq., Belfast.
>
> – *Belfast Newsletter*, 20 September 1883

William and his new bride returned to Dumbarton, Scotland, where Elizabeth gave birth to two sons—Henry Wicks Sloan in 1884 and Samuel Stuart Sloan in 1885. However, in November 1886, tragedy befell the new family when whooping cough, a life-threatening childhood illness of the time, claimed the life of the two Sloan boys within an eight-day period.

Once Elizabeth overcame her grief of the loss of her two sons and regained her strength, she gave birth to a son in 1888, whom they named Albert. Albert Sloan was soon joined by a little brother named David Livingston in 1889. Albert and David spent their childhood living at Shamrockbank and attending a boarding school which was not far from their home.

William Kennedy Sloan, having lived a full and prosperous life, succumbed to pneumonia and cardiac failure at his home on 22 October 1904. He was attended by Dr. Allen Sym, his step-son-in-law, and surrounded by Elizabeth and his surviving children from both marriages.

William was buried at the Dumbarton Cemetery in the town of

Dumbarton, Scotland, alongside his first wife, Jane Smith Harris, and his children Charles Sloan, John Campbell Sloan, Dora and Maria Sloan, Henry Wicks Sloan and Samuel Stuart Sloan. His second wife, Elizabeth, later married William Gould in 1908 in Edinburgh, Scotland.

As a young man, William's second youngest son, Albert Sloan, traveled several times between Scotland, Ireland, and Canada, starting in 1906 and ending in 1910 when he immigrated permanently to Canada. He settled in Winnipeg, Manitoba, and worked for the Canadian National Railway as a freight checker.

Albert met and fell in love with a young woman named Phoebe Patching. They eventually married on 17 April 1912 in Winnipeg, Manitoba. Soon afterward, a daughter was born to the couple on 13 February 1913. However, this child died at birth. Two years later, a second daughter was born—Eileen Mary Sloan in 1915. Eleanor Sloan was born in 1918 followed by a son in 1919 who was named Albert Sloan Junior. A fourth daughter, Noreen Sloan, was born in 1926 and the last child, Patricia Rosemary Sloan, was born on 23 July 1929 .

Albert worked all his life with the railway company in Winnipeg. In

Albert "Babba" Sloan Sr. in Winnipeg, Manitoba with his five children, two son-in-laws, and eight grandchildren (photo: 1950).

his elderly years, he spent his time equally visiting his daughters and their children. Affectionately known as "Babba," Albert would watch his grandchildren once a week which allowed his daughters to go out for the evening.

Albert Sloan developed leukemia and succumbed to the disease at the age of 77 on 6 December 1965.

Albert's younger brother David Livingston Sloan attended law school in Edinburgh, Scotland. After finishing his studies, his chosen profession was that of barrister.

David went to Ireland for a brief period where he met and married Anna Kathleen Throusen in 1913. That same year, David, Anna, and David's mother, Elizabeth Lucinda (now Gould), immigrated to Canada to the city of Calgary in Alberta.

David remained in Calgary where he practiced law until his retirement. He and Anna Kathleen had one son, whom they named Ian Hertford Livingston Sloan. Ian was born in Calgary, Alberta, on 27 July 1914.

David Livingston Sloan died in 1973 and he is buried in Calgary, Alberta.

* * *

My mother's family here in New Zealand, who are descendants of James Kennedy Sloane, have always maintained that we had a connection to Dumbarton in Scotland. When we went looking, William Kennedy Sloan was the first relative we found. This was about twenty five years ago, and for a long time William's immediate family in Scotland was the only family we could research. Ireland seemed to be such a stumbling block with little or no information available. Now, I have found we have relatives in Ireland, England, Scotland, and Canada that I keep in regular touch with. In some ways, we are now making up for the last 100 years of lost communication between "the home country" of Ireland and "the colonies" worldwide.

Ko katoa matou i tetahi e utuafare rahi – we are all one large family.

David Sloan with his infant son Ian, mother (top left), Elizabeth Lucinda Gould, and wife (top right), Anna Kathleen Throusen (photo: 1914).

Bibliography

Margaret C. Brown, *Lyell, The Golden Past* (New Zealand: Murchison District Historical & Museum Society, 1987).

R.C. Reid, *Rambles on the Golden Coast of the South island of New Zealand* (London: The Colonial Printing and Publishing Company, Limited, 1886).

Archives New Zealand, "Archway", database (www.archway.archives.govt.nz/).

Australian Newspapers Online, (www.trove.nla.gov.au/newspaper).

The British Newspaper Archives (www.britishnewspaperarchive.co.uk/).

Irish Genealogy, "Church Records", database and images, (churchrecords.

irishgenealogy.ie/churchrecords/).

National Archives of Ireland, "Census of Ireland 1901/1911," database and images (www.census.nationalarchives.ie/).

National Library of New Zealand, "Papers Past," database and images (www.paperspast.natlib.govt.nz/).

New South Wales, Australia, "Registry of Births, Deaths & Marriage," database (www.bdm.nsw.gov.au).

New Zealand Government, "Birth, Death and Marriage Historical Records," database (www.bdmhistoricalrecords.dia.govt.nz/Home/).

Public Record Office of Northern Ireland (www.proni.gov.uk).

Public Record Office, Victoria, Australia; Ships' Passenger Lists (www.prov.vic.gov.au/provguide-50).

Ros Davies' Co. Down, Northern Ireland Family History Research Site (freepages.genealogy.rootsweb.ancestry.com/~rosdavies).

The Sloan Connection website (wc.rootsweb.ancestry.com/cgi-bin/igm.cgi?db=sloanguy).

Appendix

The Descendants of Robert Sloan

We were very lucky to have found Isobel McFerran, the great-great-great-granddaughter of Robert Sloan, who had the Sloan family Bible in County Down. It was from there that the family began to emerge. Additional research has helped to fill in some of the details.

Robert Sloan of Ballyrush, Co. Down, married Elizabeth Kennedy and together they had nine children. It is not known when or where Robert and Elizabeth were born, nor have we found a record of when they died.

Children of Robert Sloan and Elizabeth Kennedy:

1. Jane Sloan, born 11 June 1808.

2. Mary Sloan, born 23 February 1810.

3. Elizabeth Sloan, born 20 August 1812; died 7 October 1852; married William Smyth ca. 1838 in Lisdoonan, Saintfield, Co. Down, Ireland.

   Children of Elizabeth Sloan and William Smyth:

   i. Elizabeth Smyth, born 1841 in Lisdoonan, Saintfield, Co. Down, Ireland; married John Hood on 5 April 1859 in Ardstraw, Co. Tyrone, Ireland.
   ii. Mary Davison Smyth, born 1842 in Lisdoonan, Saintfield, Co. Down, Ireland; died on 2 November 1926; married Alexander Hood on 26 July 1866 in Gortin, Co. Tyrone, Ireland.
   iii. William Smyth, born 1844 in Lisdoonan, Saintfield, Co. Down, Ireland; married Susanna Patterson in 1864 in Lisburn, Ireland.
   iv. Maria Smyth, born 1848 in Lisdoonan, Saintfield, Co. Down, Ireland; died 24 April 1933 in Edinburgh, Scotland;

married Hugh Frazer-Hurst in 1871 (also see "Chapter Nine").

4. Sara Sloan, born 24 April 1815 in Tullynagee, Co. Down, Ireland; died 23 October 1904 in Tullynagee, Co. Down, Ireland; married Hugh Gibson ca. 1842 in Killinchy, Co. Down, Ireland.

   Children of Sara Sloan and Hugh Gibson:

   i. Samuel Gibson, born 1844 in Tullynagee, Co. Down, Ireland.
   ii. Robert Gibson, born 1845 in Tullynagee, Co. Down, Ireland.
   iii. Elizabeth Gibson, born 18 August 1847 in Tullynagee, Co. Down, Ireland; died 1 February 1937 in Conlig, Co. Down, Ireland; married Samuel Kerr in 1884 at Gilnahirk Presbyterian Church in Belfast, Ireland.
   iv. William Gibson, born 1849 in Tullynagee, Co. Down, Ireland.
   v. James Gibson, born 1854 in Tullynagee, Co. Down, Ireland.
   vi. John Gibson, born 1856 in Tullynagee, Co. Down, Ireland.
   vii. Hugh Gibson, born 15 February 1859 in Tullynagee, Co. Down, Ireland; died 1 March 1927; married his cousin Maria Kennedy Sloan in 1895 in Newtownards, Co. Down.
   viii. David Anderson Gibson, born 1861 in Tullynagee, Co. Down, Ireland.

5. Margaret Sloan, born 12 August 1817; married James Davison Smyth on 10 December 1838 in Ballygowan, Co. Down, Ireland.

6. Robert Sloan, born 8 September 1819; died 27 May 1905 in Ballyrush, Co. Down, Ireland; married Margaret Nelson on 22 March 1855 in Comber, Co. Down, Ireland.

Children of Robert Sloan and Margaret Nelson:

i. Andrew Nelson Sloan,born 1856 in Ballyrush, Co. Down, Ireland; died ca. 1918 in Ballyrush, Co. Down, Ireland.
ii. Robert Thomas Reid Sloan, born 19 November 1857 in Ballyrush, Co. Down, Ireland; died 11 March 1875 in Ballyrush, Co. Down, Ireland.
iii. Elizabeth Sloan, born 3 July 1859 in Ballyrush, Co. Down, Ireland; married William Simpson.
iv. Margaret Sloan, born 2 February 1861 in Ballyrush, Co. Down, Ireland.
v. Mary Sloan, born 8 November 1862 in Ballyrush, Co. Down, Ireland.
vi. William Cooke Nelson Sloan, born 17 October 1864 in Ballyrush, Co. Down, Ireland; married Sara Douglas on 21 February 1896 in St. Anne's Church of Ireland, Shankill, Belfast.
vii. Jane Smith Harris Sloan, born 30 September 1866 in Ballyrush, Co. Down, Ireland.
viii. Sarah Sloan, born 5 July 1868 in Ballyrush, Co. Down, Ireland (presume died as an infant).
ix. Sarah Sloan, born 6 May 1871 in Ballyrush, Co. Down, Ireland.
x. Maria Kennedy Sloan, born 11 June 1873 in Ballyrush, Co. Down, Ireland; married her cousin Hugh Gibson, son of Sara Sloan (b. 1815) and Hugh Gibson.

7. Maria Sloan, born 8 November 1821; died in 1898 in Downpatrick, Co. Down, Ireland; married Hugh Dales on 13 August 1846 in Saintfield, Co. Down, Ireland.

Children of Maria Sloan and Hugh Dales:

i. Mary Dales, born 1849; died 3 October 1867 in Saintfield, Co. Down, Ireland.
ii. James Dales, born 22 June 1851 in Saintfield, Co. Down, Ireland.

iii. Elizabeth Dales, born 1850 in Saintfield, Co. Down, Ireland; died 2 November 1913 in Lisburn, Co. Antrim, Ireland.
iv. Margaret Stewart Dales, born 1 December 1856 in Saintfield, Co. Down, Ireland.
v. Emily Maria Dales, born 1859 in Saintfield, Co. Down, Ireland; died 6 June 1872 in Saintfield, Co. Down, Ireland.
vi. Sarah Isabella Dales, born 1865 in Saintfield, Co. Down, Ireland; died 1866 in Saintfield, Co. Down, Ireland.

8. James Kennedy Sloane, born 8 November 1824; died 1897 in Sydney, New South Wales, Australia; married Mary Horsburgh in 1856 in Heathcote, Victoria, Australia. The couple had nine children (see text).

9. William Kennedy Sloan, born 4 December 1826; died 22 October 1904 in Dumbarton, Dunbartonshire, Scotland; married Jane Smith Harris on 22 July 1852 in Glasgow, Scotland.

Children of William Kennedy Sloan and Jane Smith Harris:

i. Elizabeth Kennedy Sloan, born 5 March 1853 in Glasgow, Scotland; died 25 May 1902 in Calcutta, India; married Henry Wicks in 1877.
ii. James Kennedy Sloan, born 13 February 1855 in Dumbarton, Scotland; died 1893 in London, England; married Ethel Gillingham (died before 1888); next married Alice Rose Le Sueur on 28 March 1888 in Notting Hill, England.
iii. Robert Muir Sloan, born 29 April 1857 in Dumbarton, Scotland.
iv. William Arnot Sloan, born 27 September 1859 in Dumbarton, Scotland; died 11 April 1925 in West Kilbride, North Ayrshire, Scotland; married Mary Ferguson on 28 April 1891 in Glasgow, Scotland.
v. Jane Tait Sloan, born 27 November 1861 in Dumbarton, Scotland; died 22 March 1942 in London, England; married James Newton Harrington on 22 June 1886 in Dumbarton, Scotland.

vi. Charles Sloan, born 14 September 1863 in Dumbarton, Scotland; died 23 April 1869 in Dumbarton, Scotland; buried in the Dumbarton Cemetery.
vii. Mary Reid Sloan, born 21 July 1865 in Dumbarton, Scotland; died 13 November 1934 in Dumbarton, Scotland.
viii. John Campbell Sloan, born 11 May 1867 in Dumbarton, Scotland; died 11 February 1869 in Dumbarton, Scotland.
ix. Jessie Muir Sloan, born 23 February 1869; died 1912; married Joseph Mason on 9 June 1904 in Dumbarton, Scotland.
x. Campbell White Sloan, born 29 December 1870 in Dumbarton, Scotland.
xi. Edward Sloan, born 26 February 1872 in Dumbarton, Scotland; married Lizzie Allen Sinclair on 17 December 1897 in Glasgow, Scotland.
xii. George Scott Sloan, born 27 June 1873 in Dumbarton, Scotland; died 21 December 1923 in Glasgow, Scotland; married Margaret Hutcheson Smith on 10 April 1907 in Glasgow, Scotland.
xiii. Dora Kemp Sloan, born 21 April 1875; died 26 April 1875; buried in Dumbarton Cemetery.
xiv. Maria Dales Sloan, born 21 April 1875; died 26 April 1875; buried in Dumbarton Cemetery.

William Kennedy Sloan's wife Jane died on 3 November 1880. He next married Elizabeth Lucinda Stoeckel (formerly Livingston) on 9 September 1883 in Belfast, Ireland.

Children of William Kennedy Sloan and Elizabeth Lucinda (Livngston) Stoekel:

i. Henry Wicks Sloan, born 9 July 1884 in Dumbarton, Scotland; died 10 November 1886 in Dumbarton, Scotland; buried in Dumbarton Cemetery.
ii. Samuel Stuart Sloan, born 28 December 1885 in Dumbarton, Scotland; died 18 November 1886 in Dumbarton, Scotland; buried in Dumbarton Cemetery.
iii. Albert Sloan, born 29 January 1888 in Dumbarton, Scotland;

died 6 December 1965 in Winnipeg, Manitoba, Canada; married Phoebe Patching on 17 April 1912 in Winnipeg, Manitoba, Canada.

iv. David Livingston Sloan, born 12 November 1889 in Dumbarton, Scotland; died 1973 in Calgary, Alberta, Canada; married Anna Kathleen Throusen in 1913 in Ballymoney, Co. Antrim, Ireland.

CHAPTER FIFTEEN

My County Down Roots

The Whites of Kilbroney Parish

BY PATRICIA (WHITE) HART (NORTHERN IRELAND)

MY INTEREST IN FAMILY HISTORY started around 2007 with an old photograph that once belonged to my paternal grandparents and has always had a pride of place on my bedroom dressing table. It shows my dad, Patrick White, when he was ten years old with his parents and other siblings on the occasion of the christening of their youngest child in 1913.

All I knew about my grandfather at the time was his name (Henry White), that he was a railway signalman in Glasgow, Scotland, and that his wife (my grandmother) was Margaret Loftus. So, having reached retirement, and with access to a computer, I thought I would try this lark of tracing ancestors to find out more about my roots.

I first contacted the General Register Office (GRO) in Edinburgh, Scotland, to obtain the marriage certificate for my grandparents Henry White and Margaret Loftus. The certificate showed they were married on 18 June 1900 in Airdrie, Lanarkshire, Scotland. The certificate also stated Henry was a 29 year-old widower and that his first wife was Helen Morgan. His parents were listed as Patrick White, a farmer (deceased), and Sarah Doran (deceased).

The old photograph that was responsible for my interest in genealogy. My grandparents Henry White (far left) and Margaret Loftus (far right) with their children (left to right) Joseph (b. 1911), Patrick (my dad, b. 1902), Margaret (b. 1909), Henry (b. 1904) and Richard (b. 1913) in Glasgow, Scotland..

This was new information, and I found myself truly hooked on finding out more about this man, Henry White. My father had told me that Rostrevor, Co. Down, was where his dad had been born. Did he leave Rostrevor for Scotland because of the death of his first wife, Helen Morgan, or was there some other reason?

If Henry was 29 years old in 1900 when he married, I reckoned his birth to be around 1871. So I wrote to the General Register Office in Belfast (GRO Belfast) for a copy of his birth certificate and to the GRO in Edinburgh for a copy of his death certificate.

GRO Belfast had no record of a Henry White born to Patrick White and Sarah Doran around my date of 1871. So I trawled online and found one of interest on Emerald Ancestors[1] that had a Henry White born on 12 December 1868 and whose mother was Margaret White. I copied and filed this reference thinking that there must be a connection, but that it was not my Henry since I was looking for the birth of a child whose

[1] Emerald Ancestors (www.emeraldancestors.com/index.asp).

parents were named Patrick White and Sarah Doran.

My next line of inquiry was to look on Emerald Ancestors for Henry's marriage to Helen Morgan. I found one indexed entry for a Henry White who married an *Ellen* Morgan on 19 December 1894 in the Kilbroney Parish Roman Catholic Church, Rostrevor. I thought this was too much of a coincidence, so I sent for a transcription of this certificate. Oh, the disappointment! His father was named as Richard White, and not Patrick as I had hoped.

It was shortly after this that I found Fiona's County Down Genealogy (FCDG) Group[2] and I was very impressed with the information and input that came from the members of this group. There was mention on the group of the Public Records Office Northern Ireland (PRONI) in Belfast, and as I now live in Northern Ireland, I visited there quite a few times.

While searching for the elusive Henry White at PRONI, I did find a record that caught my attention. It was for the marriage of Patrick Whyte and Sarah Doran, which took place on 7 November 1834 in the Kilbroney Parish Roman Catholic Church, Rostrevor. However, Patrick and Sarah were too old to be Henry's parents as he was born in about 1871. It seemed I had hit another brick wall.

I asked for advice from the FCDG Group on how to get past this brickwall, and here entered the marvellous Sheila Phillips. Sheila asked a few pointed questions and also asked for copies of the certificates that I had relating to Henry from the GRO in Edinburgh. She also put me in touch with Deirdre McEvoy, who knows ever so much about Rostrevor, and asked if I had seen the baptism of Henry White on 12 December 1868 (mother Margaret). I had, but discounted it because his mother's name wasn't Sarah Doran.

Sheila offered that, the next time she was in the Newry Register Office, she would have a look at the 1868 birth of Henry. She also passed all my information on to Deirdre McEvoy. In no time at all, I had an email from Sheila who had looked at the original marriage entry for Henry White and Ellen Morgan on 19 December 1894. She noted that it looked as if the name of the groom's father was originally written as Patrick White, but had been changed to *Richard* White.

[2] Fiona's County Down Genealogy Group at Yahoo!Groups (groups.yahoo.com/neo/groups/CountyDownGenealogy/info).

Deirdre then got in touch with me with information that was mind blowing. She is descended from the Russell family of Kilbroney parish in Co. Down. Her great-great-great grandmother Bridget Russell had an older brother, named Richard Russell, who was identified in the Kilbroney Roman Catholic parish records as the father of Henry White, the illegitimate son of Margaret White born on 12 December 1868.

I now have a copy of Henry White's 1868 birth certificate from both the parish records and from PRONI. The mother is shown as Margaret White, but the entry for the father is blank. However, the person listed as registering the birth was entered as Sarah White, who I know was Margaret's mother. It appears from these events that Sarah and Patrick were not Henry's parents as shown on his marriage certificate, but in fact were his grandparents.

On a visit to the old Kilbroney churchyard, I found a headstone for Patrick White and his wife Sarah (Doran). Very close to them was a headstone for Charles Russell and his wife, Alice Carville. Charles and Alice are the parents of Richard Russell mentioned earlier. As yet, I have found no other record of either Richard Russell or Margaret White after the baptism of their son (my grandfather) in the Kilbroney Roman Catholic church.

Before I conclude, it should be mentioned that I did find a record of Henry White's marriage to Ellen Morgan dated 19 December 1894, but no record of her death. So I went back to Scotland with my search.

I found a record at ScotlandsPeople[3] that stated Ellen (Morgan) White, wife of Henry White, a railway signalman, died during childbirth on 26 June 26 1895. Her parents were given as John Morgan and Bridget Fegan. I also located the death of her premature baby son, John White. His mother was given as Ellen (Morgan) White, and his father identified as Henry White, a railway signalman. These entries made me feel very sad.

Since my grandfather Henry White had stated an incorrect age on his second marriage certificate and named his grandparents as his parents, one wonders—did he know the facts? Anyway, he didn't reckon on a nosey granddaughter and the age of computers.

My research has also enabled me to learn that my grandfather was buried in the Dalbeth Cemetery on London Road in Glasgow, and it was

[3] ScotlandsPeople (http://www.scotlandspeople.gov.uk/).

an emotional time when I was able to find his last resting place.

I have now traced the White and Doran families back to the 1790s, and I have put this information in a family file to share with anyone who is interested.

CHAPTER SIXTEEN

A Family Mystery Solved

The Wallaces of Simmy Island, Killyleagh

BY SANDRA WANAMAKER (UNITED STATES)

IN THE EARLY 1990S, MY dad gave me a list of his maternal ancestors as he was told about them. It listed his great-grandfather Hamilton Wallace (1812–1903), his wife, Mary Ann Hasson (1820–1898), and ten of his children along with the surnames of their spouses. At the time, all we knew about the family was that they had originated somewhere in Ireland.

Since then, I have researched the Wallace family and learned a great deal about Hamilton's life. However, finding where he was born in Ireland proved to be a real challenge.

This is the story of Hamilton Wallace and my journey to discover his birthplace.

* * *

Hamilton Wallace first appears in the 1850 United States census as a farmer living in Clayton, Jefferson County, with his wife, Mary Ann, and first four children (one having died in 1849). I followed him through all the subsequent federal and state censuses until his death in 1903 and found that "Ireland" was the only listing given for his place of birth.

I also obtained copies of the death certificates for Hamilton and Mary Ann with the hope that these records would provide some clues of where they were born. Although the certificates gave the names of Hamilton's parents and the name of Mary Ann's father, "Ireland" was the only indication of their birthplace. I even contacted the Jefferson County library and paid a fee to have them look for obituaries for both Hamilton and his wife, but they replied that there were none.

Hamilton Wallace (photo provided by Jill Jemison)..

Mary Ann Hasson (photo provided by Jill Jemison).

In 2003, I decided to make a trip with my husband to Jefferson County where I was able to view the land that Hamilton had farmed and to visit the cemetery where he and Mary Ann were buried. Although there are headstones for several of their children, there were none for Hamilton and his wife.

We then went to the county library and looked for obituaries on microfilms of the local newspapers. My husband found Hamilton's extensive obituary in the *Watertown Times*[1] after searching for just fifteen minutes. What a wonderful find!!

The obituary stated that Hamilton was "born on the Isle of Samms off the coast of County Down" and indicated that he had returned to Ireland seven times over the course of his long life. From his obituary, I also learned that, in 1838, Hamilton immigrated to Utica, New York; but, due to the illness of his mother, he returned to Ireland in 1841. While in Ireland, he married Mary Ann Hasson, and together they travelled back to America and settled in Jefferson County, New York.

With that information, I contacted the County Down message board on Ancestry.com and asked where the "Isle of Samms" might be. I was told that it was actually "Simmy Island", an eight acre island in Strangford Lough off of Rathcunningham, Killyleagh. So very exciting!! Sammy is apparently the way Simmy would sound to an American ear.

I next checked the online index of Will Calendars at PRONI (Public Record Office of Northern Ireland)[2] and found the following abstract:

> Letters of Administration (with the Will annexed) of the Personal estate of Thomas Wallace late of Island Simmy in the County of Down Farmer deceased who died 27 January 1858 at same place granted at Belfast to Agnes Wallace alias Carroll of Island Simmy aforesaid Widow.

It was at this point that Sheila Phillips[3] very kindly contacted me and said that she had gotten a copy of the wills for both Thomas and Agnes (Carroll) Wallace and e-mailed them to me. A true breakthrough! In Agnes' will, dated 1 March 1861, it identifies Hamilton Wallace as her son and locates him "now in the state of New York".

Once I learned where the Wallace family lived in Ireland, I began checking the internet regularly for references to Simmy Island. One day, I came across an article indicating that the island was owned by a hotelier named William Hastings and his wife, so I wrote to them. They

[1] *Watertown Times*, Watertown, New York, 5 August 1903.

[2] Public Record Office of Northern Ireland, "Will Calendars", database and images (http://www.proni.gov.uk).

[3] Sheila Phillips (1951–2012), late of Ballymartin, Co. Down, Northern Ireland.

sent me some photos of the island and an invitation to visit if we ever came to Ireland.

Three years later, my husband and I made the trip to Ireland and visited County Down for several days. Mrs. Hastings was a lovely hostess. She invited us in for coffee, gave us a tour of the house—which had been improved and extended from the original structure—and invited us to tour the island. What a wonderful moment that was to walk on the very same ground my great-grandfather had once walked on!

We researched as much as was available in County Down, visiting the Killyleagh Library, the Presbyterian graveyard, and the Linenhall Library in Belfast. We also spent a day at PRONI with the wonderful Sheila Phillips.

Upon discovering an online digital newspaper archive that covered Jefferson County,[4] I was able to fill out Hamilton's life story even more. He was a successful farmer and later owned a hotel in Cape Vincent, Jefferson County, for summer visitors to the Thousand Island area along the St Lawrence River. Unfortunately, in 1888, his home and barns burned to the ground shortly after he had let his insurance lapse. A true disaster.

The fire is probably the reason there are no family photos from prior to 1895. Very recently, I made contact with a descendant of Hamilton's second youngest daughter, and she had photos of Hamilton and his wife that were taken later in their life. These are the only pictures I have ever seen of Hamilton and Mary Ann.

Since our visit to Ireland, I have been in contact with the descendants of most of Hamilton's children and two of his sisters. Nearly every descendant that I contacted had at least a little more new information to add to the family tree.

To show the value of tracking down collateral relatives,[5] the only grandson of Hamilton's youngest daughter couldn't tell me much except that, when he was a child, his family vacationed in Bangor, Maine, and he had been told that his great-grandma (Hamilton's wife, Mary Ann Hasson) came from the town of that name in Northern Ireland. What

[4] Old Fulton New York Postcards (http://www.fultonhistory.com/Fulton.html).

[5] Collateral relatives are anyone not directly related but who share a common ancestor.

a great clue! I then started looking at Bangor, County Down, for my Hasson family and found probable family members. I've been in contact with a Hasson descendant who is likely descended from my great-great-grandmother Mary Ann's brother Henry. Perhaps someday we'll confirm that relationship.

* * *

I feel so lucky to have found the location in Ireland where my Wallaces came from, but it took a great deal of digging to get there. One thing I can't stress enough is the value of researching collateral lines rather than just your direct line descendants.

References

Baptism and marriage records for Killyleagh Presbyterian Church; viewed at Killyleagh Library, Co. Down, Ireland.

Birth records from the Raffrey Presbyterian Church, Co. Down, Ireland; provided by Nancy Schaalje.

Death records from the Town Clerk's Office, Clayton, New York.

Burial records from NYGenWeb (www.rootsweb.ancestry.com/~nygenweb/) and the Jefferson County Courthouse, Watertown, New York.

Will records for Thomas Wallace and Agnes (Carroll) Wallace of Simmy Island, Co. Down, Ireland; copies provided by Sheila Phillips, Ballymartin, Co. Down, Ireland.

Will and probate records for Hamilton Carroll Wallace; obtained from the Jefferson County Courthouse, Watertown, New York.

Census records: United States Federal (1850-1900); New York State (1865 and 1875); Ireland (1901 and 1911).

Correspondence with descendants of Thomas Wallace and Agnes Carroll of Simmy Island, Co. Down, Ireland.

Articles from Jefferson County, New York newspapers; online at Old Fulton New York Post Cards (www.fultonhistory.com/)

Appendix

The Wallace Family Tree

The earliest known ancestor in my paternal family line from County Down is my great-great-great-grandfather Thomas Wallace (born ca. 1790). Family lore says he was born on Simmy Island, but this is unconfirmed by any sources. The Tithe Applotment Books show a Thomas Wallace in 1827 who occupied land in Rathcunningham, a townland adjacent to Simmy Island in the parish of Killyleagh.

Thomas Wallace married Agnes Carroll (born ca. 1792) and they raised a family of at least seven children. When Thomas died on 27 January 1858, his wife inherited the family farm on Simmy Island which, according to the 1863 Griffith Valuation, measured 8 acres 1 rood and 24 perches. Agnes died on 16 February 1863 and the property was transferred to a John McGifford.

Children of Thomas Wallace and Agnes Carroll:

1. James Wallace (no information; identified in mother's will).

2. Agnes Wallace, born ca. 1810; died after 1863; married John McBriar (son of Hugh McBriar) of Tullymore, Co. Down, on 8 July 1828 in the Killinchy Presbyterian Church, Killinchy, Co. Down, Ireland. Resided in Belfast in 1859.

   Known children of Agnes Wallace and John McBriar:

   i. John McBriar, baptized 2 June 1834 in the Killyleagh Presbyterian Church, Killyleagh, Co. Down, Ireland.
   ii. Isabella McBriar, baptized 11 February 1837 in the Killyleagh Presbyterian Church, Killyleagh, Co. Down, Ireland.

3. Hamilton Carroll Wallace, born 6 May 1812 on Simmy Island, Co. Down, Ireland; died 28 July 1903 in St. Lawrence, Jefferson, New York, United States; married Mary Ann Hasson in Ireland.

Mary Ann Hasson, the daughter of John Hasson, was born about 1820 in Bangor or Belfast, Ireland, and died 9 April 1898 in St. Lawrence, Jefferson, New York. She and Wallace had twelve children and twenty-eight grandchildren.

Children of Hamilton C. Wallace and Mary Ann Hasson:

i. James Wallace, born September 1845 in St. Lawrence, Jefferson, New York, United States; died 26 March 1920 in Faulkton, Faulk, South Dakota, United States; married Viola Graves on 15 January 1874 in Madison, Lake, Ohio, United States.

ii. Mary Ann Wallace, born 1846 in St. Lawrence, Jefferson, New York, United States; died 18 May 1892 in St. Lawrence, Jefferson, New York, United States; married James Mooney ca. 1871.

iii. William Wallace, born 1846 in St. Lawrence, Jefferson, New York, United States; died 10 August 1849 in Cape Vincent, Jefferson, New York, United States during a scarlet fever epidemic.

iv. Henry Wallace, born 1847 in St. Lawrence, Jefferson, New York, United States; died 13 February 1907 in Seattle, King, Washington, United States; married Alice Barbour ca, 1881 in Clayton, Jefferson, New York, United States.

v. Agnes Wallace, born 1849 in St. Lawrence, Jefferson, New York, United States; died 27 August 1885 in Kimball, Brule, South Dakota, United States; married Reverend Charles William Garlock on 30 August 1880 in Cuyahoga County, Ohio, United States.

vi. Mary Jane Wallace, born 30 December 1849 in Cape Vincent, Jefferson, New York, United States; died 28 May 1922 in Clayton, Jefferson, New York, United States; married Horace Bogart.

vii. Alice Wallace, born 17 April 1852 in Clayton, Jefferson, New York, United States; died 25 October 1940 in Clayton, Jefferson, New York, United States; married Daniel Darius Butts in 1870 in Clayton, Jefferson, New York, United States.

viii. Margaret Wallace, born 1 August 1853 in Clayton, Jefferson, New York, United States; died 16 January 1912 in Sandwich, DeKalb, Illinois, United States; married William Allison Dennis on 29 March 1882 in Chicago, Cook, Illinois, United States.
ix. Althea Wallace, born May 1855 in St. Lawrence, Jefferson, New York, United States; died 18 March 1929 at Utica, Oneida, New York, United States; never married.
x. Thomas Wallace, born 11 July 1857 in Cape Vincent, Jefferson, New York, United States; died 12 April 1919 in Utica, Oneida, New York, United States; married Ida Alvaretta Hardy on 28 September 1886 in Alexandria Bay, Jefferson, New York, United States.
xi. Caroline Wallace, born 1859 in St. Lawrence, Jefferson, New York, United States; died March 1941 in Buffalo, Erie, New York, United States; married Franklin Brooks in 1885; next married Henry Affleck ca. 1910.
xii. Minnie Wallace, born December 1863 in St. Lawrence, Jefferson, New York, United States; died 20 November 1933 in Paterson, Bergen, New Jersey, United States; married Abraham Rutan ca. 1887.

4. Jane Wallace, born ca. 1814 in Ireland; died 21 June 1881 in Killinchy in the Woods, Co. Down, Ireland; married Thomas McClurg[6] on 12 March 1841 in Killinchy in the Woods, Co. Down, Ireland.

Children of Jane Wallace and Thomas McClurg:

i. Jane McClurg, born 28 May 1838 in Killinchy in the Woods, Co. Down, Ireland.
ii. Hamilton McClurg, born 12 March 1841 in Killinchy in the Woods, Co. Down, Ireland.
iii. Agnes McClurg, born 28 May 1844 in Killinchy in the Woods, Co. Down, Ireland; baptized in the First

[6] see "Chapter Six" for details on the McClurg family.

Jane Wallace (photo provided by Nancy Schaalje).

Presbyterian Church, Killyleagh, Co. Down, Ireland.

iv. Thomas McClurg, born 11 February 1847 in Killinchy in the Woods, Co. Down, Ireland; baptized in the Raffrey Presbyterian Church, Co. Down, Ireland.

v. Margaret McClurg, born July 1849 in Killinchy in the Woods, Co. Down, Ireland; baptized in the Raffrey Presbyterian Church, Co. Down, Ireland.

vi. Alice McClurg, born 17 April 1851 in Ireland; baptized in the Raffrey Presbyterian Church, Co. Down, Ireland.

vii. James McClurg, born 5 May 1857 in Killinchy in the Woods, Co. Down, Ireland; baptized in the Raffrey Presbyterian Church, Co. Down, Ireland.

viii. Susanna McClurg, baptized 6 July 1860 in Ireland; baptized in the Raffrey Presbyterian Church, Co. Down, Ireland.

ix. Christiana McClurg, born 24 May 1863 in Killinchy in the Woods, Co. Down, Ireland.

5. Susanna Wallace, born ca. 1820 in Ireland; died 19 November 1904 in Belfast Ireland; married John Morrison (farmer) of Corporation (son of John Morrison, farmer) on 24 April 1847 in the First Presbyterian Church, Killyleagh, Co. Down, Ireland. Resided in Dunmore, Co. Down in 1859.

Susanna Wallace (photo provided by N.Schaalje).

Children of Susanna Wallace and John Morrison:

i. Susanna Morrison, born 1848 in Ireland; died 26 July 1933 in Belfast, Ireland; married Joseph Orr Doran on 2 May 1872 at Berry Street Presbyterian Church, Belfast, Ireland (parents of seven children).

ii. Sara Patricia Morrison, born 20 October 1855 in Ireland; died 28 February 1944 in Belfast, Ireland; married Louis Patrick Bowler on 1 January 1874 in Belfast, Ireland (no known children).
iii. Alice Morrison, born 13 August 1860 in Dunmore, Co. Down, Ireland; died 4 March 1950 in Belfast, Ireland (never married).
iv. James Morrison.
v. Agnes Morrison.

6. Anna Wallace, born ca. 1829 in Ireland; died between 1850 and 1855 in Brooklyn, New York, United Sates; married Hugh Williamson (teacher and son of John Williamson, labourer) on 08 May 1847 in the First Presbyterian Church, Killyleagh, Co. Down, Ireland.

Child of Anna Wallace and John Williamson:

i. Agnes Edith Williamson, born ca. 1848 in Ireland; died 29 December 1919 in New York City, New York, United States; married Samuel Carlisle Cooke on 4 August 1869 in Manhattan, New York, United Sates; next married William Addy ca. 1877 in Manhattan New York, United States.

7. Alice Wallace, born before 1830 in Ireland; died before 1858 in Co. Down, Ireland; married William McClurg (mechanic and son of John McClurg)[7] of Killinchy in the Woods on 02 October 1851 in the Killyleagh Presbyterian Church, Killyleagh, Co. Down, Ireland (no known children).

[7] see "Chapter Six" for details on the McClurg family.

CHAPTER SEVENTEEN

Looking Across the Pond

Nolan(d) and Magennis (var.) *Families of County Down*

BY GENEVIEVE VAUNDELL DE HAAN (UNITED STATES)

When I first started doing my family's genealogy many years ago, I started with my mother's side and thought that my father's side would be much easier. That couldn't be further from the truth. This is a story about the difficulties and fun I have had trying to research the origins of my paternal ancestors.

I love a good mystery and, to me, the search has been very intriguing. In sharing my story, I hope to encourage you to start digging deep into your own family roots and history. You never know where it might lead.

Discovering my Irish Heritage

Growing up in North Grafton, Worcester, Massachusetts in the United States, I only remember hearing that the parents of my father's grandmother were from Scotland. My first clue that I had Irish heritage was on my grandmother's birth record that stated Sarah J. Steele was born on 6 April 1893 in Clinton, Worcester County, to Alexander Steele, born in

Scotland, and Sarah Noland, born in Ireland, both residing in Worcester.[1] I don't think it even dawned on me back then about my great-grandmother being from Ireland.

When I later found the Massachusetts marriage record for my great grandparents,[2] something began to click. It stated that, on 27 December 1888 in Grafton, Worcester, Alexander Steele, age 23, a bleacher born in Scotland to parents James and Margaret, married Sarah Nolan, age 21, a reeler born in Ireland to parents Wm. [William] and Ann E.

Imagine my surprise of never knowing I had Irish blood running through my veins and never having celebrated St. Patrick's Day.

Where in Ireland?

We are taught as genealogists to get as much information as possible on this side of "the pond"[3] before going over to the country that our relatives emigrated from. Trying to find where Sarah Nolan was from in Ireland through her American records, however, proved to be very difficult. No living relative could help me at all and most were not interested in finding their roots. Sarah's death record[4] did give me a clue as to her mother's name (Anna McGuinness) and that both her parents were born in Ireland. Since her husband, Alexander, was the informant, I thought the information could be trusted.

Sarah died on 15 August 1907 at the age of 41 years, 1 month, 25 days, and so I was able to calculate that she was born in June of 1866. I searched on the FindMyPast website[5] and there was only one Sarah "Noland" (not Nolan) whose birth was registered in 1866, and that was in the district of Banbridge, Co. Down.[6] Could this be where my paternal ancestors once lived in Ireland?

I decided to stop searching for Sarah for a while as I didn't believe I

---

[1] New England Historical Genealogical Society, "Massachusetts Vital Records, 1841-1910," Worcester Births, 1893.

[2] Town Clerk's Office, Grafton, MA; Marriage Records, Book 15, p.174, item 50.

[3] the Atlantic Ocean.

[4] Town Clerk's Office, Grafton, MA; death records, Book 16, Pg. 240, item 76.

[5] FindMyPast (www.findmypast.com).

[6] FindMyPast, "Ireland Births 1864-1958 Transcription", 1866 Quarterly returns, vol.6:225.

had enough documented evidence to make the leap over the pond yet. The research was not giving me enough clear clues, and I was not ready to think "outside the box." It was time for a rest and to work on other family history and genealogy that appeared to be easier at the time.

In 2013, since I was going to the RootsTech Conference in Salt Lake City, Utah, I decided to go over my research notes on my Irish ancestors. I did a lot of research on the FamilySearch website[7] and found that they have many records from Ireland on microfilm at the Family History Library in Salt Lake City. I gathered all the microfilm numbers and headed off to Utah in search of my great-grandmother Sarah Nolan/Noland and, hopefully, my great-great-grandparents as well. My Irish search was just about to get a big boost.

At the Family History Library, I was able to confirm that my ancestors were indeed from County Down in Ireland. I was very elated to find something at last. Here are the results, beginning with the marriage record for my great-great-gramdparents, followed by the birth records I found for four of their children:

Marriage Transcription—William Noland, age 27, bachelor, thread dyer, residing in Gilford, Parish of Tullylish, son of Daniel Noland, weaver; married Eliza Magennis, age 20, spinster, residing in Gilford, daughter of James Magennis, weaver; on 22 July 1850 at the Registers office in the town of Banbridge (both William and Eliza signed their mark).[8]

Census Transcription—James Noland, born about 1859 in Ireland, son of William Noland.[9]

Birth Transcription—Sarah Noland, born 21 June 1866 in the Parish of Tullylish; daughter of William Noland, dyer of thread, and Eliza Maguinnis.[10]

---

[7] FamilySearch (familysearch.org).

[8] FamilySearch, "Marriage records, 1845-1870, with indexes to marriages, 1845-1921," FHL film no. 101313.

[9] FamilySearch, "Census returns of Scotland for 1881," FHL film no. 203566, p. 21.

[10] FamilySearch, "Quarterly returns of births in Ireland, 1864-1955, with index to births, 1864-1921,"FHL film no. 101180, item 225.

Birth Transcription—Joseph Noland - born 20 February 1869 in Gilford, Co. Down to William Noland of Gilford, thread worker, and Anne Eliza Noland, formerly Maguinis.[11]

Birth Transcription—John M. Nolan, born 30 July 1873 at Bridge End in Lisburn to William Nolan, dryer of Longstone, and Ann Eliza Nolan formerly Maginness.[12]

I have looked for the birth of other children, but to no avail.

The Scottish Connection

About five years ago, when I was looking in the 1881 Scotland census[13] for the family of my great-grandfather Alexander Steele, I decided to look at the neighbors, not expecting to find anyone I knew. However, to my surprise, I stumbled across my great-grandmother Sarah Nolan, age 15, living at 7 Quarry Street in Johnstone, Renfrewshire, Scotland. She was working in a flax mill and living with her oldest brother, James Nolan, listed as head of the household, his wife, Mary A., and their daughter Susan, age 2. Also present in the household were James' and Sarah's father, William Nolan, age 49, and a younger brother, Joseph Nolan, age 12. All but Susan, who was born in Johnstone, were working and had been born in Ireland.

But where was William's wife, Ann(e) Eliza, and their youngest child, John M. Nolan, who I found was born in Ireland in 1873? As of yet, I still can't find any trace of what happened to them.

John M. would have been about 7 years old. Maybe he died, or maybe he and his mother, Ann(e) Eliza, stayed behind in Ireland as he wouldn't have been old enough to work. Another possibility could be that they were back in the mother land visiting relatives on the night of 3 April.

I also learned from the 1881 Scotland census that the Nolans lived on the same street as the Steele family. Residing at 4 Quarry Street in Johnstone, Scotland, were Margaret Steele (my great-great-grandmother),

[11] ibid. FHL film no.101180, p. 215, item 394.
[12] ibid. FHL film no. 255883, p. 649, item 105.
[13] FamilySearch, "Census returns of Scotland for 1881," FHL film no. 203566, p. 21.

head of household, age 52; James, son, age 22; Janet, daughter, age 19; Alexander (my great-grandfather), son, age 17; and Garvin, son, age 10. All except Margaret and Garvin (who was in school) were flax mill workers. It would appear that 17 year-old Alexander Steele and his neighbor, 15 year-old Sarah Nolan, who was also working in the flax mill, most likely knew each other.

From Scotland to the United States

My great-grandfather Alexander Steele came to Grafton, Worcester, Massachusetts, United States, with his family in October of 1881.[14] My great-grandmother Sarah Nolan immigrated later, arriving in America in 1886.[15] She and Alexander were married in Grafton, Massachusetts, on 24 December 1888.[16] Their marriage certificate states he was 23 years old and Sarah was 21.

Were my great-grandparents fond of each other before leaving Scotland, or was it an arranged marriage? I naturally want to think that it was true love; that Alexander helped Sarah come to America, and that they waited to get married until they were ready to raise children in their new adopted country.

In 1900, according to the United States census,[17] Alexander and Sarah Steele were living on Beacon Street in Worcester, Massachusetts. Alexander was recorded as born July 1864, a foreman at a thread mill, and married eleven years. Sarah was recorded as born June 1867 [sic] and a mother of five children, all living. However, only four children were listed—my grandmother Sarah Jane is not shown. Maybe she could have been staying someplace else when the census was taken, but I can't find her listed anywhere in any of the 1900 U.S. census records. Sarah Jane would have been seven years old, so I don't think she would have been out of the country.

[14] U.S. National Archives and Records Administration (NARA), "Index to New England Naturalization Records 1791-1906," film M1299, Roll 107, S340.

[15] U.S. NARA, "Passenger Lists of Vessels Arriving at New York, 1820-1897," film M237, Roll 501. Line: 47; list number 1396.

[16] Town Clerk's Office, Grafton, MA; marriage records, Book 15, p.174, item 50.

[17] U.S. NARA, "Twelfth Census of The United States, 1900." film T623, Roll 697, ED 1758.

The gravestones of my great-grandparents in Pine Grove Cemetery, Grafton, Worcester, Massachusetts.

Questions Remain

I have often wondered why my grandmother Sarah (Sadie) Steele never spoke about her mother being of Irish descent. I would like to believe it was because she was young, only fourteen years old, when her mother passed away. Also, it appears that her mother's family (the Nolans) may not have come to America, yet most of her father's family (the Steeles) immigrated and settled in North Grafton where I grew up. Thus, the family stories would have all been about life in Scotland.

I hope one day to be able to learn more about my Irish roots and to break through some of my Northern Ireland brick walls. A few important questions that need answers are as follows:

- Where and when was William Noland, the father of Sarah (Noland) Steele, born? Who is his mother? When and where was William's father, Daniel Noland, and his mother married? Who are William Noland's siblings?

- Where and when was William Noland's wife, Ann/Anne Eliza Magennis born? Who is her mother? When and where did Ann/Anne Eliza's father, James Magennis, and her mother marry? Who are Anne Eliza Magennis' siblings?
- Did William Noland and Anne/Ann Eliza Magennis have any other children? What happened to my great-grandmother Sarah Nolan's other siblings?

I really don't know where the answers to this genealogical puzzle may lie, but I probably need to look "outside the box." My next step is to do more research on this side of the pond (USA) and see where that takes me. There has to be more to the family history than I have found. It might be right in front of my eyes, and I keep looking at it and missing the clues I need.

Descendants of William Noland and Anne Eliza Magennis[18]

William Noland, son of Daniel, was born about 1823. He married Anne Eliza Magennis, daughter of James Magennis, on 22 July 1850 in Banbridge, Co. Down, Ireland. Anne Eliza was born about 1830. At the time of their marriage, William and Anne Eliza were living in Gilford, Co. Down.

Children of William Noland and Anne Eliza Magennis:

1. James Noland, born ca. 1859; married Mary A. in Ireland.[19]

   Child of James Noland and Mary A.:

   i. Susan Noland, born ca. 1879 in Johnstone, Paisley Abbey, Renfrewshire, Scotland.[20]

2. Sarah Noland, born 21 June 1866 in Banbridge, Co. Down, Ireland; died 15 August 1907 and buried in Pine Grove Cemetery, North Grafton, Massachusetts, United States;[21] married Alexander Steele on 24 December 1888 in Grafton, Massachusetts, United States.[22]

   Children of Sarah Noland and Alexander Steele:

   i. Anna Eliza Steele, born 1 October 1889 in Grafton, Worcester, Massachusetts, United States;[23] died 13 April 1974 in Grafton, Worcester, Massachusetts, United States;[24] married James

[18] Alternate spellings include Maguinnis, Maguinis and Maginness.
[19] FamilySearch, "Census returns of Scotland for 1881," FHL film no. 203566, p. 21.
[20] ibid.
[21] Town Clerk's Office, Grafton, MA; death records, Book 16, p. 193, item 26.
[22] Town Clerk's Office, Grafton, MA; marriage records, Book 15, p.174, item 50.
[23] Town Clerk's Office, Grafton, MA; birth records, Book 14, p. 259, item 99.
[24] Town Clerk's Office, Grafton, MA; death records, Book 21, p. 26, item 21.

MacDougall on 16 September 1912 in Grafton, Worcester, Massachusetts, United States.[25] They had 5 sons and four daughters.

ii. Margaret ("Maggie") B. Steele, born 20 July 1891 in Grafton, Worcester, Massachusetts, United States;[26] died 20 April 1946 in Grafton, Worcester, Massachusetts, United States.[27]

iii. Sarah ("Sadie") J. Steele, born 6 April 1893 in Clinton, Worcester, Massachusetts, United States;[28] died 8 October 1980 in Worcester, Massachusetts, United States;[29] buried 11 October 1980 in Pine Grove Cemetery, Grafton, Worcester, Massachusetts, United States; married Harry Nelson Vaundell on 26 July 1913 in Brockton, Plymouth, Massachusetts, United States.[30] They had one son and one daughter.

iv. Esther Steele, born 8 October 1895 in Worcester, Massachusetts, United States;[31] died 1985 in Grafton, Worcester, Massachusetts, United States; married John MacDougall on 14 October 1922 in Grafton, Worcester, Massachusetts, United States.[32] They had 2 daughters.

v. William Steele, born 7 June 1898 in Grafton, Worcester, Massachusetts, United States;[33] died 2 September 1910 and buried in Pine Grove Cemetery, North Grafton, Worcester, Massachusetts, United States.[34]

3. Joseph Nolan, born 20 February 1869 in Gilford, Co. Down.[35]

---

[25] Town Clerk's Office, Grafton, MA; marriage records, Book 15, p. 249 item 90.

[26] Town Clerk's Office, Grafton, MA; birth records, Book 14, p. 264, item 123.

[27] Town Clerk's Office, Grafton, MA; death records, Book 17, p. 59, item 99.

[28] New England Historical Genealogical Society (NEHGS), "Massachusetts Vital Records, 1841-1910," Worcester Births, 1893.

[29] Town Clerk's Office, Grafton, MA; death records, Book 23, p. 10, item 64.

[30] FamilySearch, "Massachusetts Marriages, 1841-1915," database and images, (familysearch.org).

[31] New England Historical Genealogical Society, "Massachusetts Vital Records, 1841-1910,"Worcester Births, 1895.

[32] Town Clerk's Office, Grafton, MA; marriage records, Book 15, p. 293, item 55.

[33] FamilySearch, "Massachusetts Births, 1841-1915," database and images (familysearch.org).

[34] Town Clerk's Office, Grafton, MA; death records, Book 16, p. 210, item 97.

[35] FamilySearch, "Quarterly returns of births in Ireland, 1864-1955, with index to births,

4. John Nolan, born 30 July 1873 in Lisburn, Co. Antrim, Ireland.[36]

1864-1921," FHL film no. 101180, p. 215, item 394.

[36] FamilySearch, "Quarterly returns of births in Ireland, 1864-1955, with index to births, 1864-1921," FHL film no. 255883, p. 649, item 105.

CHAPTER EIGHTEEN

Discovering My Irish Relatives

The O'Hare Family from Slievenaboley, County Down

BY MARY (O'HARE) HUNT (AUSTRALIA)

As a child of Irish immigrants growing up in Sydney, Australia, my knowledge of my parent's former life in Ireland was almost non-existent. I knew my mother, Anne Shea, was from Kings County (now County Offaly) and my father, Arthur O'Hare, was from County Down. My mother came to Australia in 1927 with her half-sister Kathleen Prendergast, and my father came in 1924.

Hugh O'Hare, my father's brother, also lived in Sydney, but I have no idea when he arrived in Australia. Uncle Hugh died on 27 November 1951 and is buried at Botany Cemetery in Sydney.

Occasionally, my father would talk about going to school in Legananny, which is a townland about seven kilometres north of Castlewellan in County Down. Mrs. McMullen was one of his teachers, and her son Father John McMullen, a missionary priest, used to visit us when he was in Sydney. My father also talked about working with his brother Stephen O'Hare in the grocery shop and bar at Burrenbridge, Burrenreagh, Co. Down.

Apart from these small glimpses of my father's life, I knew nothing about his family. Then, in 1982, my eldest daughter went on a trip to

Europe and met my father's sister Catherine "Katie" Murnin, who was in her eighties. I later wrote to my Aunt Katie and said I was thinking about coming to Ireland. She wrote back, "Don't think about it. Do it!"

So, in 1984, I went to Ireland for the first time.

First Visit to Ireland

Aunt Katie invited me to stay with her in Castlewellan, Co. Down. It was from Katie that I learned the names of her parents, James O'Hare and Bridget Lavery, and her siblings Stephen, Michael, Patrick, Bridget, Hugh, James, John, Francis, and Arthur (my father), who were all deceased. I also met some of my cousins and found my extended family now included the surnames Byrne, McKeown, Heenan, McKibben, and McCrickard.

Aunt Katie (centre) with her sister Bridget O'Hare (left) and mother (my grandmother) Bridget (Lavery) O'Hare (photo: 1906).

The shop and bar that was owned by my uncle Stephen when my father left Ireland was now owned by my cousin John Francis O'Hare. After my uncle Stephen died in 1930, his brother John O'Hare moved with his wife Clara and children to Burrenbridge and took over the shop. It was my Uncle John's son John Francis who was running the business when I visited.

Uncle Stephen O'Hare, proprietor of the shop and bar in Burrenbridge, Co. Down (photo: ca. 1910).

This property, which included a shop, house, bar, and mill, was sold in 2003. The *Mourne Observer* (13 August 2003) published a half-page story about my cousin John Francis O'Hare and how he had built the business up over the years. In the article, local councillor Eamonn O'Neill was quoted as saying that it was "truly sad to see the end of an era" and described the O'Hare business as "the hub of Burrenreagh life."

My cousin John died three years later in 2006. The bar is the only part of the business still operating and is known locally as the Bridge Bar. The property is situated just out of the town area of Castlewellan, on the Dublin road at Burrenreagh.

At the time of my first visit, my cousin John's brother James O'Hare, now deceased, was living in the house attached to the shop. James took me on a tour of the premises, and although I knew the O'Hare family were also undertakers, it was still quite a surprise to find the attic of the house full of empty coffins.

My cousins took me to see the old stone farmhouse at Slievenaboley, a townland in the Dromara hills. This was the home of my great-grandparents Stephen O'Hare and Catherine Burns and where my grandparents (Aunt Katie's parents) were living at the time of the 1901 census. We also visited the O'Hare family headstone at the Church of the Immaculate Conception in Leitrim, Co. Down.

This old photo of Stephen O'Hare's shop and bar in Burrenbridge, Co. Down, was found among my late father's papers. Uncle Stephen is seen standing third from the left with his wife Rose (second from the left). Others identified in the photo are my uncle John O'Hare (fifth from the left) with his wife Clara (fourth from the left), and my aunt Katie (third from the right). After Stephen died in 1930, Uncle John assumed ownership of the business (photo: 1929)

Although my cousins were happy to show me where the family lived, and to talk about living relatives, they couldn't understand my wanting to know about the past. However, they did introduce me to another cousin living in Finnis, a townland in the parish of Dromara, who was also interested in genealogy. She was a McNeill before she married and said her connection to my family was through a Catherine O'Hare. Little did I know that, many years later, I would find proof of this Finnis connection to my O'Hares.

My uncle James O'Hare sitting outside the stone farmhouse of my great-grandparents in Slievenaboley, Co. Down where my cousins took me to visit in 1984 (photo: ca. 1966).

Tracing my Family Tree

After returning home to Australia, I kept in touch with my cousins by phone and mail. Then, in 1996, my youngest daughter started travelling. She visited America and Europe, and ended up almost out of money in Glasgow and decided to stay there for a while. After obtaining a job and a flat, she started visiting her relatives in Ireland and became very friendly with Aunt Katie's granddaughter. It was Katie's granddaughter who introduced her to her future husband.

My daughter and her fiancé were married in Australia in 2001. After the wedding, they returned to County Down to live in a housing estate behind the Bridge Bar at Burrenreagh. As it turns out, the land the housing estate is built on was previously owned by the O'Hare family. Moreover, before he left for Australia in 1924, my father was living in the house attached to the shop and bar.

So, purely by coincidence, my daughter now lives in almost the same spot that her grandfather once did. Following the birth of her two daughters, my interest in finding out more about the O'Hares was reignited.

My search of the O'Hare family history in County Down began on the Internet. I soon realised what an impossible task I had undertaken as I had very little information and absolutely no genealogy research skills.

In 2008, I joined Fiona's County Down Genealogy Group[1] and was lucky enough to get help from Sheila Phillips.[2]

Sheila viewed the records for the Church of the Immaculate Conception (also known as Leitrim Chapel) and told me my paternal great-grandmother's name was Catherine Burns. She also found wills for both my great-grandfather Stephen O'Hare and my grandfather James O'Hare online at the PRONI (Public Records Office of Northern Ireland) website.[3]

Sheila also introduced me to the International Genealogical Index (IGI) on the FamilySearch website,[4] and later I found out about Ros Davies' wonderful site.[5] When the 1901 and 1911 census records for Ireland came online in 2009–2010,[6] it was amazing the information I was able to obtain working with these four websites.

Family of my Great-Grandfather Stephen O'Hare

Stephen O'Hare and his wife, Catherine Burns, had at least eight children—Hugh, Patrick, Anne, Catherine, James (my grandfather), Stephen

[1] Fiona's County Down Genealogy Group at Yahoo!Groups (groups.yahoo.com/neo/groups/CountyDownGenealogy/info).
[2] Sheila Phillips (1951-2012), late of Ballymartin, Co. Down, Northern Ireland.
[3] Public Records Office of Northern Ireland (www.proni.gov.uk/).
[4] FamilySearch (familysearch.org/).
[5] Ros Davies' Co. Down, Northern Ireland Family History Research Site (freepages.genealogy.rootsweb.ancestry.com/~rosdavies).
[6] The National Archives of Ireland, "Census of Ireland 1901/1911", database and images (www.census.nationalarchives.ie/).

Michael, and Ellen. But finding them all was not easy.

When my great-grandfather died in 1882, his sons Hugh and Patrick were already living in Finnis on separate blocks of land apparently owned by their father. In his will, Stephen O'Hare, leaves each of them the land they are living on.

So, Finnis was where I started looking for information on Hugh and Patrick.

Hugh O'Hare

Hugh was easy to find. I checked the 1901 census and found my great-uncle, then a widower, living with his mother, Catherine O'Hare, and a niece, Mary McGuinnes, in house 26 in Finnis. This was definitely the right family and finding my great-grandmother was very exciting. I had been looking for her for ages.

During my first visit to Ireland, my cousin from Finnis had told me that Hugh's first wife was Anne Owens and that they had at least three children—Anne, Catherine, and Stephen. Hugh's daughter Catherine I already knew about, as she was mentioned in the will of her grandfather Stephen O'Hare. I later found the births of the other children, Anne and Stephen, on the Irish Family History Foundation website.[7]

Hugh's second wife was Mary Ann Catherwood from Drin in the parish of Dromara. I have been unable to find a date for their wedding, but in the 1901 census, Mary Ann is single and still living with her brother Andrew Catherwood in Drin. In the 1911 census, Mary Ann is listed as a widow and living in Finnis with her four children—Mary Teresa, Stephen, Catherine Ann, and Rose Ellen. According to the online will records at PRONI, Hugh O'Hare's date of death is recorded as 30 October 1911. Three years later, in 1914, Mary Ann (Catherwood) O'Hare married Denis Keenan.

Patrick O'Hare

Great-uncle Patrick was a bit more difficult to find. That is, until one day, I was given some copies of old memorial cards. One was for a Patrick

[7] Irish Family History Foundation (http://www.rootsireland.ie).

O'Hare who died 28 March 1903. There was a will for this Patrick O'Hare at PRONI, and in it he mentions his wife, Ann Doyle, his sister Anne Magennis, and his brother James (my grandfather). I found Patrick and Ann (Doyle) O'Hare living in house 38 in Finnis when the census was taken in 1901.

Another one solved!

Anne O'Hare

I eventually found my great-aunt Anne (O'Hare) Magennis and her family in Benraw, Parish of Drumgooland. The 1901 census has the townland name transcribed as "Benrow" and the family name is recorded as "McGuinness". Anne (also known as "Nancy") was living with her husband, Patrick, and nine of their children in house 5. In the 1911 census, the name was recorded as "McGennis", but Magennis seems to be the preferred family spelling.

Catherine O'Hare

I learned that my great-aunt Catherine was single in 1882 from her father Stephen O'Hare's will which says, "my daughter Catherine is to hold the low room and the one over it as long as she remains single." I had a feeling my great-aunt might be the Catherine that connected my family to my cousin in Finnis.

I had known that my cousin's grandparents were named Catherine and Bernard O'Hare and that they were from Finnis. I later found from their marriage certificate that Catherine was an O'Hare from Slievenaboley and her father was Stephen O'Hare who was deceased. This proved to me that my cousin's grandmother Catherine was indeed my great-aunt and that she was the "connection" I first heard about in 1984.

Catherine O'Hare and Bernard O'Hare[8] were married on 24 April 1884. In 1901, they are living with their eight children in house 44 in Finnis. Their daughter Catherine ("Kate") O'Hare later married Patrick McNeill from Moybrick Upper, Dromara. Catherine and Patrick McNeill are the parents of my cousin from Finnis.

---

[8] Not related to my O'Hare family.

James O'Hare

Details about my grandfather are given in the next section.

Michael O'Hare

Michael was baptised at Leitrim Chapel on 20 February 1845 and died in 1869.

Stephen O'Hare

Stephen, the youngest son born to my great-grandparents, was baptised on 20 February 1859 at Leitrim Chapel. He was ordained a priest in 1884 and died in 1895 while a priest at St. John the Baptist Church in Yorkshire, England. His father, Stephen O'Hare, had left him land that was once owned by a Francis O'Hare. I am still trying to find out how who this Francis O'Hare was and where the land is located.

Ellen O'Hare

In 2010, I went to the Church of the Immaculate Conception (Leitrim Chapel) to look at the church records and found that Ellen was baptised on 2 February 1840. It was a complete surprise to also learn that she was the first child of Stephen O'Hare and Catherine Burns. There is no mention of Ellen in her father's will, and the date of her baptism is the only information I have about her.

Family of my Grandfather James O'Hare

On 29 January 1878, my grandfather James O'Hare married Bridget Lavery. Their witnesses were James Murray and Agnes E. McKenny.

Bridget's parents were Hugh Lavery and Margaret McGrady who lived on a farm in the townland of Legananny, Drumgooland. Her mother, Margaret, was the daughter of John and Bridget McGrady from Finnis, and PRONI has a will for Margaret's father, John McGrady, who died on 26 August 1867. Margaret also had two brothers, Felix and Laurence McGrady, who were still living in the family home in Finnis at the time of the 1901 census.

Following their marriage in 1878, my grandparents James and Bridget O'Hare had ten children—Stephen, Michael, Patrick, Bridget, James, Hugh, John, Francis, Catherine, and Arthur, my father. After his father, Stephen O'Hare, died in 1882, my grandfather inherited the family property at Slievenaboley. James, Bridget, and eight of their children are still living there in 1901. Michael was no longer at home, and my Aunt Katie told me Francis had died when he was a baby.

The 1911 census has the family living in Legananny in a much larger Georgian style house. James, Hugh, John, Kate, and Arthur are still living with their parents. James, my grandfather, has written "one in Australia" on the census form and then crossed it out. Michael would be the son he has written this about.

The house in Legananny, Co. Down where my grandparents were living in 1911 (photo: ca. 1966).

I'm not sure when my uncle Michael came to Australia. But on 14 September 1914, shortly after the start of World War 1, he joined the Australian army in Perth, Western Australia. On 22 December 1914, he sailed with the 16th Infantry Battalion "A" Company from Melbourne aboard the HMAT *Ceramic A40* to join the war in Europe. Michael was killed in action on 16 June 1915 while fighting on the Gallipoli peninsula in Turkey.

The other children missing from the 1911 census—my uncles Stephen and Patrick, and my aunt Bridget—were living in Castlewellan. Sometime after this, Stephen bought the shop and bar at Burrenbridge from the Keenan family. The McCartan family owned the property before the Keenans.

My Father Arthur O'Hare

After coming to Australia in 1924, Arthur O'Hare, my father, travelled around quite a bit and eventually settled in Sydney. This is where he met my mother, Anne Shea. Arthur and Anne were married in 1938. They moved into a house in Paddington, Sydney, where they remained for nearly forty years. Arthur died on 19 November 1976. My mother died in 1983. Sadly, neither of my parents ever returned to Ireland.

Arthur O'Hare with his sister (my aunt) Katie before he emigrated from Ireland to Australia (photo: ca. 1920).

* * *

The house connected to the shop in Burrenbridge and the fields behind the house seem to have created wonderful memories for many O'Hare family members. Over the years, I have heard many stories of family life from relations who have lived there. Now my grandchildren live behind the old house and play in one of those fields.

Auntie Katie, daughter of my grandparents James O'Hare and Bridget Lavery, lived there before she married, and this was where the family gathered to celebrate her 90th birthday in 1987. It was a wonderful celebration that my husband, youngest daughter, and myself were thrilled to be able to attend. Katie died on 24 March 1995. She was 98.

After the death of my parents, I found old photographs among my father's papers that had been sent to him over the years. I had never seen them before. Since then I have met some of the people and been to some of the places shown in these photos.

My research for information about my Irish relatives has been a very interesting and enlightening journey. Along the way, I have met relatives I didn't know I had, and fantastic cousins who have sent me photocopies of old cards and photographs. I have been helped by some amazing people such as Sheila Phillips and my friend Vik Ritelis who worked on restoring my photographs.

Over the last five years, and much to my surprise, I have gone from someone who knew nothing about genealogy to now, where I have even been able to give assistance to others in their research.

To all of the many people who have helped me along the way, a thank you seems inadequate. But I would like you to know how much your input has been appreciated.

"Thank you so much. I am so grateful to you all."

Appendix

The O'Hare Family Burial Ground

Members of the O'Hare family are buried in the cemetary next to the Church of the Immaculate Conception in Leitrim, Co. Down. During my visit to Ireland in 1984, I visited the site and transcribed the following inscription on the family headstone.

Erected
In Memory of
Stephen O'Hare, Slievenaboley
Who Departed This Life 26 August 1882
Aged 74 Years
Also His Son Michael
Who Departed This Life Oct 1869 Aged 24 Years
Also His Beloved Wife Catherine
Who Departed This Life Jan 1904 Aged 82 Years
Also Their Son James
Who Departed This Life 12 Jan 1912 Aged 64 Years
Also His Beloved Wife Bridget
Who Departed This Life 5 July 1920 Aged 63 Yrs
Also Their Son Patrick
Who Departed This Life 27 Feb 1920 Aged 35 Yrs
Also Their Daughter Bridget
Who Departed This Life 10 July 1920 Aged 32 Yrs
Also Their Son Stephen
Who Departed This Life 7 July 1930 Aged 52 Yrs
Also Michael O'Hare
Died 17th June 1915 Aged 32 Years
James O'Hare
Died 22nd June 1934 Aged 2 Yrs
Mary Catherine O'Hare
Died 8th May 1939 Aged 5½ Yrs
Hugh O'Hare
Died 27th Nov 1951 Aged 61 Yrs.

CHAPTER NINETEEN

A Family from Ballyalgan, County Down

The Morrows

BY NANCY MCCORMACK SCHAALJE (CANADA)

THERE WAS AN ARTICLE SOME time ago showing how to calculate what percentage of your heritage is Irish. I was born in Canada, but since my parents, grandparents, and all eight great-grandparents were born in Ireland, I figure I qualify as 100% Irish—a fact in which I take great pride. As a result, and following about forty years of off and on research, I have several binders of information on my Irish roots. This is more than enough to fill a book, so I will narrow my story here to the Morrows of Ballyalgan, Killyleagh, Co. Down.

Gathering the Evidence

The Morrows are my most recent research project, and it all started with a handwritten note that was sent to me by a McClurg third cousin living in Raffrey, Co. Down. It was a transcription of the baptism for Robert McClurg that took place on 4 June 1821 in the Killyleagh Parish Church of Ireland (see overleaf).

I had already found proof that Robert was the brother of my great-grandfather Thomas McClurg (see "Chapter Six" for details on the

McClurg family), so this important piece of information gave me some new leads; specifically, the names of my great-great-grandfather James McClurg and his wife, Ann. The amazing part is that Ann's maiden name of "Morrow" was also given. This information is very frequently left out by the clergy in the 1800s, so finding it brought on a huge "aha" moment for me.

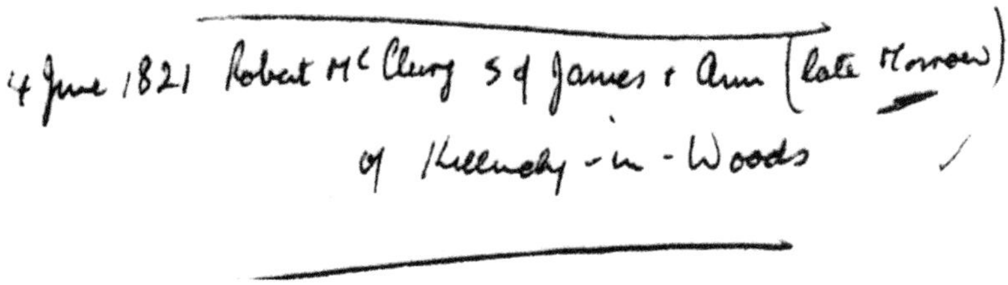
4 June 1821 Robert McClurg s of James & Ann (late Morrow) of Killenchy-in-Woods

Baptism of Robert McClurg transcribed from Killyleagh Parish Church (Church of Ireland) records by Ethel McClurg Murdock (PRONI Film MIC/1/58/A/1).

I then went to a loose scrap of paper in the McClurg family Bible. It still amazes me that this six by eight inch piece of paper hadn't fallen out and been lost many years ago. On it was written the following:

> *Aunt Jane Morrow died 1841 aged 64*
> *Cousin Joseph Morrow March 13, 1856 aged 51(?)* [torn]
> *Hugh Morrow March 26, 1833*
> *Mother December 11, 1871 aged 86*
> *Sergeant Brown died December 18th 1871 aged 68*
> *Jane Coulter, Grove, died November 28th 1877*
> *John Coulter [ditto] March 9th 1878*
> *William Cleland died December 1881*
> *My Wife died June 9th 1881 …* [cont.]

Who, I had wondered, were the Morrows?

Through research on the entries for "Mother" and "My Wife," I had found that the author of the document was my great-grandfather Thomas McClurg. I had also known that his daughter Christiana McClurg, my grandmother, married Thomas Robert Morrow in 1884. However, I had never understood why Thomas McClurg was recording information about the Morrows long before his daughter married into the family. Now that I had the transcription of his brother Robert McClurg's baptism, it made sense. Thomas McClurg's mother was Ann Morrow, and these were his blood relatives

My next step was to check a book of gravestone inscriptions edited by Clarke (1999).[1] There were two notable matches to the information in the family Bible.

On page 132, under "Killyleagh Presbyterian Graveyard," is the following inscription for Hugh Morrow:

> Morrow [Rough Granite Stone] Erected in memory of the late Hugh Morrow of Ballyalgin who departed this life March the 26th 1833 aged 66 years.

And further on the same page is an inscription for Joseph Morrow:

> Morrow Erected by John Morrow of Ballyalgin to the memory of his Mother Elizabeth Morrow who departed this life the 18th July 1841, aged 64 years. Also his brother Joseph Morrow who departed this life on the 12th March 1856 Aged 51 years.

This is how I discovered where this line of Morrows lived, and thus began my search for all I could find about the Morrows from the townland of Ballyalgan, Co. Down.

Ballyalgan, also spelled "Ballyalgin", is a townland of about 644 acres in the parish of Killyleagh, County Down. It is bounded by the townland of Killinchy in the Woods to the southwest, Ballywillin to the southeast, and the parish of Killinchy to the northwest. All of these areas figure prominently in my County Down research.

My next approach was to comb through the wills available online at the Public Record Office of Northern Ireland (PRONI) website.[2] I was able to match some wills to the gravestone inscriptions in Clark (1999)

[1] R.S.J. Clarke, *Old Families of Downpatrick and District From Gravestone Inscriptions, Wills and Biographical Notes* (Belfast: Ulster Historical Foundation, 1999), Volume 21.

[2] Public Record Office of Northern Ireland, PRONI (http://www.proni.gov.uk/).

and to start fleshing out the families.

I then used available church records for Killyleagh, Raffrey and Killinchy on microfilm at the Family History Library in Salt Lake City.[3],[4],[5],[6],[7] I have also viewed filmed copies of the Tithe Applotment Books available at the Family History Library[8] and the online copies of Griffith's Valuation.[9] The 1901 and 1911 Ireland census records[10] have been helpful with the later generations.

Putting it all Together

Beginning with the baptismal transcript showing that Ann Morrow was the wife of my great-great-grandfather James McClurg, and researching through many Irish records, I have determined that Ann may be the second youngest of six children born to unknown parents in the townland of Ballyalgan, Co. Down:

- Hugh Morrow (ca. 1767–1833)
- Thomas Morrow (ca. 1770–1847)
- Jane Morrow (ca. 1777–1841)
- William Morrow (ca. 1780–)
- Ann Morrow (ca. 1785–1871)
- Robert Morrow (ca. 1787–)

---

[3] Public Record Office of Northern Ireland (PRONI), "Parish of Killyleagh, Diocese Down, Co.," 1813-1896, microfilm, PRONI Reference: MIC1/58A/1).

[4] Ibid, "1840-1968: Baptism register of 2nd Killyleagh," microfilm, PRONI Reference: MIC1P/261/1.

[5] FamilySearch, "Baptisms in the congregation of Killyleagh, 1835-1881, and marriages in the congregation of Killyleagh, 1835-1871," transcribed by David Stewart, FHL film no. 928510.

[6] ibid, "Raffrey Presbyterian church, County Down, marriages, 1845-1877 and births, 1843-1885", transcribed by David Stewart, FHL film no. 990494.

[7] ibid, "Killinchy Presbyterian Church : list of births 1835-1900, list of marriages 1835 to 1845", transcribed by David Stewart, FHL film no. 824373.

[8] Family History Library, Salt Lake City, Utah.

[9] AskAboutIreland, "Griffith's Valuation," database and images (www.askaboutireland.ie/griffith-valuation/index.xml)

[10] The National Archives of Ireland, "Census of Ireland 1901/1911", database and images (www.census.nationalarchives.ie/).

The remainder of this chapter summarizes my research and provides details on what I have been able to learn so far about each of the children and their descendants.

Hugh Morrow (ca. 1767–1833)

Hugh died on 26 March 1833 at the age of 66 years in Ballyalgan, Co. Down. I have no evidence that he is related to the other members of the Morrow family except for his mention in the McClurg family Bible. His birth is too close to the others in the family to be considered as the father, so I have placed him as the eldest son.

Hugh's name appears in the Tithe Applotment Books of 1827 but not in Griffith's Valuation. I also found a Hugh Morrow of Ballyalgan listed in the "Name Search" section of the PRONI website. There it lists a pre-1858 will for Hugh Morrow of Ballyalgan dated 1834 and the executor was Janet Morrow. The record is a very good match to the Hugh Morrow I am seeking as it is shortly after his death in 1833. Unfortunately, there is a notation that the "document does not exist". A later check of the "Index of Irish Wills 1484-1858" online at FindMyPast[11] indicated there is a will for Hugh at the National Archives dated 1834. I am currently attempting to get a copy of this document.

Thomas Morrow (ca. 1770–1847)

Thomas died on 6 June 1847 in Ballyalgan, Co. Down, at the age of 77 years. His will, dated 24 May 1847, [12] has an important clue about the structure of the Morrow family. Although there is no mention of a wife or children, it does state that "I bequeath unto my brother William's Joseph Morrow ..." which I have interpreted as meaning that Thomas had a brother William who had a son named Joseph. He also leaves to his brother Robert £7 per year for the rest of his life, and to Robert's son Thomas, £10 when he comes of age. He bequeathed to his sister Ann the sum of £20 and a heifer, and to Ann's son Thomas McClurg, the sum

[11] FindMyPast (www.findmypast.com).

[12] Public Record Office of Northern Ireland (PRONI), "Legal papers of Thomas Morrow," 1848-1856, PRONI Reference: D1538.

of £20. This was an important link for me since Thomas McClurg is my great-grandfather.

Jane Morrow (ca. 1777–1841)

Jane Morrow died in 1841 at the age of 64 years. She is recorded by Thomas McClurg on the loose sheet of paper in the McClurg family Bible as "Aunt Jane Morrow." No further information has been found about Jane. She may have been unmarried, or perhaps had married, but was still known in the family by her maiden name. It is also possible that she was the spouse of a Morrow.

William Morrow (ca. 1780–)

No date of death has been found for William, and his year of birth is estimated. A wealth of knowledge was gleaned from the will of his son Joseph,[13] who is mentioned in the McClurg family Bible as "Cousin Joseph Morrow" with a death date of 12 March 1856. His will is dated 1 March 1856 and the following is an extract giving the names of family members and their relationships (emphasis mine).

> … I Joseph Morrow of Ballyalgin, farmer, finding myself sick and weak, but of sound and disposing mind and judgement, do make, ordain and publish my last will and testament.
>
> … Next I give and bequeath to *my brother John* now in America all the rest and residue of my property . . . on the following condition forever that he comes and resides on it and further that he pay to *my father, William Morrow* and to *my three brothers, William, Robert and James*, and to *my two sisters, Anne and Jane* to each one hundred pounds and provided my brother John does not choose to have my said farm and houses on said condition . . . to sell my said property to the highest bidder at public auction and the amount realized after defraying all necessary expenses be

[13] Public Record Office of Northern Ireland (PRONI), "Legal papers of Thomas Morrow," 1848-1856, PRONI Reference: D1538.

> equally divided among my foresaid friends in America, viz, my father, my four brothers and two sisters before named.

As noted earlier, the inscription on Joseph's gravestone came from his brother John Morrow, and it also mentions their mother, Elizabeth, who died on 18 July 1841 at the age of 64 years. So from this and the contents of Joseph's will, I learned that Elizabeth was the wife of William Morrow (b. ca.1 770). Also from Joseph's will, I have the names of the seven children born to William and Elizabeth.

It would appear that, after the death of his wife in Ireland in 1841, William Morrow and some of his children immigrated to America. Joseph remained in Ireland.

The children of William Morrow and Elizabeth[14] were:

1. Joseph Morrow (born ca. 1805) died on 12 March 1856 in Ballyalgan, Co. Down. His year of birth is calculated from a lease document dated 1813 which included the names William Morrow, Joseph Morrow, Robert Morrow, Hugh Morrow, John Morrow, Robert Cleland, Samuel Cleland, John Cleland and Robert Ward.[15] The lease was for the life of "Joseph Morrow, eldest son of said William Morrow of Ballyalgin aged eight years." Again, no mention is made of Joseph's wife or children.

2. John Morrow (born ca. 1807) was living in America at time of his brother's death in 1856 and may have returned to Ireland in order to fulfill the requirements of his brother's will.

3. William Morrow (born ca. 1809) immigrated to America.

4. Ann Morrow (born ca. 1812) immigrated to America.

---

[14] After preparing this story, I found a baptismal record for the youngest child of William Morrow which records the mother's name as Elizabeth Cleland.

[15] Public Record Office of Northern Ireland (PRONI), " Notice of serving memoranda to Lord Dufferin," D1071/A/J/2/4.

5. Jane Morrow (born ca.1815) immigrated to America.

6. Robert Morrow (born ca. 1817) of Ballyalgan, Co. Down, married Ann Trimble of Killinchy in the Woods, Co. Down, on 21 May 1842.[16] By 1856, according to the will of his brother Joseph, it would appear that Robert was in America. However, he may have subsequently returned to Ireland since I have found a death record dated 25 July1866 for Robert Morrow of Ballyalgan that was registered by John Morrow.

   Robert Morrow and Ann Trimble had seven known children, all of whom are mentioned in Robert's will dated 19 July 1866 (available online at PRONI):

   i. Catharine Morrow (ca. 1848–1923) married William Woods on 19 March 1869 in the Raffrey Presbyterian Church and died on 3 May 1923 in Ballyalgan, Co. Down. William was born about 1843 and died in Ballyalgan, Co. Down, on 25 March 1919.

      The known children of Catharine Morrow and William Woods were:

      – Robert Woods, born 24 November 1869 in Ballyalgan, Co. Down; died 1869 Ballyalgan, Co. Down.
      – Anna Woods, born 25 June 1871 in Ballyalgan, Co. Down; died 1 September 1897 in Ballyalgan, Co. Down; buried in the Raffrey Presbyterian Church graveyard.
      – Sarah Jane Woods, born 3 May 1873 in Ballyalgan, Co. Down; died 20 February 1925; buried in the Raffrey Presbyterian Church graveyard.
      – Mary Woods, born 1875 in Ballyalgan, Co. Down; died 26 November 1896 in Ballyalgan, Co. Down.
      – Elizabeth Woods, born 5 March 1877 in Ballyalgan,

[16] FamilySearch, "Baptisms in the congregation of Killyleagh, 1835-1881, and marriages in the congregation of Killyleagh, 1835-1871," transcribed by David Stewart, FHL film no. 928510.

Co. Down.

- Ellen Morrow Woods, born 25 March 1879 in Ballyalgan, Co. Down.
- Robert Woods, born 21 June 1881 in Ballyalgan, Co. Down.
- Agnes Woods, born 26 October 1883 in Ballyalgan, Co. Down.
- Thomas Joseph Woods, born 2 October 1887 in Ballyalgan, Co. Down.
- Catharine Woods, born 6 May 1889 in Ballyalgan, Co. Down.

ii. Joseph Morrow (ca. 1852–1887) married Jane Orr Gill on 2 November 1877 in the Raffrey Presbyterian Church and died on 5 December 1887 in Ballyalgan, Co. Down. Jane was born on 22 March 1852, the daughter of Thomas Gill and Jane Orr.

Joseph Morrow's will was probated in 1888, eleven years after his death, and was proved by his brother Francis Morrow. The will mentions his wife, Jane, and four children:

- Anne Morrow, born 18 August 1878 in Ballyalgan, Co. Down.
- Jane Morrow, born 19 June 1881 in Ballyalgan, Co. Down.
- Robert Morrow, born 22 April 1883 in Ballyalgan, Co. Down.
- Mary Smyth Morrow, born 17 June 1885 in Ballyalgan, Co. Down.

iii. Francis Morrow (1853–) seems to be the same Francis/Frank Morrow residing in Ballyalgan, Co. Down at the time of the 1901 and 1911 censuses, although the ages do not match. There is also a Francis Morrow whose death was registered in Downpatrick, Co. Down in 1919.[17] Francis was recorded

[17] FamilySearch, " Ireland, Civil Registration Indexes, 1845-1958," index (https://

as unmarried in both census records

iv. Mary Ann Morrow (ca. 1855–) is in both the 1901 and 1911 censuses living with her brother Francis Morrow and is recorded as unmarried.

v. Eliza Morrow (ca. 1856–) married Joseph Coulter on 18 November 1881 in the Raffrey Presbyterian Church. She appears in the 1901 census living in Killinchy in the Woods, County Down, but is not in 1911 census where her husband is listed as a widower. She died 13 March 1902 in Killinchy in the Wood.

The children of Eliza Morrow and Joseph Coulter were:

- John Coulter, born 7 October 7 1883 in Killinchy in the Woods, Co. Down; married Catherine Shaw on 3 January 3, 1906.
- Robert Coulter, born 17 April 1885 in Killinchy in the Woods, Co. Down.
- Jane Lowry Coulter, born 12 May 1887 in Killinchy in the Woods, Co. Down.
- David Stewart Kerr Coulter, born 7 July 1889 in Killinchy in the Woods, Co. Down; married Matilda Rogan on 26 November 1913 in Killyleagh, Co. Down.
- Joseph Coulter, born 21 June 1892 in Killinchy in the Woods, Co. Down.
- William Coulter, born 21 April 1894 in Killinchy in the Woods, Co. Down.

vi. Robert Morrow (ca. 1857–) was baptised in the Raffrey Presbyterian Church on 30 November 1857. He appears with his brother Francis and sister Mary Ann in both the 1901 and 1911 census and is recorded as unmarried.

---

familysearch.org).

vii. Jane Morrow (ca. 1859–)

7. James Morrow (born 1819) was baptised in the Killyleagh Presbyterian Church on 20 July 1819 and his mother's name is recorded as Elizabeth Cleland. He immigrated to America.

Ann Morrow (ca. 1785–1871)

Ann married James McClurg about 1810 and died on 11 December 1871 in Killinchy in the Woods, Co. Down. Ann and James are my great-great-grandparents.

So far, I have six possible children for Ann Morrow and James McClurg:

1. Thomas McClurg (ca. 1814-1888)
2. Hamilton McClurg (ca. 1818–)
3. Robert McClurg (1821–1908)
4. Mary Ann McClurg (ca. 1823–1896)
5. Joseph McClurg (1826–1898)
6. William McClurg (ca. 1830–)

I have extensive information about the McClurg family, especially the descendents of the eldest child, Thomas McClurg, who was my grandfather (see "Chapter Six" for details on the McClurg family).

Robert Morrow (ca. 1787–)

Robert is identified in the 1847 will of his brother Thomas, which mentions that Robert has a son named Thomas who is to receive his inheritance when he comes of age. There is also a will dated 1844 for a Robert Morrow of Ballyalgan that did not survive, but which may refer to the

Robert Morrow discussed here. It would be too early for the other Robert Morrows of Ballyalgan that I have documented so far.

In Reverend David Stewart's transcriptions of the Killinchy Presbyterian Church records (page 142) is a list of marriages with the entry "Robert Morrow of Ballyalgin to Agnes, daughter to Isaac Patterson of Ballymacreely" (no date).[18] I have not yet found a record giving the date of this marriage, but it may have been about 1816.

The known children of Robert Morrow and Agnes Patterson, who appear in the Killyleagh Presbyterian Church baptismal records as born in Ballyalgan, were:

1. Ann Morrow (1817–) was baptised on 19 October 1817.

2. Thomas Morrow (1830–) was baptised on 1 November 1830.

* * *

This narrative accounts for what I have been able to discover so far about the Morrow family of Ballyalgan, Co. Down. I have found the availability of the wills on the PRONI website to be particularly helpful.

There are obviously other avenues to explore in discovering more about this family. I have not had access to all of the church records that I would like to see. I have also not been able, as yet, to trace William Morrow (ca.1780–) and his family in "America", which could mean either the United States or Canada.

I want to acknowledge the help of Ethel McClurg Murdock for providing the baptismal record of Robert McClurg which identified his mother as Ann Morrow. This was the piece of information that started the quest for information about this Morrow family. I am also indebted to Peter Gibson who has extracted church records for me at PRONI.

I would be interested in hearing from anyone who may have further information on the Morrows of Ballyalgan (email address: schaaln@shaw.ca).

---

[18] FamilySearch, "Killinchy Presbyterian Church : list of births 1835-1900, list of marriages 1835 to 1845 ", transcribed by David Stewart, FHL film no. 824373.

CHAPTER TWENTY

A Weaver from Bleary, County Down

Mary McConville (1854–1895)

BY FRANCES DONNELLY IGARASHI (ENGLAND)

"I think I have brothers and sisters. Will you help me find them?"

MARY (MULLEN) NEWCOMBE SAT IN her little cottage in Cambuslang on the outskirts of Glasgow, Scotland, talking to her grandson William Francis Donnelly. She had just revealed to him a secret that she had kept very close to her heart and had never revealed, not even to her own children. She had been adopted when she was nine years old to a wonderfully loving couple and vaguely remembered having had brothers and sisters. She knew very few details, except the name of a Catholic church in Glasgow—St. Mary's on Abercrombie Street—that had stayed in her memory. Unfortunately, there was very little that William Francis could find for her, and she died in 1968 not knowing her own story or the story of her siblings.

In 2013, her great-grandson Mark sat in the Mitchell Library in Glasgow and came across a reference in the poorhouse records of a family that seemed to fit Mary's hazy recollections. And so began our journey to find our lost family. What follows is the story we have discovered about Mary's early life.

Mary (Mullen) Newcombe's cottage in Cambuslang, Lanarkshire, where she revealed to her grandson that she had been adopted at the age of nine years.

* * *

The year was 1854 and in Bleary, a small village of weavers in County Down east of Portadown, Felix McConville and Betty McDowel brought a new child into the world—Mary McConville. Meanwhile, in Drumnakelly, Drumcree, Co. Armagh, a young 5-year old James McMullan helped his father and mother, James and Ellen Clarke, on their farm. Some years later, Mary met James and on 4 January 1879, they were married in the beautiful Catholic church of St Peter's in Lurgan, Co. Armagh, by Father J. McKenna. The couple settled in the townland of Cornakinnegar, Lurgan, where they were blessed with their first child, John Mullen, on 1 November 1879.

In 1881, the Mullen[1] family moved to Bellshill in the parish of Bothwell, nine miles north of Glasgow. It isn't clear why James and Mary decided to take a chance on starting a new life in Scotland, or whether there was any family waiting for them. Whatever the reason, James Mullen had given

[1] The surname "McMullan" was used by the families living in Ireland. When James and Mary immigrated to Scotland, the "Mc" was dropped and they were known as "Mullen".

up the hard life of a farmer for a much more dangerous occupation as a brusher[2] in the booming coal mining industry in the west of Scotland.

Family life seemed to be going well, and on 3 October 1885, a daughter named Sarah Mullen was added to the family. Tragedy, however, was about to strike.

In December 1885, at the age of 38, James died, leaving Mary and their two young children fatherless and homeless. James may not have realised it, but Mary was yet again pregnant with their third child.

That child was my great-grandmother Mary Mullen, and she was born in Bellshill on 9 July 1886 having never met her father. Two years later, whether from desperation or love, her mother Mary (McConville) Mullen met and married William Kelly in Bellshill on 1 April, 1888. It must have been difficult to take on a wife with three young children, but this is exactly what William Kelly did.

William, the son of Cornelius and Mary Kelly, was a labourer and the family moved to Govan, a district of Glasgow, possibly in search of work. They lived close to William's mother in a cramped tenement on the banks of the River Clyde where there was an abundance of work for young, strong men in the shipbuilding industry.

The family seemed settled and a son, also named William, was born on 9 March 1891. However, Mary's life was soon to change for the worse when her husband, William, began to show his true colours.

She made her first application for poor relief as a result of William being sent to prison. Mary (McConville) Kelly, a very feisty character, had reported him to the police for assault and he received a two-week prison sentence. The family was left destitute as a result and were awarded a small sum of money to tide them over until William was working again.

After he was released from prison, William moved back home and a daughter Catherine was born on 29 November 1892. All was not well, however.

A second application for poor relief was made by Mary on 7 December 1893. She was destitute once more because William had deserted her and the family. His whereabouts was known; and although he had been ordered by the court to pay maintenance, he did so only occasionally. Mary, it seems, was not averse to taking her wayward husband to court.

[2] A brusher is a miner employed to widen passages.

William's mother was interviewed and agreed that he had a bad character and was well known for "going with other women". With five children to feed and the only income being from Mary's son John who was working as a newsboy, life must have been very tough.

On 9 March 1895, Mary (McConville) Kelly died of tuberculosis at the age of 41 years, leaving her children with no means of support and no family to care for them.

At this time in Glasgow, the Catholic Church was rather progressive in how it dealt with destitute children. After two years in the poorhouse, arrangements were made to board Mary's youngest children, William and Catherine Kelly, out to a family in the village of Tomintoul in Aberdeenshire. It was seen as better to have the children grow up in a clean, healthy environment in the countryside rather than on the crowded streets of the rapidly growing city of Glasgow. However, this also meant the family was separated. The eldest son, John Mullen, worked as a newspaper boy according to the poor relief records. His sister Sarah Mullen disappeared from the records, and Mary Mullen, my great-grandmother, was adopted by the McCleary family, who also adopted another young girl named Kate. Only William and Catherine kept in contact with each other as they grew older. The others never met again.

While living with the McCleary family, Mary worked as a power loom weaver in the mills of Bridgeton near Dalmarnock in Glasgow, running to work every morning in wooden clogs to catch a ferry across the River Clyde. She was proud of the fact that she could operate five looms at the same time. Did she realise that her mother's family, too, had been weavers in Bleary, Ireland?

Mary Mullen eventually met a kind and gentle man named James Newcombe, and they were married on 28 June 1912. Her step-sister Kate was a witness at the wedding and Mary had insisted that her widowed step-father come live with them after the wedding. It was a happy marriage.

Mary was tough on her daughters while they were growing up, possibly trying to protect them from a fate that befell her own childhood. She never explained to them just how unhappy and clearly terrifying her childhood must have been. It is interesting that she could recall very little of it. She passed away on 9 July 1968 in her little cottage in Cambuslang surrounded by a loving and happy family.

Six months ago, whilst trying to fill in the gaps of Mary's life, I was contacted by the granddaughter of William Kelly asking if he was related to Mary. She had seen a message I posted on a forum discussing Glasgow orphans who had been boarded out to Tomintoul. I replied back, and from the information we shared, the question of missing siblings was finally answered for both our families.

What I learned, and what Mary (Mullen) Newcombe wasn't to know, was that her half-brother William Kelly remained in Tomintoul and had a very contented life as a farmer. His sister Catherine had moved back to Glasgow and she kept in touch with William until her death on 1 January 1957.

William's granddaughter also told me about the beautiful cloth that Catherine used to send them every year and thought that she had some connection to the weaving industry in Glasgow.

* * *

People often emigrate to provide a better future for their family, and I don't think we always appreciate just how much is given up to provide us with that better future. Mary's story of her journey from the village of Bleary in County Down to the sadness and courage of her life in Glasgow, and ultimately to her dream of giving her family a secure future, has shown me where my strength comes from.

Take, if you must, this little bag of dreams;
Unloose the cord, and they will wrap you round.

– William B. Yeats.

I am very proud of Mary McConville, a weaver from Bleary, Co. Down.

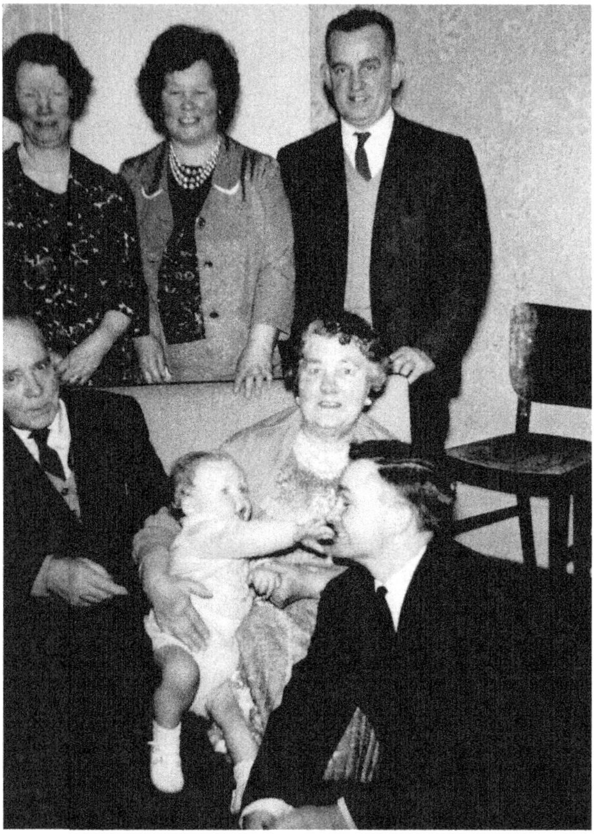

This photo was taken in 1963 in Rutherglen, Lanarkshire, at the first birthday of Mary (Mullen) Newcombe's first great-grandchild.

Mary is seated in the front with (left to right) her husband James Newcombe, great-grandson Jim Donnelly, and grandson William Francis Donnelly.

Standing in the back are (left to right) Mary Speirits, Mary Donnelly (Mary Newcombe's daughter), and Terry Donnelly (Mary Donnelly's husband).

Mary (Mullen) Newcombe and her grandson Jim Donnelly in Cambuslang, Lanarkshire. She always wore an apron! (photo: 1962)

Mary (Mullen) Newcombe (left) with her daughter Mary (Newcombe) Donnelly at the marriage of her granddaughter May Donnelly to John McIntyre in St Cadocs Catholic Church, Halfway, Cambuslang, Lanarkshire (photo: 1967).

CHAPTER TWENTY-ONE

My Irish Heritage

The Ancestors of George Frederick Lilburn (1899–1969)

BY THERESA ANN (LILBURN) MAHORTOFF (CANADA)

I REMEMBER MY GRANDFATHER GEORGE Frederick Lilburn, or "Paddy" as he liked to be called, as a charismatic Irishman with a strong brogue, pure white hair, and a slight hump of his shoulders. He was forever wearing a red vest. He died when he was 70 years old, and although I was only 13, I remember him well. He asked his grandchildren to call him "Granddad," and we did.

Granddad owned a restaurant in Vernon, British Columbia, and always seemed to be working. He was very well known in our community and to this day, when I mention his name, people remember him. Some recall him as a bit of a rogue, remembering how much he loved the "garls" as he called women.

We learn a little bit about Granddad from an excerpt taken from a column written about him after his death on 26 July 1969, which reads:

> Paddy was born near Belfast, Ireland and came to Canada in 1923, living at Regina and Vancouver before moving to Vernon, B.C. in 1942 as a service man. His military career had an interesting beginning, when he ran away from home at the age of 14 and

joined the Imperial Army, serving a number of years in the Near East during the First World War. At the outbreak of hostilities in the Second World War, he joined the Canadian Scottish Regiment and was posted to Vernon as Regimental Sergeant-Major and in charge of advanced commando training at the Coldstream Battle Drill School.

Sgt. Maj. George "Paddy" Lilburn on leave from advanced commando training at the Coldstream Battle Drill School in the Okanagan region of British Columbia (photo: ca. 1942).

When the war ended, Paddy liked the Okanagan so much he decided to make his home there. On his discharge, he went to work for Canada Safeway Limited and later took a position with Boultbee Sweet and Nutter Real Estate and Insurance Firm as a salesman and appraiser until 1962, when he took over the management of Okanagan Cafe Limited. Business commitments kept him from taking an active part in community affairs although he was a member of the Gyro Club of Vernon. He is well known for his kindness and support for young people's activities, in particular for organizations such as the Vernon Girls Trumpet Band and the MacIntosh Pipe Band of which his granddaughter Theresa was a member."

– *Vernon Daily News*, 28 July 1969

Granddad immigrated to Canada in March of 1923 with his father, Hugh, and siblings Adam and Mary, settling in Regina, Saskatchewan. His mother, Mary, his brothers Walter and Hugh James, and his sister Dosia followed in 1929. He met and married his wife, Grace Arkle Cameron, in 1925 in Carlyle, Saskatchewan. Grace's grandparents Angus Cameron and Flora McLeod had immigrated to Canada from the Isle of Skye, Scotland, in 1829 and settled in Glengarry, Ontario. They eventually moved west to Carlyle, Saskatchewan, being one of the early pioneer settlers in the area.[1]

George Frederick Lilburn in his office at the Okanagan Cafe in Vernon, British Columbia (photo: ca. 1968).

[1] Carlyle and District Historical Society, Prairie Trails to Blacktop: Carlyle and District, 1882-1982 (Carlyle, Saskatchewan: 1982).

I think that knowing Granddad and wondering where exactly he was from in Ireland is what got me interested in researching my family's history.

I have now been researching my family off and on for some thirty years, and in the last ten years I really began to dig my heels in, especially with the internet there to help me. At first I asked family members for our history. My dad was helpful, but my granddad's sister Dosia, who'd been back to Ireland, was even more so and gave me a good starting point. About the time I became more serious about seeking the Lilburn family history, I received a letter from Bernie Koltun and Greg Lilburn, two cousins of my dad, asking for information on our side of the family. They were also working on the Lilburn family tree and further along than me. They sent me a circular pedigree chart of the Lilburns, which I still use as a reference to this day.

When I first began to use the internet, I found many free sites helpful, such as Ros Davies,[2] FamilySearch,[3] and the National Archives of Ireland.[4] I also subscribed to Emerald Ancestors,[5] which provided many of the records I sought. I joined Fiona's County Down Genealogy Group[6] and found the members there to be fantastic. Whenever I had a question, someone was there to help; and their emails are full of valuable information. In 2009, I subscribed to the Ancestry website[7] and was able to find even more documents and records.

* * *

In October 2012, a group of family members[8] headed off to Ireland, and while they were there, they did some research on our family history. in County Down. My brother Graham wrote about their arrival into the

[2] Ros Davies' Co. Down, Northern Ireland Family History Research Site (freepages.genealogy.rootsweb.ancestry.com/~rosdavies).

[3] FamilySearch (familysearch.org).

[4] National Archives of Ireland (www.nationalarchives.ie).

[5] Emerald Ancestors (www.emeraldancestors.com).

[6] Fiona's County Down Genealogy Group at Yahoo!Groups (groups.yahoo.com/neo/groups/CountyDownGenealogy/info).

[7] Ancestry (www.ancestry.com).

[8] Martin Lilburn, Juhli (Lilburn) Taylor, Graham Lilburn, Syndi Prokopich Lilburn, Tim Lilburn, Ryan Lilburn, Carmen (Lilburn) Riguedell, and Tim Riguedell.

town of Banbridge, which proved to be a very moving experience.

> We (myself, my wife Syndi, Dad & Auntie Juhli) were getting excited as we were about 20 K [kilometres] south of Banbridge, the first time we were setting our eyes on the town. You could see the village in the distance through the sunny green hills. Then at that moment, a full rainbow appeared directly over the village where our forefathers lived.
>
> We went silent. I had a lump in my throat. We hid our tears in silence. It was an emotional moment - my dream of bringing my father back to his and my roots, where it all began ... was coming true. It was a magical moment for all.
>
> When we finally pulled into town after passing by the famous bridge[9] and parked our car, we all got out and I gave my father a big hug with tears in my eyes.
>
> We were home.
>
> – Graham Lilburn, October 2012

Although I didn't go to Ireland with them, it was still exciting for me. They would send me emails with pictures of homes and gravestones of our ancestors, and I would piece them together. It solved many mysteries; but at the same time, it created others.

One example is their discovery of a marriage record for our ancestor Isabella Lilburn. Her father was Hugh Lilburn, and she had married a Samuel Lilburn whose father was also named Hugh Lilburn. The helpful Genealogy and Heritage Officer at the Banbridge tourism office thought they might be second cousins, which brings in an entire new line of Lilburns. Further research into this other branch of the Lilburn family has been my latest project.

Another bit of information the family group learned from the heritage officer was that brick lintels around door frames, fireplaces, and windows are a sign of wealth. At the homestead of my great-great-grandmother Mary Ann Jamison, wife of Adam Lilburn, you can see lintels around the windows of the house. The stables at the Jamison estate, however, had slits instead of windows to provide air circulation and light for the

[9] The town of Banbridge derives its name from the bridge spanning the Bann river.

animals. The reason they didn't build actual windows is because of how the property taxes worked. The tax man would pass by and the more windows you had, the wealthier you were seen to be, and the more you would be taxed. So to avoid paying more taxes, they put fewer windows in the walls. This was an ingenious method of being both smart and frugal.

The old Jamison estate house in Banbridge, Co. Down (photo: 2012).

I heard many wonderful stories of how friendly and helpful the people of Banbridge are, such as the time my dad and his family were driving up and down Skillyscolban Road looking for an old family homestead. They spotted two women out for a stroll and stopped to ask them if they knew the location of this particular property. During the conversation, they discovered one of the women knew my dad's second cousin Vera, and she offered to take them to her home and introduce them. Vera welcomed them with open arms.

Although it was a rainy, mucky day, Vera had insisted my family members enter her home and go right into her living room—with their boots on. Pictures were taken, stories were exchanged, and Vera showed them old photos and the family bible. They were invited back the very next day to meet Vera's daughter Jennifer. I later learned that Jennifer's grandmother was Elizabeth Alice May Lilburn, the daughter of Adam

Lilburn and Mary Ann Jamison, my great-great-grandparents.

Vera also introduced my dad and the others to a wonderful gentleman named Cecil, who was an excellent guide and became a great friend. Cecil took them round to the old schoolhouse, where my grandfather and his siblings went to school, as well as to the Jamison estate, where my great-great-grandmother grew up. They also visited the Adam Lilburn Estate, the home built by Adam Lilburn and his wife, Mary Ann Jamison (which, incidentally, had many windows—one reason they were considered gentlemen of wealth). Later, after Adam and Mary had died, their daughter Elizabeth Alice May and her husband, James Baird, lived there.

My dad, Martin Lilburn (right), and his sister Juhli standing outside the ruins of the stables at the former home of their grandparents Hugh and Mary Lilburn in Banbridge, Co. Down. (photo: 2012).

Near the end of that day, their guide Cecil took them to his place and showed them his garden, his greenhouse, the chickens that he raised for food, and even his collection of miniature soldiers. A lovely and interesting man who my father still talks about.

Top: My brother Tim standing on the ruins of the home of Hugh and Mary Lilburn where our grandfather Paddy Lilburn grew up in Banbridge, Co. Down.

Bottom: The former home of Paddy's grandparents Adam Lilburn and Mary Ann Jamison in Banbridge. After Adam and Mary died, their daughter Elizabeth Alice May Lilburn (shown in inset) and her husband, James Baird, lived there (photos: 2012).

Through Vera, they found out about another relative in the area, Dr. William McCandless. His grandmother was Eleanor Jamison Lilburn, and the family group was able to set up a meeting with him. What was really serendipitous about the whole thing was the fact that the farmhouses they had booked to stay in while in Banbridge were on the Banbridge golf course where Dr. McCandless was the captain of the men's golf club. He stopped by on a Saturday morning on his way to his tee time. He brought his family tree "map" with him, and it literally rolled out to about 5-6 feet long. He held one end and Graham held the other as he tried to show them what he had so far.

Because Dr. McCandless was on his way to his golf game, they had only enough time to take a few pictures and shake his hand. In the meantime, he had called his wife, Robina, to come and stop by and see the group, which she did. According to Robina's husband, she was the one who was more involved with the family tree than him and could explain it better. Unfortunately, they did not have much time, so again they took a few pictures and that was the end of the visit.

A couple the family met in an Irish pub were over from Britain for the big soccer match between Germany and Ireland. My brother Graham, Tim, Ryan, and Syndi had walked down to the arena hoping to buy some scalped tickets to get in, but there were none to be had. So they walked back to where they were staying in Dublin (The Townhouse) and on their way stopped in at this tiny pub where a local musician was singing and playing on his guitar—mostly Beatle music if you can believe it. The place was packed and they sat at a booth with Mary and John from England. She had Irish roots and when they told her the story of trying to find their own roots, she got very emotional and talked about her family as well. It was a lot of fun for my brother and the others, meeting this couple and sharing their stories.

As part of their visit to Ireland, Tim, Dad and the others went to the parish churches looking for gravestones. It was getting late one day, and the sun was starting to go down. Everyone was spread out over the graveyard; and in the near darkness, someone would yell, "I found a Lilburn," or "Here's a Baird," or "Got a Jamison over here," or "Found a McCandless," all the while wondering if these were our ancestors. So they took pictures and sent them back to me to see if I could make a connection.

The earliest ancestors that they were able to find, and that I am still researching, were Jane Lilburn (1818–1906) and her daughters Matilda (1869–1892) and Eliza Jane (1858–1909). I also have Elizabeth Alice May (1893–1969) and James Baird (ca. 1888–1970) with their sons Joseph (1895–1996) and William John (1929–2007), as well as Eleanor Jamison Lilburn (1877–1935) and William McCandless (1872–1952) with their daughter Hilda (1915–2004) and other members of the McCandless family. Hopefully, there will be another trip to Ireland in the future to visit more cemeteries.

A summary of all my research to-date on my grandfather's ancestors is provided in the Appendix. I have done my best to make sure that the information is correct, but I expect it's not 100% accurate. My brick walls are Hugh Lilburn (born ca 1773) and his wife Jane. It is very difficult to find information from the 1700s, but I intend to keep working at it.

Appendix

Ancestors of George "Paddy" Frederick Lilburn

First Generation

1. George Frederick Lilburn, son of Hugh Lilburn and Mary Eliza Jameson Graham, was born on 22 December 1899 in Tullinisky, Co. Down, Ireland, and died on 26 July 1969 in Vernon, British Columbia, Canada.

   George married Grace Arkle Cameron on 25 February 1925 in Carlyle, Saskatchewan, Canada. Grace was born on 12 March 1906 in Carlyle, Saskatchewan, Canada, and died on 18 August 1981 in White Rock, British Columbia, Canada.

Second Generation *(Parents)*

2. Hugh Lilburn, son of Adam Lilburn and Mary Ann Jamison, was born on 20 August 1875 in Skillyscolban, Co. Down, Ireland, and died in 1947.

3. Mary Eliza Jameson Graham, daughter of William John Graham and Agnes Graham Hutton, was born on 4 February 1876 in Tullinisky, Co. Down, Ireland, and died in 1953. Another name for Mary was "Minnie".

   Hugh Lillburn and Mary Eliza Jameson Graham were married on 14 October 1898 in Banbridge, Co. Down, Ireland. Children from this marriage were:

   i. George Frederick Lilburn - see "First Generation".
   ii. Adam Lilburn, born 6 September 1903 in Tullinisky, Co. Down, Ireland; died 4 October 1971 in Surrey, British Columbia, Canada; married Mercy Victoria Jevons on 2 August, 1931 in Estevan, Saskatchewan. Canada

iii. Mary Lilburn, born September 1906 in Ednego, Co. Down, Ireland; died 20 February 1985 in Regina, Saskatchewan, Canada; married George Turner Henry in Regina, Saskatchewan, Canada.

iv. William Henry Lilburn, born 13 December 1908 in Ednego, Co. Down, Ireland; died 31 August 1963 in Regina, Saskatchewan, Canada; married Charlotte Hildrew on 19 December 1936 in Surrey, England.

v. Elizabeth Theodosia Lilburn, born 9 May 1914 in Ednego, Co. Down, Ireland; died 13 January 1989; married John Junor on 27 November 1943 in Regina, Saskatchewan, Canada.

vi. Walter Lilburn, born 10 December 1915 in Ednego, Co. Down, Ireland; died 4 September 1976 in Regina, Saskatchewan, Canada; married Winnifred Blaylock on 22 September 1945 in Regina, Saskatchewan, Canada.

vii. Hugh James Lilburn, born 6 May 1918 in Ednego, Co. Down, Ireland; died 1948; married Elizabeth Ita Gavin on 27 March 1943 in Islington, Middlesex, England.

Third Generation *(Grandparents)*

4. Adam Lilburn, son of Hugh Lilburn and Sarah Anne Lilburn, was born about 1832 in Skillyscolban, Co Down, Ireland, died on 15 May 1905 in Co. Down, Ireland, and was buried in the Dromore Non Subscribing Presbyterian graveyard.

5. Mary Ann Jamison, daughter of William Henry Jamison and Eliza Jane Strong, was born about 1852 in Ednego, Co. Down, Ireland, died on 13 March 1942, and was buried in the Dromore Non Subscribing Presbyterian graveyard.

Adam Lilburn and Mary Ann Jamison were married on 24 September 1874 at Dromore First Presbyterian Church, Banbridge, Co. Down, Ireland. Children from this marriage were:

i. Hugh Lilburn - see "Second Generation".

ii. Eleanor Jamison Lilburn, born 1 January 1877 in Dromore, Co. Down, Ireland; died 2 December 1935 in Dromore, Co. Down, Northern Ireland; married William McCandless on 24 May 1898 at Dunmurry Presbyterian Church, Co. Antrim, Ireland.
iii. Sarah Carrothers Lilburn, born 18 August 1879 in Banbridge, Co. Down, Ireland; died June 1905 in Ireland; married William Reid.
iv. Thomas Henry Lilburn, born 11 October 1881 in Dromore, Co. Down, Ireland; died 31 May 1964 in Yakima, Yakima, Washington, United States; married Mary Campbell.
v. Walter Lilburn, born 26 April 1884; died 23 April 1984; married Jessie Sanders on 25 December 1912.
vi. William Lilburn, born 1886 in Ireland; died 25 June 1961 in Co. Down, Northern Ireland; married Margaret Baird.
vii. Maude Lilburn, born September 1889 in Ireland; married John Baird on 30 July 1918 in Dromore parish, Co. Down, Ireland.
viii. Elizabeth Alice Lilburn, born December 1893 in Banbridge, Co. Down, Ireland; died 4 May 1969; married James Baird on 26 June 1928 in Newry parish, Co. Down, Northern Ireland.

6. William John Graham

7. Agnes Graham Hutton

William John Graham and Agnes Graham Hutton were married. A child from this marriage was:

i. Mary Eliza Jameson Graham - see "Second Generation".

***Fourth Generation** (Great-Grandparents)*

8. Hugh Lilburn, son of Hugh Lilburn and Jane, was born about 1799 in Skillyscolban, Co. Down, Ireland, died on 14 April 1858 in Skillyscolban, Co. Down, Ireland, and was buried in the

Dromore Non Subscribing Presbyterian graveyard.

Sarah Anne Lilburn was born about 1810, died June 1889 in Banbridge, Co. Down, Ireland, and was buried in the Dromore Non Subscribing Presbyterian graveyard.

Hugh Lilburn and Sarah Anne Lilburn were married. Children from this marriage were:

i. William Lilburn, born 1829; died 29 April 1903 in Belfast, Ireland; married Isabella Russell on 11 April 1898 in Ireland.
ii. Isabella Lilburn, born ca. 1831 in Dromore, Co. Down, Ireland; married Hugh Lilburn on 1 April 1851 in Dromore Presbyterian Church, Co. Down, Ireland.
iii. Adam Lilburn - see "Third Generation".
iv. Eliza Jane Lilburn, born ca.1836 in Ireland; died 2 March 1878 in Ireland; married George Hammond on 7 May 1863 in Seapatrick parish, Co. Down, Ireland.
v. Thomas Patterson Lilburn, born about 1841; married Matilda Corry on 7 November 1861 at Moira Presbyterian Church, Co. Down, Ireland.
vi. Hugh Miniss Lilburn, born ca. 1843 in Newtownards, Co. Down, Ireland; died 6 August 1896 in Bangor, Co. Down, Ireland; married Anna Kent on 11 January 1872 at Dunmurry Presbyterian Church, Co. Antrim, Ireland.
vii. Sarah Ann Lilburn, born 1845; died 11 June 1917 in Ballylintagh, Co. Down, Ireland; married James Patterson on 21 January 1869 in Banbridge, Co. Down, Ireland.

9. William Henry Jamison was born about 1828 in Banbridge, Co. Down, Ireland, and died on 7 October 1881 in Banbridge, Co. Down, Ireland.

10. Eliza Jane Strong was born about 1825 and died on 14 July 1906 in Banbridge, Co. Down, Ireland.

William Henry Jamison and Eliza Jane Strong were married on 27 June 1848 in Banbridge, Co. Down, Ireland. A child from this marriage was:

i. Mary Ann Jamison – see "Third Generation".

***Fifth Generation** (Great-Great-Grandparents)*

11. Hugh Lilburn was born about 1773 in Dungannon, Co.Tyrone, Ireland.

Hugh Lilburn married Jane. Children from this marriage were:

i. Hugh Lilburn – see "Fourth Generation".
ii. Jane Lilburn, born 17 October 1818 in Dromore parish, Co. Down, Ireland; died 27 February 1906 in Belfast, Ireland.

CHAPTER TWENTY-TWO

Immigrants to Australia

The Lennon and McGee Families of Portaferry

BY JENNI GAY (AUSTRALIA)

THIS IS THE STORY OF my great-great grandparents William Lennon and Margaret McGee, who I have been researching for nearly 30 years.

Seven years after Margaret's father (James), sister (Susan), and brother (Patrick) came to Victoria, Australia, she and William left their home in Portaferry, Co. Down, and immigrated to Melbourne with their young family. I imagine they sailed from the shores of Ireland filled with hopes and dreams of a promising future. What I learned, sadly, is that they would suffer more than their fair share of tribulations, starting soon after arriving in their newly adopted country.

Ireland ... the Beginning

According to the records I've been able to examine, my great-great-grandparents were born in County Down. William Lennon was born about 1825, and his father was also named William, which suggests my great-great-grandfather was the eldest son of the family. His future wife, Margaret McGee, was born about ten years later to James and Margaret McGee in Portaferry. Again, the fact that she is named after her mother suggests that she was the eldest daughter.

William and Margaret were married on 20 June 1852 in St Patrick's Catholic Church, Portaferry, in the parish of Ballyphillip on Strangford Lough. The witnesses were Thomas Convery and Ann Lennon.

William and Margaret had six children in Portaferry before they left Ireland for Melbourne, Australia. The first five children were born prior to the start of civil registration in 1864, so records of their births do not exist. However, due to the kind help of the late Sheila Phillips of Ballymartin, Co. Down, I have their baptismal dates and the names of their sponsors.[1]

All the children were baptized in St Patrick's, the same church in Portaferry where their parents were married. The sixth child, Mary, was born in 1866, after civil registration, so I was able to purchase her birth certificate.[2]

- William Lennon, baptized 5 July 1857; sponsors were Thomas Lennon and Susan McGee.
- Margaret Lennon, baptized 10 March 1859; sponsors were Pat McGee and Marianne McLea.
- Thomas Lennon (my great-grandfather), baptized 1 September 1861; sponsors were James Mason and Margaret Lennon.
- Susanna ("Susan") Lennon, baptized 7 June 1863; sponsors were William and Rose Lennon.
- Rose Lennon, baptized 6 November 1864; sponsors were Henry Lennon and Mary McManus.
- Mary Lennon, born 4 May 1866 and baptized 10 May 1866; sponsors were William Fitzsimmons and Marianne Falloona.

My assumption is that the Lennon and McGee sponsors were siblings and/or cousins of the parents, William and Margaret, but I have yet to prove that.

---

[1] Sheila Phillips found the baptisms in the parish registers for St Patrick's Catholic Church on microfilm at the Public Records Office of Northern Ireland (PRONI) in Belfast in 2009. I will be eternally grateful to her for her generous help.

[2] The General Register Office for Northern Ireland (GRONI), Oxford House, Belfast, Northern Ireland.

Immigration and Life in Australia

Margaret and her six children travelled to Melbourne, Australia, on the *Alumbagh*,[3] arriving on 30 October 1870 with 412 other immigrants.[4] Her husband, William, was not listed as a passenger, so I presume he travelled out to Australia first. So far, I have only found two persons named William Lennon as possibilities. One arrived from the island of Mauritius in October 1868 on the *Thames*,[5] and the other arrived from New Zealand in March 1869 on the *Mary*.[6] However, I am unable to confirm that either of these is definitely Margaret's husband.

Also aboard the *Alumbagh* in 1870 was a Peggy McGee with her two children Henry and Mary. I wonder if this was a sister-in-law of Margaret. Interestingly, all of the Lennons and McGees came out as unassisted immigrants, which suggests they had some money behind them.

I don't know exactly where the Lennon family lived on their arrival in Melbourne. But as I was preparing this story, the Royal Women's Hospital Archives and their volunteers made available online both an index and scanned copies of the midwifery records of their first institution—the Melbourne Lying-In Hospital. I was thrilled to discover the details of Margaret's first delivery in Australia and her seventh child, John Alexander, on 20 October 1871.[7]

According to the newly discovered records, Margaret was in the hospital for two days before she had a half-hour labour! Sadly, six days later, she was diagnosed with "puerperal mania", a mental illness that follows childbirth. On 28 October 1871, Margaret was moved from the Lying-In hospital and admitted to the Yarra Bend Lunatic Asylum (north of Melbourne) by her sister Susan McGee of Barkly Street in St Kilda.[8] In late December, she

---

[3] Public Record Office Victoria "Index to Unassisted Inward Passenger Lists to Victoria 1852-1923," database (www.prov.vic.gov.au).

[4] "Shipping Intelligence", *The Argus*, 31 October 1870, p. 4.

[5] Public Record Office Victoria "Index to Unassisted Inward Passenger Lists to Victoria 1852-1923," database ((www.prov.vic.gov.au).

[6] ibid.

[7] The Royal Women's Hospital, Victoria, Australia, "Melbourne Lying In Hospital, Midwifery Record Book No. 1, from 19th Aug 1856 to 15th Mar 1879," database and images (www.thewomens.org.au)

[8] Public Record Office Victoria, "Yarra Bend (Asylum 1848-1905; Hospital for the Insane 1905-1925)," Agency VA 2839.

was listed as "Out on Leave" from the Asylum, and on 6 May 1872 she was pronounced "Cured" and discharged from Yarra Bend.[9]

By November 1872, the Lennon family was living well out of Melbourne in Doncaster where William was renting land from John Jobson.[10] In 1873, William is listed in the rate book for the local municipal council as farming seventy acres on Doncaster Rd. He is also listed as a carter when their eighth child, Hugh Patrick, was born on 6 November 1872.[11] This area of the country was being cleared for orchards at the time, and William may have worked to help support his family by hauling the cut wood to the markets in Melbourne where it was being used for cooking and heating.[12] He was used to farming as he and his father farmed in the townland of Craigaroddan, Co. Down, a couple of miles from Portaferry.

On 4 February 1874, the ninth child, Agnes, was born in Doncaster,[13] but by the middle of that year tragedy struck when two-and-a-half-year-old John Alexander died of croup on 5 June.[14] His father, William, may have taken his little coffin by cart along the Mitcham road for several miles to the Airhill cemetery at St John's Catholic Church in Mitcham. There he was buried on 6 June by William, John Quilan (Secretary of the Airhill Burial ground), and Thomas Larkins. Unfortunately, that burial ground has been built over by the current school and church, so I am unable to locate his grave.

Earlier that year, the first school chapel was opened at St John's Catholic Church. Who knows, perhaps some of the older children attended school there. However, I have yet to find relevant school records.

Making ends meet must have been difficult as the Lennon family moved again—and much further this time. By 1875, the family had relocated from Doncaster to Sandhurst (now known as Bendigo) north-west of Melbourne. It was here where yet another tragedy befell the family when the youngest child, Agnes, died as a result of "scarlatina" (now known

---

[9] Public Record Office Victoria, "Yarra Bend (Asylum 1848-1905; Hospital for the Insane 1905-1925)," Agency VA 2839.

[10] Archivist at Doncaster Templestown Historical Society (email message).

[11] Births Deaths Marriages Victoria (www.bdm.vic.gov.au).

[12] Archivist at Schramm's Cottage Musuem, Doncaster (personal communication, March 2011).

[13] Births Deaths Marriages Victoria (www.bdm.vic.gov.au).

[14] ibid.

as scarlet fever) on 7 December 1875. She was buried in the Sandhurst cemetery the following day.

William and Margaret's last child was born around 1877 and she was named Agnes Therese.[15] I haven't been able to locate her birth certificate, but assume she was born in Sandhurst from her age as listed on her mother's death certificate.

On 7 September 1877, Margaret's 35-year-old sister Susan McGee married a sailor named Travers Gilmore in St. Ignatius Catholic Church, Richmond, Victoria.[16] I now believe that Susan and her husband knew each other from their earlier days in Ireland as they both stated on their marriage certificate that their birthplace was in County Down. Also, I have found a record of both families living in the townlands of Derry and Portaferry.[17] They both died in Melbourne—Susan in 1912 and Travers in 1898—and left no descendants.

After having given birth to four more children in Australia, burying two of them, and struggling to make ends meet, it is hardly surprising that Margaret was readmitted to the Yarra Bend Lunatic Asylum on 20 April 1880, this time by her husband, William.[18] Her "Form of Insanity" was described simply as "D", which I presume meant depression. She is described as experiencing "incoherency and delusions".[19] Her home address in the asylum case book was given as 12 Lothian Street in North Melbourne, which was a crowded slum area at the time.

On 12 July 1880, Margaret was sent out on leave from the asylum, but died on 27 August 1880 as a result of "Cerebral Disease and Phithis" (now known as tuberculosis, or TB).[20] The 44 year-old mother and wife was buried two days later by her husband in the Melbourne General Cemetery in Parkville, Victoria. It is surprising to me that her illnesses are not mentioned in the Yarra Bend Lunatic Asylum case book, even

[15] Births Deaths Marriages Victoria (www.bdm.vic.gov.au).

[16] ibid.

[17] Public Record Office of Northern Ireland, "Valuation Revision Books," database and images (www.proni.gov.uk).

[18] Victorian Archives Centre, North Melbourne, Australia; Yarra Bend Lunatic Asylum: admission register.

[19] Victorian Archives Centre, North Melbourne, Australia; Yarra Bend Lunatic Asylum: case book.

[20] Births Deaths Marriages Victoria (www.bdm.vic.gov.au).

though it must have been obvious that she was extremely ill.

I assume that the older girls—Margaret (age 21), Susan (age 17), Rose (age 15), and Mary Lennon (age 14)—would have cared for the two youngest children before and after their mother's early death. They were 8-year-old Hugh and 4-year-old Agnes Therese.

The eldest son, 23-year-old William Lennon, must have left Melbourne around the time of his mother's death. This information I gleaned from his death certificate[21] which was issued after he died in 1933 while a patient at the Orange Mental Hospital in New South Wales (NSW). It states that he had lived for two years in Queensland, and fifty-one years in NSW. At this stage, I don't know how long he had spent in the mental hospital prior to his death. His death certificate also states he was unmarried.

Life must have been extremely difficult for my great-great-grandfather William Lennon Sr. after the death of his wife. In the next seven years, he lost three of his older daughters while still living on Lothian Street in North Melbourne.

Susan, who was a tailoress and aged 19 years, died on 23 May 1883 in the Melbourne Hospital from "Febris Enterica" (now known as enteric fever, and related to typhoid fever).[22] Two months later, on 2 July 1883, 16 year-old Mary died at home from "Phithis Pulmonaris" (tuberculosis).[23] And in 1887, on 16 February, Rose, also a tailoress and aged 24, died at home from "Typhoid Fever".[24] All three girls were buried in an unmarked grave in the Melbourne General Cemetery with their mother.[25]

The only good news during this time must have been the wedding of the eldest daughter, Margaret Lennon, to John Cox in 1884, and the marriage of the second eldest son, my great-grandfather Thomas Lennon, to Mary Prendergast on 4 January 1888 in St Brigid's Catholic Church, North Fitzroy. St Brigid's was used for many Lennon baptisms, weddings and, presumably, funerals too, as they remained in that area for several years. In fact, my mother was baptised there in 1918.

Margaret and John Cox were only married for twelve years when John died in 1896, leaving his wife with three children under the age of

[21] NSW Registry of Births Deaths & Marriages (www.bdm.nsw.gov.au).
[22] Births Deaths Marriages Victoria (www.bdm.vic.gov.au).
[23] ibid.
[24] ibid.
[25] Melbourne General Cemetery, Roman Catholic section (grave no. 464).

11 years in an era when there wasn't a widow's pension. Margaret died in 1935 at the age of 76. She and John are buried in an unmarked grave in the Melbourne General Cemetery with Margaret's father and my great-great-grandfather William Lennon, who died in 1907.

My great-grandparents Thomas and Mary Lennon had four daughters: Mary Winifred, Elsie, Alma Margaret (my grandmother) and Vera Rose (who died at the age of 4 years in 1902). Thomas died in 1923 and Mary died in 1942.

Hugh Lennon, the second youngest child of my great-great grand-parents William and Margaret, doesn't seem to appear in any Victorian records. The youngest child, Agnes Therese Lennon, married a widower with nine children, Thomas Banks, in 1909 in St Ignatius Catholic Church, Richmond, Victoria. [26] This was just eighteen months after her father's death in 1907. She and Thomas had a daughter together named Carmel who didn't marry or have any children. All three are buried in the Faulkner Cemetery, Faulkner, Victoria.[27]

Epilogue

I often wonder why my great-great grandparents William Lennon and Margaret McGee left their home country, but I assume it was for a better life in Australia for their children, which is still the main reason people immigrate to Australia. I am in absolute awe of their decision to come here. To leave family and friends to come so very far, knowing there was no possibility of going home, must have taken a lot of courage.

Despite William and Margaret having ten children, only two of those children—Margaret and Thomas—had children of their own. Most known descendants still live in Melbourne, while some of us live in South Australia and others in Queensland. Having only known life in Australia, I am keen to understand what it was like for my great-great-grandparents in Ireland and have great hopes that one day I will be able to walk the streets of Portaferry, Co. Down and attend mass at St Patrick's Catholic Church as my ancestors once did. It looks like this dream may come to fruition next year, and I can't wait.

[26] Births Deaths Marriages Victoria (www.bdm.vic.gov.au).
[27] ibid.

Surname Index

B

C

D

G

I

J

K

L

M

P

Q

R

S

T

Y

Printed in Great Britain
by Amazon

36256120R00175